100 THINGS
A's FANS
SHOULD KNOW & DO
BEFORE THEY DIE

100 THINGS A's FANS SHOULD KNOW & DO BEFORE THEY DIE

Susan Slusser

TRIUMPH
BOOKS

This book is available in quantity at special discounts for your group or organization. For further information, contact:

Triumph Books LLC
814 North Franklin Street
Chicago, Illinois 60610
(312) 337-0747
www.triumphbooks.com

Printed in U.S.A.
ISBN: 978-1-62937-068-2
Design by Patricia Frey
Photos courtesy of Getty Images unless otherwise indicated

In memory of Joyce Slusser, a true A's fan

Contents

Foreword

The history of the A's is filled with characters and stories as rich and colorful as nearly any organization in sports. From Connie Mack through Charlie Finley and from Sandy Alderson through the teams of the 2000s and today, each generation of A's baseball has put its stamp on history in a unique way.

Some of the greatest teams of all time were the A's of the early '30s under Connie Mack. From 1929 to 1932, Mack's teams averaged more than 101 wins and dominated the game even more than the famed Yankees teams of that era. Though, in a precursor of things to come, Mack was the first one to have to sell off players for financial reasons. History repeated itself in the early '70s, when Charlie put together three World Series champions, only to see many of his players go elsewhere via free agency. When the Haas family took over and Sandy was running the team, the personality of the club changed from the mustachioed gang of Catfish and Rollie to the rock stars of the '80s that were Rickey and Jose and McGwire. But, the success of the franchise continued. That team, led by Hall of Famer Tony La Russa and on which I was lucky enough to be a player for a brief moment, went to three straight World Series and set the standard for excellence over the course of almost a decade.

The game began to change when I moved from the field into the front office in the early '90s, but the circumstances were the same as they'd always been. The A's were always trying to compete with bigger clubs that had more than we did; whether in Philadelphia or Kansas City or Oakland, that's been the case. Now in this era, where new stadiums and huge TV contracts create seemingly unlimited revenue streams around the game, we still face those same challenges.

And, with those challenges come solutions that have to be inventive and creative. Mack, Finley, and Alderson—all three were considered great innovators during their time with the A's. We've tried to further that innovation in my 17 years here as general manager. I've done some things differently than those who came before me, but always tried to keep the spirit of the franchise intact. To some extent we've taken on the personality of the Bay Area and the tech boom around us, using whatever information we could capture to help put a winning team on the field. But, the players on the field and the personalities they bring remain the heart of the A's.

My first year as GM in 1998 was Rickey's last year in Oakland. There's no doubt Rickey is the best player in Oakland A's history; an incredibly complete player who could impact the game in every way. And there have been some great players who've followed in his footsteps over the last two decades. Jason Giambi was the first star to play here in Oakland during my tenure. Eventually, Miguel, Tim Hudson, and Eric Chavez joined Jason and were then followed by Zito, Mulder, and Ramon Hernandez to form those great teams of 2000–2003. That group gave way to guys like Dan Haren and Nick Swisher, who were joined by Hall of Famer Frank Thomas for his magical season in 2006. And then you have the most recent collection of personalities, led on the field by Bob Melvin, who provided the most enjoyable season of my term as GM in 2012. That team went almost entirely unnoticed until the last day of the season when we won the AL West after never having led the division for a single day.

Whether in Philadelphia, Kansas City, or Oakland, the A's have never lacked for color. There's a reason our rabid, knowledgeable, and loyal fan base has connected so much with these teams over the years. The players tend to take on the personality of the fans, whose own creativity and passion spills out of the stands and onto the field. It's not uncommon to hear opposing players say that Oakland is one of the toughest places in the game to play.

The A's, and those of us who love the organization, never quite know what tomorrow will bring. We take it day by day and have learned to enjoy the team we have in the moment. But, no one can take away the incredible history of this team—the stories, the personalities, the fans, and the characters are what have made the A's one of the greatest franchises in sports.

—Billy Beane

1 Rickey Henderson

Leading off, of course: No. 24, Rickey Henderson.

On June 24, 1979, the A's dropped a doubleheader to Texas, forgettable enough in a terrible season, except for the fact that one of the greatest baseball players of all time made his debut in left field. In the first game, the 20-year-old went 2-for-4 with a double and a stolen base, a statistic that became synonymous with Henderson.

The one-time Oakland Tech football star would soon team with a new A's manager to turn the franchise's fortunes around— saving major-league baseball in the East Bay.

From his first moments, Rickey Henderson was in a hurry. He was born in the back seat of an Oldsmobile en route to the hospital in Chicago on Christmas Day, 1958.

In Henderson's autobiography with John Shea, *Off Base, Confessions of a Thief,* he credits his speed to chasing chickens as a small child at his grandmother's home in Alabama; after moving to Oakland, he raced city buses.

Baseball wasn't his early passion, though. Football was Henderson's game, and he had to be dragged to the diamond by his brother and by some neighborhood coaches who realized they needed the area's top athlete on their teams, even if they had to bribe him.

"I hated baseball," Henderson said from a distance of more than 40 years. "I played because of my brother; he loved it, but I hated the game. A baseball player was nowhere near what I wanted to be.

"But I had a couple of father figures who kept me playing. Because I was good at it, I was playing on two teams—they got me to play by bringing me cocoa and donuts to get me out of bed, or I never would have gone to the field. I'd play in Oakland and Berkeley, one game at 10:00 AM and the next one at 2:00."

Henderson wound up playing with Louis Burrell, who like his brother, Stanley "MC Hammer" Burrell, worked in the A's clubhouse; Oakland players of the mid-70s remember Louis Burrell bringing Henderson around and telling them that here was a future big-leaguer. Another A's connection: Dave Stewart, the future Oakland star right-hander, was the catcher on Henderson and Burrell's Connie Mack team.

Henderson was, famously, cut from the varsity baseball team as a sophomore. He was a high school All American in football, however, and he received 20 scholarship offers, with USC and UCLA among the suitors.

"I was going to go to Arizona State because of Reggie Jackson and because I could play football and baseball," Henderson said. "My mom was the one who decided against football. She said, 'I want you to play baseball.' I said, 'Mom, I don't like baseball, I just did it to get away from my chores.'

"One scout told me I had a better chance at baseball. He said I was the best athlete he had ever seen and I was going to make it. A lot of teams didn't like me, though, because I hit right-handed and threw left-handed."

That's an unusual combo, with only a few dozen in the fraternity (including, lore has it, Eddie Gaedel, though the undersized pinch hitter never threw a baseball at the big-league level).

"When I got into baseball, I just looked to see what everyone else was doing, and they all hit on the right side," Henderson said. "So I did it from the right side, even though I'm left-handed. People to this day wonder why I wasn't a left-handed hitter, but it's only because I was watching the other kids.

Rickey Henderson holds third base aloft after stealing it against the Yankees on May 1, 1991, giving him 939 career steals, and putting him one ahead of Lou Brock.

"In single-A, they talked about having me switch hit, but Tom Trebelhorn was my manager and he said, 'You're hitting .380. Why mess with your swing?' We're talking a lot more hits if I'd hit left-handed because it always took me awhile to get out of the box. I'd have been two steps closer to first. Batting right-handed, I never got any infield hits because I got so tied up with my swing and getting out of the box."

The A's overlooked this oddity and selected Henderson in the fourth round of the 1976 draft.

In A-ball, in 1977, Henderson stole 95 bases. He was still perfecting his craft, however. He credits Trebelhorn with helping him learn to steal bases, but Henderson kept working on finding the right sliding style.

"When I went feet first, with all the pounding, it was wearing my legs down," Henderson said. "I asked [teammate] Mike Rodriguez to show me how to slide like he did and I ran down to second and pow! I crushed my behind. I hit the ground so hard, I hurt my butt. So I tried sliding head first and that hurt more than feet first."

Pitcher Mike Norris, on a rehab assignment at Double-A Jersey City, was an observer.

"The first day I got there, they had Rickey in the outfield and they're teaching him to slide head first on the wet grass," Norris recalled. "But he couldn't get it right, and come game time, he steals second base head-first and it's bumpety-bumpety-bump all the way; he arced and slammed down and almost stopped. Later, he got so when he slid head-first, he picked up speed, like throwing a rock on the water, but not then—he couldn't do it.

"Then he stole third, and his belt-buckle tore his stomach open. So he was scared to slide on his stomach, and he was afraid to go feet first because he didn't want to break an ankle. But he came back and, with his stomach bandaged up, he did it right head-first."

Always trying to better himself, Henderson could find inspiration anywhere.

"Four or five years later, we were on a flight to Chicago and I was sleeping when we started to land," he said. "It was windy and when we hit the ground, there was a big bounce, boom, boom. It was a rough one.

"Then, when we landed in Oakland, it was smooth. We hit the ground no problem, everyone was clapping. So I went to the pilot and asked him, 'What was the difference? That landing in Chicago was so bouncy, this one was nice.'

"He said, 'It's about coming in smooth and low to the ground—if you don't, you bounce a lot.'

"So I thought, 'I'm going to get low to the ground.'"

Only one problem with the new technique: Henderson had trouble stopping. He slid way past the bag, and had to back up his low approach until he was five strides from the bag.

Henderson continued his tutelage under A's teammate Davey Lopes, the former Dodgers star.

"I had speed, but I had to learn something more. If you get a better jump, you make it easier on yourself," Henderson said. "Davey said he always watched what the pitchers did when the slowest guys were on base, because they're not worried about those guys. So what did they do when they went to the plate [versus] when they threw over? What was the key to tell they were going to go home?

"Davey said if you're worried about getting picked off, you'll never steal a base. Look for one thing the pitcher is doing different when he gets ready to throw to the plate."

Even late in his career, with the Padres in 1996, Henderson was getting tips from Lopes, who coached first.

"He'd say, 'Hey, Rickey, you don't know the NL pitchers, you can't read them,' and bang, bang, I'd be out." Henderson said.

"Lopes said, 'Let me pick a pitch and I'll yell and you go.' I said, 'How can you do that?'

"He'd say, 'Can't you see that pitcher flinch with his glove on his breaking ball?' And I say, 'What are you talking about?' So he said, 'Just listen to my voice and if you get thrown out, I'll take the blame.' I said, 'That sounds like a good deal.'

"The first time he said, 'Go!' it scared the hell out of me. I forgot. I panicked. I said, 'Oh. What?' And it was too late.

"He said, 'Okay, just relax and listen.' Two pitches later, he saw something and said, 'Go!' And I paused and took off. I got the worst jump of my career—but I was at second base, no contest. I thought I'd be out by a ton. Davey said, 'No—he hadn't even thrown the ball yet when you went.'"

The most important figure in Henderson's development was hired on February 21, 1980, days before spring training opened. Owner Charlie Finley had found his new manager, one-time Kansas City A's infielder and West Berkeley native Billy Martin. Martin loved letting his speedy guys run—especially Henderson. The "Billyball" team was bunting, stealing home, flashy, exciting. That was reflected in the attendance, which increased by more than 500,000 in Martin's first season and hit 1.3 million his second— remarkable considering that was a strike year. In 1982, the total was up to 1.7 million.

"We went from no one at all to drawing like crazy," starter Matt Keough said. "It was a fun team to watch with Rickey."

The fun factor increased in 1982, as Henderson was approaching Lou Brock's single-season record for stolen bases and Martin was abetting him.

"He gave me the green light to go whenever I wanted to, but he also had a sign for me to go whenever he knew a breaking pitch was coming. He knew. He was a genius at picking pitches," Henderson said. "He told me that spring training, 'You're going to break the record this year. Between you and me, we're going to do it.' I'd get to first base and he'd read the breaking ball, I'd peek over [at Martin] and I'm gone."

Martin was determined that Henderson nab record-tying No. 118 at home, and he had one last chance against the Tigers on August 24.

"It was Billy vs. Sparky Anderson, the most exciting manager matchup at that time, I thought," Henderson said. "They were always anticipating each other's moves, strategywise."

Jerry Ujdur walked Fred Stanley to open the eighth, Henderson followed with a single, and Stanley stopped at second.

"We were going on the road after that," Henderson said, "so Martin told Chicken Stanley to steal third base. Chicken wondered why, because he was the slowest guy in the team, but he was like, 'I'll do it.' Either way, it works for me. Either he makes it, or he's out, and second base is open.

"Martin was yelling to Stanley, 'Get a big lead! Get a big lead!' Sparky heard and he knew what Billy was doing. He yelled to Ujdur, 'If Stanley gets a big lead, don't pick him off! Concentrate on Rickey!'

"Chicken takes a big lead, bigger lead, and Ujdur wouldn't throw down there. Finally, he took off and they threw him out."

Anderson was furious, yelling, "That ain't the way the game is played!"

He found an ally in third-base umpire Durwood Merrill, who told Martin, "You can't do that," according to Henderson.

"So Sparky kept throwing over to first base and throwing over," Henderson said. "I knew I had a chance, and I'm thrown out or I'm not, but I have a shot. So I took my lead, I read the move, and I got a great jump. Everyone knows I'm going and Sparky had Ujdur pitch out. I slid into second base and the throw was good, but the tag hit me on the back leg.

"Durwood said, 'You're out!' I said, 'No way! He got my back leg!' And Durwood said, 'You can't do it this way. That's why you're out.'

"Durwood made a bad call, but he said he didn't want the record to go like that. We were fuming. Billy was furious. He wanted to do it for the home fans, and so did I."

Henderson finished the season with 130 steals, still the all-time mark. On May 1, 1991, he added the career stolen-base crown, sliding safely into third in the fourth inning of a game against the Yankees at the Coliseum for No. 939 overall. (The home plate umpire: Durwood Merrill.)

Henderson hauled the base up and held it aloft, then, after thanking his family, Trebelhorn, Martin, and the A's owners, he said, "Lou Brock was the symbol of great base stealing. But today, I'm the greatest of all time."

A wave of criticism followed that speech, with Henderson branded arrogant and self absorbed. That still stings Henderson, who had no intention of causing a fuss.

"I went through a week or something trying to steal that base, and Lou Brock was traveling with us," Henderson said. "I was a big, big fan of Lou Brock, and a big fan of Muhammad Ali and all the things he had been through. Lou and I were talking and I was trying to figure out what to say when I broke the record. I told Lou I wanted to say, 'I'm the greatest,' to honor Muhammad Ali, and Lou thought there was no problem with that.

"It didn't get across very well. I think everyone thought I meant I was the greatest player, but I said the greatest basestealer. And I was. I had achieved the biggest thing—and I added on 500 after that.

"It ended up getting so blown out of proportion, and I just wanted to do the right thing. I took a lot of grief, but I wouldn't change it. I did it because Lou Brock was with me and he knows why I said it. But it did hurt me when people took it negatively.

I felt bad, like what am I out here busting my butt for? To be the greatest! And if someone breaks my record, they can say they're the greatest—and if they don't, I'll say it for them even if I have to take the microphone away from them."

Rene Lachemann was coaching third when Henderson broke the mark, and he said, with a laugh, "When Rickey held up the base and claimed he was the greatest—well, he was right. That record will never be broken."

Oakland general manager Sandy Alderson traded Henderson to the Yankees in 1984 and then reacquired him in 1989. He dealt him away again in the middle of 1993 and he re-signed Henderson that off-season as a free agent. Henderson had four different stints with Oakland in all.

"I went to a 25-year college reunion and they asked us to list our hobbies in a questionnaire and I put 'Trading Rickey Henderson,'" Alderson said with a laugh. "I kind of liked Rickey. You had to take into account his background and experiences. He was frustrating at times because he might have more than one agent speaking on his behalf and he changed his mind a lot.

"He mellowed some, that's why we brought him back—combined with his ability and his relationship with Oakland. This is the entertainment business, you're always looking for that hook. Sometimes he was a challenge, but that's what made it fun."

"I love Rickey. How could you not? He's so great with kids and with people," said Wally Haas, son of former A's owner Walter Haas. "Our last Sunday of owning the team in 1995 was a very emotional day. Instead of Fan Appreciation day, they made it 'Haas Appreciation.' My dad was too ill to attend and he died three days later.

"And Rickey did a Rickey game. He single-handedly won the game. I went down to the clubhouse and I said, 'Hey, Rickey, thank you for a great game,' and he said, 'Well, I wanted to win one for the old guy.' I was very touched. But I do remember thinking, 'What about all those other games you played in for him?'"

Henderson finished his 25-year career, which included an MVP award in 1990, with 1,406 steals and 2,295 runs, all-time records that still stand. He was elected to the Hall of Fame in 2009 in his first year of eligibility, and he works with the A's as a special instructor.

"In my opinion, Rickey is the best player ever to play the game," former teammate Carney Lansford said. "I hit behind him for a number of years, played with him for a number of years, saw how he affected the game in so many ways, whether it was putting a run on the board to start the game or stealing a couple of bases, making a great play in the outfield. My all-time idol was Willie Mays, and I'm not sure he affected the game as much as Rickey did."

2 Charlie Finley

Charles Oscar Finley was born in Ensley, Alabama, on February 22, 1918, and as a youngster, he exhibited the same interests that would make him famous: baseball and salesmanship. He was a batboy for the Birmingham Barons minor-league team while also winning awards for selling *The Saturday Evening Post* door-to-door, and he later played semi-pro baseball in Indiana while working at a steel mill in Gary, Indiana, where his father and grandfather were steelworkers.

During World War II, he worked in an ordinance plant. At the same time, Finley began selling insurance on the side and set a company record for policies sold. He didn't have health insurance of his own, however, when he came down with a severe case of tuberculosis and pneumonia that nearly killed him and reduced his weight to 96 pounds. So during his 27 months of convalescence, he devised a group insurance plan for professionals, including doctors. He sold the coverage to the American College of Surgeons, among other high-profile medical associations.

That made Finley a multi-millionaire. He decided to spend his newly minted fortune on a baseball team…. and became one of the most flamboyant and controversial owners in major-league history.

First, Finley attempted to buy the Philadelphia A's in 1954, then he failed to purchase the Tigers, the White Sox, and the expansion Angels.

When Kansas City owner Arnold Johnson had a stroke and died after watching a spring game in March 1960, Finley targeted the A's. On December 19, 1960, he went to probate court and made a high bid of $1.975 million for a 52 percent controlling interest in the team, and he shelled out an additional $200,000 to pay debts owed by the Johnson estate. He also began to buy up the local shares of the franchise, spending $4 million to gain the A's outright.

"I'm here to stay," Finley announced on a local radio station. "This team is not moving out of Kansas City, regardless of attendance."

That, like many of Finley's statements, turned out to be far from the truth. First, he reneged on a promise to strike a clause that he could move the team if attendance dropped—a ceremony in which he lit a match to burn that clause turned out to have been faked.

Almost immediately, Finley began flirting with other municipalities. By August 1961, he was exploring Dallas as a possibility, even while calling rumblings about a move "disgusting." The list of potential targets eventually expanded to include Louisville, Seattle, Milwaukee, New Orleans, San Diego, Toronto, Montreal, Atlanta, and Denver.

"He'd been threatening to move basically since he'd been there," longtime A's broadcaster Monte Moore said. "Once when he visited Kansas City, he had a press conference and told all the people, 'Hey, all these rumors about moving, it's not going to happen, we're here to stay.' That Saturday morning, I had him on my talk show there in Kansas City and he said the same things. Then he went to the airport, flew to Louisville, and offered to move the team there."

Nevertheless, the A's remained in Kansas City for seven more seasons while Finley was running the show—emphasis on *show*. He was innovative, perhaps to an extreme. He was energetic. He was impatient. He was demanding. He was combative and at times downright unpleasant. And he was contradictory, known for sudden bursts of generosity as well as for extreme stinginess, candor one moment, lies the next.

The first sign that Finley had some different ideas came in 1963, when he introduced new uniforms. Out went the Athletics' red, white, and navy blue, and in came some decidedly nontraditional colors, which Finley gave official names, as if they were paint swatches. The "Kelly green," "Fort Knox gold," and "wedding-gown white" uniforms were considered garish at the time, particularly with their green belts, but the ensemble inspired other teams to adopt a brighter approach in the next decade, culminating in the Astros' rainbow-striped tops in 1975.

Finley became known for a range of novelties, some of which caught on—like the DH and night games—and many that didn't, such as orange baseballs and mechanical rabbits to deliver baseballs to umpires.

"A lot of people called Charlie O. crazy," said pitcher Blue Moon Odom, who has remained one of Finley's staunchest supporters. "They'd ask, 'How do you like your crazy owner?' But he was just creative. He put ideas out there, and some of them stuck."

"I'm not trying to be popular," Finley told author Bill Libby. "I'm trying to make my team and my game popular."

He might be best remembered for wacky stunts, but Finley had another trademark. He ticked off all of his managers and most of his players at one time or other—and some of his run-ins changed the team and baseball.

Managers and front-office personnel didn't have much job security with Finley around. He fired two general managers in his first nine months as owner, and he'd given the second of those, Frank Lane, an eight-year contract. Halfway through the 1961 season, he promoted Hank Bauer to replace manager Joe Gordon, who'd dared to show reporters a lineup card with changes penciled in by Finley and which Gordon had marked "approved by COF."

Bauer learned this over the loudspeakers at Municipal Stadium, according to Tom Clark's *Champagne and Baloney*.

"Hank Bauer, your playing days are over," Bauer heard the PA announcer say while he was standing in the outfield. "You have been named manager of the Kansas City A's."

Bauer quit the next fall, to be followed by Ed Lopat. Lopat lasted a year, then Mel McGaha came in for less than a season. Haywood Sullivan finished out 1965, and Alvin Dark made it through 1966 and most of 1967 before being replaced by Luke Appling.

"When a man invests $5 million in a team, he has the right to name his own manager," Finley told reporters.

Dark's firing angered the players, who briefly threatened a strike. It was reported that first baseman Ken Harrelson had called Finley "a menace to baseball," and though Harrelson told Finley he hadn't actually used the word "menace," Finley fired Harrelson outright—rather than waiving him and getting a $50,000 fee when he was claimed. Harrelson later said it was the only time Finley's temper got the better of his wallet.

The future White Sox broadcaster hooked up with Boston for $75,000 and wound up helping the Red Sox to the American League pennant. Bauer and Dark, undaunted by their experiences with Finley, would make repeat appearances as manager when the team was in Oakland.

In seven years in Kansas City, Finley employed seven managers and five general managers. The longest serving GM, Pat Friday, was one of Finley's insurance company employees; he lasted three years. And in reality, Finley was acting as the team's general manager. He turned out to have a knack for some aspects of the job, especially when it came to building the organization via the minor leagues and the new amateur draft.

Johnson hadn't invested much in developing players—the A's were busy filling that role for the Yankees, anyway. Finley ended the association with the Yankees, pronto, going so far as to burn a bus pointed toward New York in a grand symbolic gesture. Meanwhile, on a practical level, he began beefing up the minor-league operations.

He and the Athletics also benefited from the major-league draft, which began in 1965. By virtue of finishing last, Kansas City had the top pick and took outfielder Rick Monday from Arizona State; third baseman Sal Bando, another ASU product, in the sixth round; and catcher Gene Tenace in the 20th round. Monday received a $104,000 bonus, as Finley demonstrated a commitment to improving the team.

Poor seasons ensured more high picks, and Finley and his handful of baseball people exhibited savvy in their selections. Reggie Jackson was the team's choice in 1966, going second overall. The following year, the A's took a left-handed pitcher from Louisiana, Vida Blue, in the second round, even though other teams had been scared off by the possibility that Blue—a tremendous high school quarterback—might accept a football scholarship; Notre Dame, Grambling, and Houston were especially interested,

Tiny Turnouts

The nadir of the Charlie Finley era came on Tuesday, April 17, 1979, when a crowd of 653 showed up at the Coliseum for a game against the Mariners. The assembled few were grouped into two sections by security guards, and kids had to race enormous distances for foul balls.

"That crowd was so small, I could hear a guy yell from the back of the bleachers and he sounded like he was on second base," A's pitcher Mike Norris said.

The tiny gathering wasn't the smallest to see a professional baseball game in Oakland's history: In 1905, a Pacific Coast League between the Oakland Commuters and Portland drew one paid fan, prompting the umpire who was announcing the lineups to turn to the grandstand and begin, "Dear Sir...," according to Dick Dobbins' *Nuggets on the Diamond.*

The meager support at the Coliseum was noted. One columnist offered this trivia question: "On April 17, an Oakland-Seattle game drew 653 people..... Name them."

and one college coach had gone so far as to say that Blue would be the first great black quarterback.

The A's had done well with their amateur signings even before the draft came along. Under Finley, they'd signed Joe Rudi, Dave Duncan, Paul Lindblad, John "Blue Moon" Odom, and two future Hall of Famers in pitchers Roland Glen "Rollie" Fingers and James Augustus "Catfish" Hunter.

Odom and Hunter were good examples of Finley's involvement in acquiring young talent. Finley was determined to sign Odom, a star in his native Georgia—and while other clubs' scouts were at Odom's high school graduation, hoping to make a good impression, Finley went a step further. He bought groceries, went to Odom's house and cooked dinner. For that, Odom's mother urged him to sign with Finley, and he did, for $75,000. Finley signed Hunter despite a hunting accident that cost the pitcher a toe; Finley sent Hunter to the Mayo Clinic for repairs, gave him a $75,000 bonus, and had himself an ace.

When the team moved to Oakland in 1968, Finley's front office remained a bare-bones operation, and there wasn't even a real work space, per se. "When we got there, the team didn't have offices," broadcaster Monte Moore said. "It was two rooms at the Edgewater Hotel. Eventually the offices moved to a storage company down the street."

The staff was in constant flux. Finley fired some employees, while others quit on their own—one World Series opener in Oakland wasn't a sellout, for instance, because the ticket manager had resigned and hadn't been replaced.

Finley kept tabs on everything—the phone bill in the training room, the money spent on every bit of equipment. He counted bats. He lectured Reggie Jackson for giving away too many baseballs to fans and tried to charge the outfielder for them.

"Anything Finley did was a direct reflection of his pocketbook," longtime equipment manager Steve Vucinich said.

And yet Finley could show unexpected generosity; outfielder George Hendrick said that Finley paid for his mother's funeral in 1971 and did so with no fanfare, then still paid Hendrick a scheduled bonus. "He was a very hard businessman, but always very fair to me," Hendrick said.

Jackson—among the most vocal critics of Finley's cheapness—bashed the owner for the team's budget travel (they never had non-stop flights), for terrible tickets for players' families (in the upper deck) and for his insignificant pay raises. Throughout his entire time in Oakland, Jackson said in his biography, *Reggie,* the clubhouse was uncarpeted because Finley wouldn't splurge on the players' comfort. The experience left an impression: Jackson recalled being horrified after leaving the A's to discover that on other teams, players sometimes used half a roll of athletic tape—and threw the rest away.

Jackson acknowledged that Finley's penny-pinching made the A's that much tougher. They were a little rag-tag band, making do

with the bare minimum, with an ethos of us-against-the-world...
and sometimes against the owner; Blue and Jackson were among
those who engaged in holdouts during the Oakland years.

And Finley always had a wandering eye. After the 1972 season,
disappointed that only 400 additional season tickets had been sold,
he considered a move to Seattle, New Orleans, or Toronto. Not
even a championship could bring stability to Finley's franchise.

Finley never stopped being cheap. Employees complained they
had to get permission to get paper clips. Turnover remained high.
In 1973, Finley went through three ticket managers, two traveling
secretaries, two public relations men, two comptrollers, and eight
receptionists.

"It was a staff of seven people, the entire office," PR man Bob
Fulton said. "We'd even have to man the gates when there were
giveaways. Finley didn't want anyone getting extra bats or balls."

"The traveling secretary and the equipment manager had to
do everything," said Don Baylor, who arrived in 1976. "There
was really no office at all. Midway through the season, I was in the
stands, looking for the team offices and I ran into Chuck Tanner,
the manager. I said, 'I'm trying to find the office,' and he said, 'I'm
trying to find the office myself.'"

Contracts were always protracted disputes, and players learned
to be creative.

"One year, I was making $10,000 and I wanted $18,000,"
Bando said. "Finley was at $17,000 and I'd just gotten married so I
said, 'Charlie, we're trying to buy bedroom furniture.' Charlie said,
'Okay, I'm going to give you $18,000—but you've got to carve my
name in the headboard.'

"When we were in New York for the 1973 World Series, I'd
had gotten some extra tickets from him. People wanted to buy
them, but I was only selling them for what they cost. Charlie called
me and said, 'Sal, are you scalping those tickets? If you are, I want
half.'"

The core group of players sickened of the bickering. After the 1973 season, nine of them took Finley to arbitration, with five winning.

Finley, angry at players he felt were "ungrateful," skimped on the World Series rings after the 1973 and 1974 titles.

"I guess we were winning too many World Series," Odom said. "The rings were getting less gaudy. We got cracker box rings."

And then Finley, unhappy with the advent of free agency and rising contracts, began to break up the team. After the Red Sox swept Oakland in the 1975 ALCS, the A's dynasty—the third in franchise history—was over. Finley fired manager Alvin Dark and hired Tanner.

Not surprisingly, several players, including Bando, Campy Campaneris, Rudi, Tenace, and Fingers, decided they wouldn't sign deals for 1976, making them free agents after the year.

"One time, Rollie and I were walking down the tunnel to shag flies, and back then, to become a free agent, you had to give up [15 percent] of your previous year's salary," Vida Blue recalled. "So Rollie said, 'Another day, another 85th of a dollar.'"

On April 2, 1976, Finley traded Jackson, the team's biggest star, and starter Ken Holtzman to Baltimore for Baylor and two other players.

"Charlie called once to ask me, 'How do you pitch to Don Baylor? And by the way, he's just become your teammate. One Reginald Martinez Jackson is now a member of the Baltimore Orioles,'" Blue recalled. "Charlie would sell his grandmother for the right price. He was a combination of Ted Turner and George Steinbrenner."

With his stars scattered all over baseball, Finley's fortunes sank, and so did the A's. They finished last in 1977, second-to-last in 1978, and last again in 1979, when they lost 108 games. Finley went through three more managers. Or was it four? Bobby Winkles replaced Jack McKeon during the 1977 season, and when Winkles resigned the following year, McKeon replaced him.

"Bobby Winkles finally couldn't take it anymore, Charlie calling all the time at 4:00 AM after a tough night game," said Larry Baer, a team broadcaster in 1978. "So Jack McKeon went from third base to the manager, and the first-base coach became the third-base coach.

"But Charlie didn't want to bring anyone additional on, so he told Bobby Hofman, the traveling secretary, to do it. Bobby's making reservations and lining up buses—and all of a sudden, he's also coaching first."

With the A's struggling, Finley's cost-cutting grew more extreme.

"One day at the Coliseum, all of a sudden it was quieter than usual," Baer said. "We looked around, and three booths over, the organist was packing up his stuff and leaving. Someone went over to see what was going on, and he said, 'Mr. Finley just called and fired me.'

"That was in the middle of the game—in the second inning, there was music, in the third inning, none. Finley told him, 'I've got expenses I've got to trim. And I'm not paying you for the whole game, either.'"

Though it was no secret that Charlie Finley had considered selling the A's dozens of times—he twice had deals in place that would have moved the franchise to Denver—when he finally completed a $12.7 million sale with Walter Haas before the 1981 season, the transaction was hush-hush.

"Charlie was so completely unpredictable, and when we made the offer, we didn't want him to shop it around, because that was his MO," said Haas' son, Wally. "So the last week of negotiations, my job was to babysit Charlie. We told him, 'Charlie, if this deal remains a secret until the press conference, we'll take you to dinner the night before.' So what, right? But to him, that was a big deal.

"We couldn't figure out where to take this guy because we couldn't be seen with him before the announcement and everywhere he goes, it's like a billboard—he wants to be recognized."

Finally, Walter Haas settled on a private club in San Francisco as the safest bet.

"We get there and there's no one there, and I think, 'Oh, no, he's going to think we brought him someplace unpopular,'" Wally Haas recalled, chuckling. "But Charlie said, 'You two guys have more class than I thought. You bought out the entire restaurant for me.'

"I spent the rest of the night looking at the door every 10 minutes, hoping no one else would come in. No one did and the deal was announced the next day."

The new owners were stunned by the state of the A's offices after years of Finley's cheap ways. For one thing, the phone system was an outdated switchboard.

"It was one of those old-fashioned ones where you pull out one line, put in another one, like in a comedy show," Wally Haas said. "It literally blew up one day. We'd won 11 in a row to start the season, a Hollywood start, and the Yankees were coming to town. The switchboard went up in smoke, it just couldn't take it."

Other areas were just as obsolete. There was no computer system for ticket orders—just 81 drawers, one for each home game.

"You hear those stories about not selling out home games during the World Series with Finley? Now I understand it," Haas said. "As part of pulling my chin off the floor as we walked around the place, I remember going into Finley's office and seeing two of the three World Series trophies gathering dust as bookends."

The other championship trophy was being used to sort mail.

Finley died in Chicago in 1996, and despite his three championships, numerous innovations, and remarkably colorful ownership, he is not in the Hall of Fame, although the Veterans Committee considered him as recently as 2011.

"Charlie Finley should be in the Hall of Fame, absolutely," Hendrick said. "All those great teams, this guy drafted and signed all those guys himself, even if it was because he wasn't going to pay scouts.

"And the talent he found, the talent we had, had he decided to pay those players, we'd have won every World Series in the '70s, that whole decade. You looked around the league 10 years later, all of his players were everywhere, still stars. It was truly amazing. He was truly amazing."

3 Connie Mack

Cornelius Alexander McGillicuddy was born in East Brookfield, Massachusetts, on December 22, 1862, during the Civil War. Neighbors referred to the family as the Macks, and the shortened version was affixed to young Connie when he took up baseball because his full name wouldn't fit in a box score.

Mack's father, an Irish immigrant who'd fought for the Union army, was a wheelwright by profession, but he was often out of work, and the family was poor. Starting at the age of nine, Mack worked 12-hour days in a cotton mill during the summer for 35 cents a days. Later, he moved to a shoe factory, where he quickly became assistant foreman. He lost the position seven years later, and that's when he took a $90 a month job playing for Meriden of the Connecticut State League.

It was against his mother's wishes; Mary McGillicuddy worried that her boy would take to drinking and fighting. He promised her he would not.

"There's room for a gentleman in every profession," Mack said later, "and my profession is baseball."

The tall, thin catcher (his nickname during his playing days was "Slats") worked well with another lanky sort, pitcher Frank Gilmore, and when Washington came calling for Gilmore, he insisted on bringing his catcher along.

So at 23, Mack was in the National League, where he was noted for his ability to distract batters with his chatter and other tricks, such as faking foul tips. He was never a great hitter, however, and when he broke his ankle in a home-plate collision with Boston's Herman Long in 1893, the end of his playing career was near. He became Pittsburgh's manager on September 3, 1894, and was known there for freezing baseballs to deaden them. Famous for his polished manners, Mack incurred the only ejection in his managerial career when he was tossed from a game in 1895 while with the Pirates.

In 1897, he moved on to Milwaukee in the Western League before agreeing to take on the fledgling Athletics in 1901.

He held that post until October 18, 1950, when he was almost 89.

Mack remained a stockholder until the team was sold in 1954. He received $604,000 for his 302 shares in the club and he died less than two years later, on February 8, 1956, in Philadelphia.

Mack was beloved by his players, who found him fatherly and courteous and who referred to him as "Mr. Mack" long after they had retired. He generally did not call his players by their nicknames or last names—he used Chief Bender's given name, Albert, for example. He called Rube Waddell "Eddie," which Waddell preferred.

"He always had troubles with names, anyway," recalled outfielder Gus Zernial, who was with the A's in the early '50s. "When we played the Yankees, they had Phil Rizutto at shortstop and Joe

DiMaggio in center field, and he'd go down the lineup and say, 'This fellow Dah-mahg-eye-ee," or "Rizz-oo-tu.'"

Mack seldom swore and he did not drink. He preferred that his players avoid profanity and alcohol, too, though his A's teams wound up featuring some notorious boozers. Many credit Mack for elevating the sport from one that was considered rough and uncouth, full of gamblers and carousers, to a more dignified activity—the national pastime.

"In my opinion, Connie Mack did more for baseball than any other living human being—by the example he set, his attitude, the way he handled himself, and his players," Rube Bressler said in Lawrence Ritter's *The Glory of Their Times*. "You know, like you're playing a great game and you're heroes to the children of this country. Live up to it, conduct yourself accordingly."

Mack's signature was his natty attire: a dark three-piece business suit and hat, straw in the summer and a fedora in the cooler months. Early in his managerial career, he had worn a uniform, but he began showing up on the bench in his high-collared clothes, waving his rolled-up scorecard to position infielders. Without a uniform, he could not step on the field of play during a contest.

Like Mack's suit, the scorecard drew lots of comments. Some players, such as Hall of Famer Al Simmons, swore Mack wasn't indicating anything at all with the scorecard, but merely was fanning himself.

Ty Cobb refuted that. According to Leonard Koppett's *Man in the Dugout,* one day Mack started moving Cobb over in right, then moved him a bit more, more, more—and the veteran, though reluctant, followed instructions.

When the batter hit it right to him, Cobb didn't have to move an inch. He got back to the dugout and said to Mack, "I've heard a lot about your scorecard, and from now on, I'm going to believe it."

Mack put together two of baseball's greatest dynasties, the 1910–14 A's—who won three championships—and the 1929–31 team, which is considered one of the best clubs of all time. Mack had to break up both dynasties, though, because he was unable to continue paying his superstars, a trend that would continue with the Oakland A's 1970s championship teams and right into the present day.

After losing to the Cardinals in the 1931 World Series, the A's finished near or at the bottom of the league for the next nine seasons, and they never again got higher than fourth while in Philadelphia. From 1935 to 1954, they had six seasons in which they lost 100 games or more.

There was speculation after the 1934 season that Mack would step down. His club had been disbanded, again, and he was 72 years old. He was a principal owner, he easily could have retired and let others handle the daily work.

He stayed on for 16 more years, however. His family was involved in every aspect of the team, and he enjoyed what he was doing, so leaving the game wasn't an issue. It wasn't until after the 1950 season that Mack retired, at the age of 88, although by that point, the coaches and players themselves were doing most of the managing. Mack's successor was one of his favorite former players, Jimmy Dykes.

That same year, 1950, Mack's sons, Roy and Earle, maneuvered to get 52 percent of the club—a transaction that would eventually drive the A's out of Philadelphia.

Most of Mack's players had an anecdote or two about him—often revolving around salary issues, not surprising for a man who once took only two pitchers to a one-game series at Cleveland in order to save train fare.

First baseman Lou Limmer, who signed with the A's after a tryout, recalled in late 2006 that when discussing terms with Mack, he had mentioned some of the other salaries recently signed. Robin Roberts had received a $10,000 bonus from the Phillies, for instance.

"No sooner did I say that than Mr. Mack grabs his heart, has palpitations," Limmer said. "I was scared. I thought he'd die. So he signed me for $200 and didn't even give me the bus fare home.

"A Giants scout told me, 'Oh, gee, I'm sorry, we would have given you $1,000.' I got back home and my mother said, 'You stupido!'"

Limmer also recalled second baseman Pete Suder's unsuccessful negotiations after the 1952 season, when Mack used a line he hauled out for some other players as well.

"Suder went to ask Mr. Mack for a raise," Limmer said, "and Mr. Mack said, 'Mr. Suder, do you remember what place we ended up?'

"Suder said, 'Last.'

"Mr. Mack said, 'Well, we finished last with you, we'll finish last without you.'"

Mack's sons took a similar tack: Gus Zernial led the league in homers in 1951, with 33. When he hit 29 the next year, his pay was cut.

"I said, 'Why'd you cut my salary?'" Zernial remembered. "Earle Mack said, 'Well, you didn't hit as many home runs.'"

Shortstop Eddie Joost had his own versions of tales often told about Mack.

"In 1947, I'd come over from the National League and Bob Feller was pitching against us," Joost said. "About the eighth inning, I was coming up for my fourth time, and Mr. Mack called me back and said, 'What did you do your first three times?' I said, 'Well, Mr. Mack, he's struck me out three times.'

"He said, 'I tell you what, I don't want you to set any record, I'll take you out for a pinch hitter.'"

Another well-known story involves fiery first baseman Ferris Fain, who played for Philadelphia at the end of Mack's tenure.

"Fain had a bunt play he would do, where he'd sneak in and really get in there, 10 feet away from the batter, and man, did he have a great arm," Joost said. "But the first time he did it, his throw sailed into left field and two or three runs scored."

The next game, at Detroit, Joost was holding a runner at second when he saw Fain creeping in toward the batter again.

"Don't you know, he fires it into left field again and they score three or four unearned runs after that and we lose the ballgame," Joost said. "After the inning, Mr. Mack stood up and said, 'Boy, come here.'—He called all of us boy—'I just want to let you know, I don't think that's a very good play. Every time you do that, you throw it into left field. I don't think you should do that again.'

"Ferris said, 'What do you want me to do, stick it?'

"And Mr. Mack said, 'I think that would be the safest place for it.'"

In 1953, Shibe Park was renamed Connie Mack Stadium, but by then, the Phillies were the hot ticket in town and Mack's sons had run the team into the ground. They often feuded with each other and other relatives and they had mortgaged the team heavily.

"The owners were in dire straits financially, and there were so many people living off the team that there was no money to put back into it," Joost said. "I knew it was a bad situation, we all did."

Joost, who managed the team in 1954, realized how severe the problems were that spring when he got a call that the team couldn't meet its payroll. He had to contact a team lawyer to get things settled and keep the club afloat, but, Joost concluded, "It just wasn't going to work."

Joost was unhappy when a trade he'd attempted to swing with the Yankees fell through—and then Roy Mack orchestrated a much worse deal, in which Philadelphia took on a lot of the Yankees' dead weight, saddling the manager with a bunch of players he had little use for. The A's finished in last again that year, scoring the fewest runs in the league.

"We were a disaster," Zernial remembered.

Making this worse, the Phillies were enjoying a good run, and the hometown fans turned on the Athletics. One day in 1954, Zernial tripped over a sprinkler that had not been covered, breaking his shoulder—and as he lay on the field, the fans booed and heckled the team's most popular player.

When his sons sold the team after that season, Mack collapsed and his blood pressure dropped; he recovered but required hip surgery after a fall the following year. He died on February 8, 1956, at the age of 93, and commissioner Ford Frick, both league presidents, all 16 team owners, both Pennsylvania senators, the governors of Pennsylvania and Missouri, and the mayors of Philadelphia, Pittsburgh, and Kansas City served as pallbearers, along with Grace Kelly's father, John B. Kelly, a longtime friend of Mack's.

In his remarkable tenure, "the Tall Tactician" won more games (3,731) and lost more (3,948) than anyone in baseball history. He was elected to the Hall of Fame in 1937, while he was still managing.

His teams won nine American League pennants and five World Series.

They also finished last 17 times.

"Mr. Mack was always a wonderful gentleman, that's fair to say," Joost said. "I never saw him get flustered. The last couple of years, he wasn't the manager, he was just sitting on the bench, so the entire ballclub was running things, really, but all in all, it was just a pleasure to play for that man, a real treat to know him. He had patience beyond belief, but if someone wasn't doing their job, he'd tell them what he thought.

"He was such a great person and all the people around him appreciated that fact. The history of the Athletics is Mr. Mack."

4 Billy Beane

As the 1990s came to a close, a major figure emerged who hearkened back to those other brilliant architects of great Athletics teams: Like Connie Mack and Charlie Finley, Billy Beane had to tear things down, build the club back up, and do so with smarts and with limited finances.

He did so not by looking back, but by looking ahead—way, way ahead—and in the process, Billy Beane and his front office helped change the way all baseball teams operate.

Beane was, at one time, a terrific outfield prospect, a first-round pick by the Mets, but he hadn't been able to stick as an everyday player in the major leagues, including a stint with the A's. Despite his lack of success on the field, he made a strong impression with his intelligence. When Beane decided his playing days were over, the A's were quick to find a way to keep him around.

"Billy played on that World Series team in 1989 and then he jumped on an incredible fast track," former owner Wally Haas said. "He clearly could have played a few more years, but he realized he wasn't as good as he wanted to be. We made him an advance scout and he ascended so quickly—what a talent."

"To his credit, when the advance scouting position opened up, Billy jumped at it," said former A's general manager Sandy Alderson, who eventually made Beane his right-hand man. "With his background, he knew his stuff. He was a natural. Over time, it became clear how smart and how enthusiastic he was about the game, and Billy learned very quickly.

"He adopted the quantitative approach we'd been using and understood what it was all about. At that point, the only question was if we could hold on to him in Oakland."

When Alderson stepped down after the 1997 season, the 35-year-old Beane took over. The Moneyball period of A's history had begun.

As detailed in Michael Lewis' bestselling book *Moneyball: The Art of Winning an Unfair Game*, Beane took much of what Alderson had done in using quantitative analysis (including some theories espoused by statistics expert Bill James) and applied those principals to developing a contender despite the club's limited means.

Financial constraints meant that Beane had to exploit any market discrepancies he could find, often by employing statistical information and computer analysis. If other teams were overpaying for power, the A's would focus elsewhere, say, on high on-base percentage or defensive ability. And with a small budget, Beane needed to reduce risk: For some time, one avenue the club took to do so was to draft college pitchers. That led to the Big Three of Tim Hudson, Mark Mulder, and Barry Zito.

The so-called Moneyball philosophy was not, as some believe, about placing a premium on on-base percentage or OPS, or any other stat. It was about reacting to the market to find bargains and taking advantage of other clubs' spending patterns.

"We were just trying to find a way of doing things in a difficult situation, in a two-team market and with a lower payroll," Beane said. "We were trying to find a way to compete. Ultimately, what we were trying to figure out was what other teams weren't paying for, trying to exploit market inefficiencies. We never felt we needed to explain ourselves."

In 2011, *Moneyball* was turned into a successful feature film starring Brad Pitt as Beane.

"Billy is very, very smart, very competitive; he has a commanding presence and he is so charismatic—he's got everything," one-time A's first baseman Scott Hatteberg said. "My God, Brad Pitt played him—what more can you say?"

Under Beane and the most diverse front office in baseball, the A's made the playoffs eight times in a 15-year span through 2014, despite puny payrolls, with the team often near the bottom of the league in spending. Beane, who now owns a small percentage of the team, twice has been named the Major League Executive of the Year by the *Sporting News* and he has won similar honors twice from Baseball America.

"Billy and the rest of the front office, they changed the game, they really did," former A's third baseman Eric Chavez said. "All the things that everyone does now, they were at the forefront of it way back when."

5 The First of Three: 1972

With Vida Blue tearing up the league and Sal Bando turning in a career year, the A's went 101–60 in 1971, winning the AL West by 16 games over Kansas City. The Athletics were back in the postseason for the first time in 40 years, since Connie Mack's great 1931 club lost a terrific World Series to St. Louis.

This time, the A's bowed out quickly, falling to pitching-rich Baltimore in a three-game sweep. Still, the 1972 season looked promising after such a terrific 1971 campaign—and then Blue, the reigning MVP and Cy Young winner, held out well past Opening Day.

There was little argument that Blue was underpaid, considering his accomplishments. Still, he and owner Charlie Finley were far apart on terms, and when Blue introduced an agent, Bob Gerst, into the equation, it hardened Finley's stance; he hated agents and always wanted to deal with players directly.

"I lived with Tommy Davis at 10th and Adeline and he introduced me to his attorney," Blue said. "I was one of the first players to get an attorney to represent myself, and Charlie Finley took offense to it."

Finley, who according to Ron Bergman's *Mustache Gang*, promised Catfish Hunter that Blue wouldn't make more than the $50,000 Hunter was getting that season, initially offered $45,000; Gerst countered with a request for $115,000. Finley went up to $50,000—and stayed there, despite Gerst's assertions that one in every 12 major-league tickets purchased the year before was for a game Blue started. Forty three percent of the A's total home and road attendance came with Blue on the mound.

Gerst requested a sale or trade if Finley didn't accede and Blue went home to Louisiana while negotiations dragged on.

One month into spring training, Blue announced at a press conference in Oakland that he was retiring from baseball after being hired as a vice president for a toilet fixtures firm called Dura Steel Products, which led *Sports Illustrated* to dub the affair "a bathroom farce." Blue went so far as to go to work in Santa Fe Springs, a town between Los Angeles and Anaheim.

"Since Mr. Finley was playing hardball, the attorney introduced me to the president of Dura Steel," Blue recalled. "I went behind a desk and made some calls for them for about a week."

Finley sent Gene Tenace, who was often Blue's catcher, to smooth things over.

"Gene Tenace and I came to the big leagues at the same time and we were close. So he takes a cab from LAX all the way to near Knott's Berry Farm to talk to me," Blue said. "And I said, 'With all due respect, [take a flying leap]. I've got to take care of myself.' I was trying to be nice, because he came all that way and I know he wanted to help get the thing done."

With Blue missing from camp, the A's traded for veteran Denny McLain, who was on his last legs. Further complicating things was baseball's first labor stoppage, a 13-day strike over the players' pension that Finley helped to resolve.

The season finally got underway on April 15. The A's lost seven games to the strike, and even with the delay, Blue wasn't back yet.

Oakland's attendance dipped to an average of 6,000 per game. Fans clamored for Blue's return, even in visiting parks, where the team bus was met with shouts of "We want Vida!" No less than the President weighed in; when asked by a reporter his take on the situation, Richard Nixon replied, "Blue has got so much talent, maybe Finley ought to pay."

The impasse didn't make the commissioner—Finley's archenemy, Bowie Kuhn—very happy, and he summoned all parties for a stormy meeting in Chicago on April 27. A compromise followed: Finley stuck to his $50,000 offer but included a $5,000 bonus plus $8,000, the estimated value of a college scholarship stipulation in Blue's original contract in the event he ever wanted to get a degree.

Finley blasted Kuhn for meddling and he was fined $500 for denigrating the commissioner. Blue, now a major celebrity, announced he'd accepted the offer on Howard Cosell's national TV show and he officially signed the deal on May 2.

Before the season, Blue had been able to joke about his low wages in a comic exchange on Bob Hope's USO tour.

"How come you weren't paid more money for pitching?" Hope asked.

"Mr. Finley pointed out I only used one arm," Blue responded.

Hope: "If you don't get a big raise, will you keep pitching?"

Blue: "Sure—with my right arm."

Blue was soured by the experience, though. Asked about the contract issue when he rejoined the team, he said, "The first two games I pitch, he's got his money back. I'm not happy, but I signed."

Without any spring training, Blue was placed on the inactive list until he was in shape, a process that took three weeks. A lengthy holdout hadn't helped Reggie Jackson in 1971 and Blue would be no different: He went 6–10 and his ERA rose from 1971's 1.82 to 2.80.

"I believe Vida would have kept going like [1971] if he hadn't held out the next year," Bando said. "He was still a dominant pitcher, but he really was never the same again."

Several other things had gone on besides Blue's holdout, though none with the same kind of national cache. Over the winter, Finley had traded former No. 1 draft pick Rick Monday to the Cubs in exchange for left-hander Ken Holtzman, and during the season, he'd made deals to bring in two veterans, Orlando Cepeda and Matty Alou.

Also before the start of the season, steady second baseman Dick Green announced his retirement—for the fourth season in a row. He again changed his mind.

Meanwhile, mustaches had become the norm in Oakland and the young club took on a slight air of rebellion. The A's also were making quick work of their division: They reeled off 33 wins in their first 46 games and led the AL West by five games on June 10.

But by late August, with Jackson out of the lineup with a muscle strain incurred in an on-field fracas and Green absent much of the year with a back problem, the White Sox had overtaken Oakland. The A's dropped an eight-game lead in just three weeks and Dick Williams' job was rumored to be in jeopardy.

Finley, never predictable, offered Williams a two-year extension at that point, and he accepted.

A couple of five-game winning streaks pushed Oakland's advantage back to five games. They officially clinched the title on September 28 by beating Minnesota 8–7 with a run in the bottom of the ninth.

In August, when Green briefly returned from the disabled list, Williams—acting at Finley's request—began to do something unheard of. Back in 1969, Finley had suggested using four catchers per game, pinch hitting each time one of them came up. Now he wanted Williams to follow that same plan, but with the club's second basemen. Williams' job security wasn't the best at the time, and he agreed.

"It was Charlie's idea, and I had to go along with it," Williams said 35 years later.

As a result, the A's used 11 different players at second—even Sal Bando and Gene Tenace made brief appearances there late in games when Williams ran out of other options.

None of the participants liked the idea. At one point, veteran Dal Maxvill, added late in the season, started five straight games and he didn't hit in any of them.

On September 19 against the second-place White Sox, the second-base rotation was especially notable. The game went into extra innings, and all four regular second basemen had played in the field but had not hit. Tenace took over at second in the 10th and when he failed to cover first base on a bunt play, Chicago scored twice. Oakland tied it up again however—and with Tenace moving to right (instead of pinch runner Catfish Hunter), third-string catcher Larry Haney had to man second base.

It was the first time in major-league history a team had used six second basemen. By the end of the game, when Ken Holtzman pinch hit, Williams had used all 30 men at his disposal, another record. The A's lost, 8–7.

The second-base ploy would continue, however. And it nearly cost Oakland big in Game 4 of the ALCS against Detroit when, with the score tied 1–1 with two out in the seventh, Williams pinch hit for defensive whiz Green.

Already missing a major part of the infield in Campy Campaneris, who'd been suspended, Williams now was out of second basemen because he'd used three of them to fill in at short as the game wore on. Tenace was sent out to second base for the bottom of the seventh.

In the 10th, Oakland took a 3–1 lead and looked ready to claim the pennant. But in the bottom of the inning, Detroit loaded the bases, and when catcher Bill Freehan hit a bouncer to third, Bando went to second for the double play rather than throwing home for the force. Tenace dropped Bando's low throw, and one run scored on the error. (Afterward Tenace said, "Was it a difficult play? It was for me.") Norm Cash walked to tie the game, and Jim Northrup singled in the winning run.

"The rotating second basemen nearly cost us a chance to go to the World Series," Williams said. "I had to put Gene Tenace out there. It wasn't too good of an idea."

The A's went on to beat the Tigers 2–1 in Game 5 of a chaotic series that featured Campaneris' bat-tossing incident, fans storming the field, fights in the A's clubhouse, and a bomb threat.

Compared to the Detroit series, the A's first World Series appearance in more than 40 years was expected to be a sedate affair. Sparky Anderson's Reds were so clean-cut compared to the shaggy A's that the series was referred to by some as "The Hairs vs. the Squares."

The series went the distance and was dominated by pitching— especially by the A's Hunter, Holtzman, and closer Rollie Fingers. Oakland remained without Jackson, sidelined by his hamstring tear, but Campaneris had been reinstated. Commissioner Kuhn announced that he would suspend Campaneris without pay for the first week of the following season rather than to punish his teammates by holding the shortstop out of the World Series.

The A's offensive star, however, was a surprise: Tenace, 1-for-17 in the ALCS, became the first man ever to homer in his first two World Series at-bats, and he drove in all of his team's runs in a 3–2 Game 1 victory. He also called for a pitchout in the seventh and threw out Dave Concepcion at second base, a call the Reds disputed vehemently and that Anderson called the turning point of the game.

Finley gave Tenace a $5,000 bonus afterward, calling it a retroactive raise. Tenace hadn't hit two homers in the same game once during the regular season.

There was another Oakland hero in Game 2. Joe Rudi hit a homer in the third inning, then in the ninth, with the A's up 2–0 and a man at first, he made an unforgettable catch in left, turning and dashing for a deep drive by Denis Menke. He jumped and slammed into the fence, still facing away from the plate, and he back-handed the ball while fully stretched out—one of the most famous plays in World Series history. Williams called it the greatest catch he'd ever seen. Rudi said it was the exact same catch he'd perfected while working with Hall of Famer Joe DiMaggio.

"I was in center field, coming over to back it up, and I said, 'Wow! Wow!' It was pretty impressive," outfielder George Hendrick said. "But then so was Joe. So you expected it from him. Probably the most fundamentally sound player I've ever seen."

First baseman Mike Hegan recorded the second out with another terrific play, a diving stop of a low liner by Cesar Geronimo, and Fingers took over from Hunter for the final out, getting Julian Javier to pop up foul to Hegan. On the flight back to Oakland, Finley gave out more "raises," to Rudi, Hegan, and Williams. An estimated 8,000 fans met the team plane at the airport.

Stung by Blue's comment that the A's were handling the Reds more easily than they had the Texas Rangers (who'd finished 38-½ games out that year), Cincinnati came out and took Game 3, 1–0. Oakland still provided the best highlight, though: With a man at second and a 3–2 count on dangerous Johnny Bench, Dick Williams went to the mound, and everyone expected that Fingers would issue an intentional walk.

Tenace stuck out his glove as if that's what was coming—and Fingers uncorked a perfect slider down the middle to strike out the Reds catcher. Fingers called it the best slider he'd ever thrown.

"Why me?" Bench asked reporters with a laugh.

"Bench said he couldn't have hit it even if he'd known it was coming," A's TV announcer Monte Moore said.

Tenace homered again in Game 4, and, with the Reds leading 2–1, he singled in the bottom of the ninth to put two on for pinch hitter Don Mincher, who drove in Allan Lewis with the tying run. Another pinch hitter, Angel Mangual, bounced a single past Joe Morgan with the infield in, and Tenace came in with the winning run.

In Game 5, Tenace smacked a three-run homer, joining a select list of men to homer four times in the same World Series (Babe Ruth, Lou Gehrig, Duke Snider, and Hank Bauer).

Pete Rose gave the Reds a 5–4 lead with an RBI single in the ninth off Fingers, who had pitched in every game of the series, but Tenace walked to lead off the bottom of the inning and pinch runner Blue Moon Odom went to third on a base hit by Dave Duncan. With one out, Campaneris hit a foul pop down the first-base line, and Odom took off for home, figuring second baseman Joe Morgan would have his momentum going the other way and also would be contending with turf slick from recent rain. Morgan slipped, but he still managed to get off a throw, and Bench did the rest, blocking the plate and swiping Odom with the tag to end the game.

Odom, who protested so strongly he was fined $500, hasn't changed his stance at all.

"I still think I was safe," he said in 2007. "A bunch of people think I was safe. Morgan had to go to his left, and he made a perfect throw, but I still think I was in there. I'm always going to think that."

Game 6, an 8–1 Reds win in Cincinnati, had little drama, but it did even things up.

The day of the big finale started off when a woman in line at the ticket booth overheard a man say, "If Tenace hits another homer, he won't walk out of this ballpark." Police were alerted, and the man, who was carrying a loaded gun, was apprehended outside the stadium.

Jackson joked to Tenace, "Well, Geno, if you've got to go, at least it will be on national TV."

Because of continued concern over Tenace's safety, the team bus was escorted to the stadium by unmarked FBI vehicles, with two FBI agents on board the bus, too.

The belief at that point was that the Reds had momentum in their favor. Williams moved Tenace up to the cleanup spot and put him at first base to take away the extra stress of catching. Tenace drove in the first run with an RBI bouncer over third, and with the game tied in the sixth, he connected on a two-out double to drive in Campaneris. Williams gambled by taking out Tenace for pinch-runner Lewis at that point, and Bando followed by doubling home Lewis.

In the eighth, with Rose at third, Morgan at second, and one out, Williams went against the grain by ordering Bench—the potential go-ahead run—walked intentionally. Rose scored on a sacrifice fly, and after Bench stole second, Fingers got Menke to fly to left on a 3–2 pitch. Duncan talked Williams into leaving Fingers in with two out and a man on in the ninth, and Fingers managed to get Rose to fly out to Rudi in left.

The A's were world champions, and Williams and Finley were spotted on the roof of the dugout, kissing their wives. Tenace was an easy choice as MVP, and there was another star, albeit one who was virtually unknown: Scout Al Hollingsworth had provided such a detailed breakdown of the Reds and their predilections that the A's often anticipated their moves, especially when it came to situational hitting and the running game.

Finley, in one of his rare bursts of generosity, sprang for $1,500 World Series rings for his players, complete with one-carat diamonds, and he even included a half-carat diamond for the players' wives.

It was the first championship of any kind for a major professional sports franchise in Northern California. Oakland mayor John Reading, who'd received 50 condolence letters from citizens of Kansas City when the A's moved west, gleefully announced that he'd sent all those letters back to the mayor of Kansas City the day the A's won the title.

Reggie Jackson

Reginald Martinez Jackson, a complicated superstar, wasn't always liked by his teammates. They always loved having him at the plate, though.

"I don't care what you say about Reggie, none of us would be standing here right now if it wasn't for him," outfielder Billy North said during the 40th anniversary of the 1974 championship team.

While waving his World Series ring, North added, "See this? We wouldn't have this without him. All the moaning my teammates do about Reggie? I tell you this, when everyone was watching, he was the biggest hitter I ever saw. When they had all the cameras on, the biggest hitter for the moment I ever saw. He loved the limelight. He relished it."

Jackson was a first-round pick in 1966, second overall, out of Arizona State, a school he attended on a football scholarship despite a devastating high-school tackling injury that had left him in traction for six weeks, uncertain if he'd walk again.

He first made his presence felt in 1969, going on a homer tear that included a memorable blast at Kansas City. The drive nearly cleared the scoreboard, and Jackson said it would have gone 700 feet if the scoreboard hadn't been there. On June 14, he had an astonishing day at Fenway Park, driving in 10 runs with five hits, including two more homers, in Oakland's 21–7 victory. Afterward, he received one of the rarest of baseball tributes: His teammates gave Jackson a standing ovation when he walked into the clubhouse.

On July 2, the 23-year-old outfielder banged three homers against Seattle at the Coliseum. The A's were in first place, and Jackson's 33 home runs led all of baseball. Jackson was 23 games ahead of Babe Ruth's 60-homer pace in 1927 and 10 games ahead of Roger Maris' 61 in 1961. He referred to the targets he was chasing as a mythical lady named "Ruth Maris." He was the talk of baseball, not something Jackson ever shied away from. So many reporters were following him at one point, the team tried to limit access to him, especially when he started to get calls in the middle of the night.

Pitchers began working him way inside and Jackson was hit often enough that owner Charlie Finley complained in a letter to umpire supervisor Cal Hubbard that it was a "criminal attack." Jackson was walked with increasing frequency, and he was wearing down in just his second full season. Jackson hit five homers in August, then missed nine days in September because of a rash (possibly stress related, although Jackson said it was a reaction to a flu shot) that required hospitalization. He managed two homers in September, and Harmon Killebrew passed him for the home run title, with 49. Frank Howard hit 48 and Jackson 47.

"I just died in September," Jackson told Mike Lupica in *Reggie*. "I was a wreck by the time the season was over, tired and beat up."

His salary more than doubled, to $45,000, but it was a bitter fight to get to that point—Jackson held out until April 2, and his 1970 season suffered with no spring training. He hit .237 with 23 homers, and Finley cut his salary.

In 1971, Jackson made headlines again, clobbering a homer off a light tower at Tiger Stadium during the All-Star Game at Detroit, the longest homer in All-Star Game history. Howard, one of the top sluggers of the day, estimated that the ball would have gone 600 feet.

In 1972, the A's played in the postseason for the second year in a row, and this time, they advanced to the World Series by beating the Tigers, with Jackson stealing home in the second inning of the decisive Game 5 to tie it 1–1; Oakland went on to a 2–1 victory. Jackson tore his hamstring on the play, knocking him out of the World Series.

The A's took that series against the Reds in seven games, but Jackson, sidelined the entire time, was the forgotten man—by all

Charlie Finley hugs Reggie Jackson and Dick Green after the A's won the 1973 American League Championship Series. (AP Photo)

but Johnny Bench, Cincinnati's top player. Before the series began, Bench told the A's star he wished Jackson could play so the Reds would be playing Oakland at its best, a sentiment that Jackson appreciated greatly. Then, according to Jackson's autobiography, Bench asked him what his plans were that night. Jackson said he'd probably just watch TV in his hotel room, and Bench responded that that just would not do.

"This is my town," Bench said. "You're coming to dinner with me."

Jackson said he never forgot that kindness. And when the series was over, and Jackson stood leaning on his crutches in the A's dugout, it was Bench who came over again, this time to offer both congratulations and commiseration.

Jackson swore that would never happen if his team made it back to the playoffs. Glory would not elude him again. Not only did he keep that promise to himself, but Jackson also became known as one of the best postseason performers in history. Before the 1973 season even began, Jackson announced, "We got to do it all over again so I can be a part of it…. I want to be the big man in the league. I want to be Most Valuable Player. I want to be a $100,000 ballplayer."

When the ALCS opened, though, Jackson had more on his mind than just Baltimore's terrific pitching staff. He'd received a threat in September warning that if he participated in the play-offs, he would be killed. The threat allegedly was signed by the Weathermen, a violent radical group, prompting the FBI to assign Jackson full-time protection. Jackson added a hefty bodyguard of his own and he tried not to dwell on it—after all, he wanted more than anything to play in the postseason.

With that hanging over him, plus some rust from missing much of September with another hamstring injury, Jackson hit .143 in the ALCS and he did not drive in a run. He admitted later that the death threat had rattled him.

Even without much production from Jackson, the A's moved on to the World Series against the Mets, and Jackson homered in Game 7 and was named the series MVP.

"In '73 against the Mets, especially after missing '72 you could see him thinking, 'Hey I missed it once, now I'll show you what I can do,'" A's catcher Ray Fosse said. "Like Reggie said, he was the straw that stirred the drink. Reggie got the nickname 'Mr. October' for a reason. He loved the spotlight, he loved the big stage. You could see him stepping up a level. In October, if you ever wanted someone to put the team on his back, it was him. He walked the walk and talked the talk—and he definitely talked it."

And yet the man known for his enormous ego and for his longing to come through in the postseason said he actually would have voted for teammate Campy Campaneris, who also homered in Game 7, as the MVP.

After the season was over, Jackson earned the regular-season MVP award. He'd led the league with 32 homers and 117 RBIs.

"People think about him as an offensive player, but he had a strong arm and great range, too," Fosse said. "He was a five-tool player. And he was perfect for the club because he accepted the role of team spokesman. It helped all of us, because if anything happened, the media would go straight to Reggie and he handled it. And he loved it. He was the quote master. He could take an 0-for-4 with four strikeouts and turn it into the greatest game in the world, make it an interesting story."

That didn't always go over so well with his teammates.

"Reggie at that time was arrogant," A's starter Blue Moon Odom said. "He's mellowed out a little bit since then, but in those days, it was tough to get along with him. That was Reggie. We were family so long, you learn to deal with it, but he was someone who would let you know if he made a big play. He'd pat himself on the back before you would. He was very outspoken. He wanted to make sure he was seen or heard. He was not going to be out of the spotlight."

Jackson famously battled with numerous teammates during his time in Oakland. He and North brawled in the clubhouse in Detroit in 1974, leaving Jackson with a shoulder injury—and Fosse, who tried to break it up, with shattered vertebrae in his neck.

"Me and Reggie mixed it up a little, but that's between me and Reggie. It's cool," North said 40 years afterward.

Jackson hit another homer in the World Series that year, as the A's beat the Dodgers, but by 1976 he was gone, traded to Baltimore in April along with starter Ken Holtzman. In his autobiography, Jackson said emphatically, "I did not want to leave Oakland. Did. Not."

Two months later, his home in the Oakland hills burned down and he lost everything, including his MVP trophy.

In 1977, Jackson, a free agent, was off to New York, where he had running feuds with manager Billy Martin and owner George Steinbrenner. When Jackson got off to a rough start in the postseason that year and was still spatting with Martin, Yankees catcher Thurman Munson mockingly called him "Mr. October," but the name proved to be apt. Jackson went on a tear in the World Series against the Dodgers, homering in Games 4 and 5—and then three times in Game 6, off three different Dodgers pitchers. He hit the third almost 500 feet, going deep to dead center at Yankee Stadium.

In 27 World Series games, 12 of them with Oakland, Jackson hit 10 homers, batted .357, and drove in 24 runs.

He was elected to the Hall of Fame in 1993.

"I will say this about Reggie: When the red light went on the camera, this guy was a Hall of Famer," former teammate and occasional combatant George Hendrick said. "When the spotlight came on, he could rise to an occasion better than anyone I've ever seen."

1989: The Earthquake Series

By going to the World Series three years in a row, the A's earned comparisons to the great Oakland teams of the early '70s, as well as clubs like Cincinnati's Big Red Machine. When Rickey Henderson was reacquired in 1989, the A's were particularly dominant.

Just one title went to Tony La Russa A's, however, and that was overshadowed by a major natural disaster.

Right before Game 3 of the only Bay Area World Series in history, at 5:04 PM on October 17, 1989, a 7.1 magnitude earthquake shook the region, causing one section of the Bay Bridge between San Francisco and Oakland to fall. A freeway known as the Cypress Viaduct collapsed in Oakland, killing 42, and San Francisco's Marina District suffered damage from structure failure and from fire.

At Candlestick Park, the light standards swayed and there were cracks in some sections of the stadium, but few people initially realized what had happened.

"I was in left field running sprints and I had no idea what was going on," third baseman Carney Lansford said. "I heard the crowd roar and I thought the Giants were coming out on the field. I actually thought, 'It must be Will Clark or Kevin Mitchell.' A fan there had a portable TV and he mentioned that the bridge had collapsed. I thought he was joking, and then I saw on his TV that the Marina was on fire. I was like, 'Wait a minute, this is serious.'

"I was the player rep at the time so Sandy Alderson came to me and said, 'Hey, I want you to get the families out of the stands, get them down here, get all your stuff out of the clubhouse, get them on the bus, we're going back to the Coliseum, it's a lot worse than people realize.'

"It was very surreal. It took us hours to get to the Coliseum, we had to go all the way around the Bay. We were going the opposite way on freeways, we couldn't go over the bridges, so we were going the wrong way on off-ramps, on-ramps. We took 101 all the way around Mountain View and then went back up 880. No one had cell phones, so we had to wait to get to the Coliseum to use a phone and find out how our kids were, our kids were with a babysitter and we didn't know what was going on, so the whole ride it was just panic, not knowing if everything was okay.

"We were 10 minutes from starting a World Series game and a few minutes later, we're back on the bus, like, 'What in the world is going on?' It was like a nightmare."

Players in the clubhouse knew something was happening, but they didn't realize it was an earthquake initially, either.

"I was in the clubhouse and there was dirt pouring out of the vents—we all thought something was on fire," pitcher Curt Young said. "And then the lights went out and people were yelling to get the heck out. The first thing I saw when we got outside was the light standards going back and forth like someone was shaking them.

"I drove on that Cypress structure every day. I knew what it would have been like that time of day if it hadn't been for the World Series going on."

Pitcher Mike Moore was still getting dressed when the rattling began.

"I'd finished my workouts and was getting ready for TV introductions, I had one shoe on and my pants on, and someone said, 'Earthquake,'" he said. "I didn't really know what was going on. I ran out into the back parking lot and just assumed everything was on until I got to home plate and stopped and started talking to Will Clark, and Will was talking to a San Francisco police officer who had a radio, so he knew what was going on. The Bay Bridge was down, the Marina District was on fire, and you got perspective on what was going on."

Two players were particularly affected: Pitcher Bob Welch, who'd been scheduled to start Game 3, had a home in the Marina that sustained damage, and Oakland native Dave Stewart visited the collapsed Cypress structure repeatedly to offer support.

"Being from the area, born and raised, and going through areas I'd played in and seeing the destruction...to see an accordion-like structure instead of the freeway I drove on every day, watching those people work and struggle to help, I wanted to do whatever I could," Stewart said. "Because of the safety issues, I wasn't able to do anything with the [professional] relief efforts but I did organize people and vendors to bring clothes and food to keep spirits up and keep the relief workers fed. I was there every day until we went to Arizona, three or four times a day."

The World Series did not resume for 10 days, and there was talk of cancellation.

"It got to the point where resuming it was what everyone wanted, what the community wanted," Dave Parker said. "The World Series helped things get back to normal, or seem more normal."

With rain in the forecast in the Bay Area, La Russa decided to take his club to Arizona to work out for two days during the break in action, while the Giants remained in the Bay Area. The A's were greeted by throngs of fans at the Phoenix airport and an intrasquad game drew thousands.

"We realized the rest of the country was waiting for the World Series. It gave us a different view of things," Lansford said.

The A's returned home and finished off a sweep of the Giants. Out of respect for the victims of the earthquake, there was no champagne celebration.

Rube Waddell

On June 26, 1902, one of the great wild men of Athletics history—baseball history, really—joined the A's, spirited away from the California League in the company of bodyguards. Waddell, age 25, went on to win 24 games that season despite his late arrival.

Waddell, who had pitched for Connie Mack's Milwaukee team in the Western League, was more than just a wonderful pitcher with a hard fastball and super curveball. He was also the Athletics' first bona-fide character—a big, strong fellow renowned for showing up to games drunk. (This never has been verified, according to Dan O'Brien, who has studied Waddell extensively in order to write a screenplay based on his life.) One story that he'd spent his entire signing bonus on alcohol led the *Sporting News* to call Waddell the "sousepaw."

According to reports of the day, Waddell occasionally rushed out of the stadium, even mid-windup, to chase passing fire trucks. Such accounts are wildly exaggerated, but Waddell did have a fascination with fires and he helped bucket brigades extinguish several. Mack once said that he constantly worried about Waddell joining local fire departments when the team was on the road. He described Waddell as always wearing a red undershirt so that he could "gallop off to the blazes."

It is true that Waddell would arrive late to games because he was playing marbles with street kids and that he sometimes didn't show up at all because he was fishing. Once he went missing for several days before he was discovered tending bar in nearby Camden, New Jersey.

Waddell wrestled alligators in a circus during the off-season; he also played rugby and, after being suspended by Mack in 1903, he toured with a theater group, acting in a play called *The Stain of Guilt*. That same year, according to Cooperstown historian Lee Allen, Waddell "saved a woman from drowning, accidentally shot a friend through the hand, and was bitten by a lion." He once picked up teammate Danny Hoffman, knocked unconscious by a pitch, put him over his shoulder, and raced him out of the stadium, flagging down a carriage for a ride to the hospital—and was credited with saving the man's life. He was married three times in four years while he played for the A's.

After pitching 20 innings in a storied victory over Boston great Cy Young in 1905, Waddell did cartwheels off the mound, and according to O'Brien, he is said to have bartered the game ball for drinks...repeatedly. Dozens of "game balls" from the famed contest showed up in bars around Philadelphia in the following years.

Waddell iced his pitching arm before starts, telling teammates he'd "burn up the catcher's glove" if he didn't. Lore has it that he once sent his outfielders off the field against Detroit, then struck out the side; O'Brien said this did happen, but it was in an exhibition game.

Opposing players tried to distract Waddell by putting rubber snakes or mechanical toys on the field while he was pitching, often successfully. Some baseball historians have theorized that Waddell was mildly autistic or may have had a developmental disability.

"He had a room-temperature IQ and no impulse control," said Major League Baseball's official historian, John Thorn, "but fans loved him. He was the Peter Pan of baseball, and an amazing amount of the stories about him are verifiably true."

Mack had had difficulty getting Waddell for his Milwaukee club two years earlier. Pittsburgh had released Waddell after the 1900 season because of his poor behavior, despite his league-best 2.37 ERA, and Mack went to work, sending letters and telegrams for two weeks before Waddell finally sent an answer: "Come and get me."

Mack went to Punxsutawney, Pennsylvania, to find him, and Waddell hauled Mack all over town and had him pay off his debts at each stop, including $25 to get his watch out of the pawnshop. A group of men saw the two off at the train station—and they thanked Mack for taking Waddell away.

Despite their extreme differences in temperament and deportment, Mack recognized Waddell's worth, saying in 1953, "I have seen all the great left-handers and there was none greater than Waddell." Mack's granddaughter, Ruth Mack Clark, said that Waddell was always one of her grandfather's favorites and he enjoyed telling stories about him.

Needing players for his new team in 1902, Mack tracked Waddell down again, this time playing for the Los Angeles Looloos. According to the first volume of Norman Macht's Connie Mack biography, Waddell told Mack to send him $100 and a train ticket—then did not show in Chicago. Mack hired the Pinkerton Detective Agency to locate Waddell, and two agents found him pitching in San Francisco that June, and they hauled him as far as Dodge City, Kansas.

There, Macht writes, Waddell insisted on stopping. There was a boxing match he wanted to see, and afterward, Waddell wandered off to Kansas City with featherweight Young Corbett and his trainer. The Pinkerton men sent Mack a telegraph: They'd had enough, Mack needed to get Waddell himself. So Mack left the A's, who were en route to Baltimore, and found Waddell in Kansas City, preparing to pitch in a minor-league game. Mack packed Waddell's things up and prodded him to the train station instead.

At one point during Waddell's time with the A's, Mack paid the pitcher's entire $2,200 salary in dollar bills, hoping that would make it last longer.

Some histories of the Athletics state that Waddell died of alcoholism at the age of 37, but the circumstances were far more complicated.

In 1911, he won 20 games in the minors for Minneapolis, and that winter, while visiting his manager, Joe Cantillon, in Kentucky, Waddell volunteered to help when the Mississippi flooded and threatened the town. He stood in icy water for hours piling sandbags, then came down with a severe case of pneumonia that turned into tuberculosis.

Waddell was sent to recover at a sanitarium in San Antonio, near his parents, and Mack and Philadelphia A's owner Benjamin Shibe paid all his medical expenses. Waddell never improved and he died on April 1, 1914. As many have noted, one of baseball's true originals was born on Friday the 13th and died on April Fool's Day.

Several obituaries declared that Waddell's popularity in the second year of the American League saved the new venture from bankruptcy. There was some truth in that; the Athletics' attendance doubled after Waddell joined them. Crowds arrived early when he was scheduled to pitch, Macht writes, because crazy things happened: Once he wrestled Boston first baseman Candy LaChance for 30 minutes before finally pinning him, and afterward, he threw a complete game.

Waddell's personal catcher, Ossee Schreckengost, also died in 1914, aged 39, three months after his friend. The two were roommates for six years; once, Schreckengost (known as "Schreck") refused to sign his contract until he received a stipulation that Waddell would no longer be allowed to eat animal crackers in bed.

According to Macht, there was a popular story that Waddell jumped out a hotel window because he thought he could fly, and wound up in the hospital. "Why didn't you stop me?" he's alleged to have asked Schreck, who responded: "What, and lose the hundred dollars I bet you could do it?"

Schreckengost was known for one repeated prank at restaurants—he would send steaks back, claiming they were too tough—and when his order again did not arrive to his satisfaction, he'd nail the meat to the floor.

Waddell wound up a major factor in the A's first ever World Series—because he could not play in it. The nutty left-hander went 27–10 with a 1.48 ERA during the regular season, but he was hurt late in the year in a mishap: While wrestling on the train with teammate Andy Coakley in a good-natured tussle over a straw hat, Waddell fell over a suitcase and hurt his left shoulder.

Years later, this "Straw Hat incident" was portrayed as a possible attempt to throw the series, but the truth was that Waddell had "declared war" on the wearing of straw hats after September 1, a popular ritual of the day. According to Bob Warrington of the Philadelphia Athletics Historical Society, Waddell and other baseball players tried to punch out the tops of every straw hat worn after that date each year.

In 1920, with baseball still reeling from the Black Sox scandal, Horace Fogel, a former president of the Phillies, claimed that Waddell had invented the 1905 injury after he was approached by gamblers who offered him $17,000 to stay out of the World Series. Waddell had died six years before the allegations were made, but Connie Mack called the claim "silly and ridiculous." As Warrington points out, it's unlikely that Waddell would have been contacted by gamblers with a month left in the season, especially when the pennant was undecided. And why would he concoct an injury with so much time remaining?

Baseball historians still consider the matter in doubt, even though Coakley, then the baseball coach at Columbia, confirmed every detail of the original incident after the controversy arose. Macht writes that Mack always believed Waddell's arm trouble was the result of sitting next to an open window on the train that night—the next morning, Mack said, "the Rube came up and told me he could not raise his left arm. It was stiff as a pine board."

Waddell expert O'Brien said that there is no evidence to suggest Waddell's injury was anything other than the result of horsing around. He also noted that Fogel was banned by baseball in 1912 for accusing umpires of unfair treatment.

There was also a lot of incentive to win the 1905 Series, rather than throw it: The victors received 70 percent of the players' pool, the losers just 30 percent. And as Macht writes, Waddell never would have missed the chance to shine on the big stage of the World Series, especially opposing Giants star Christy Matthewson.

Macht cites the *Sporting Life* account at the time, which said, "Waddell is childishly tricky, but not crooked."

No matter what his eccentricities, Waddell was an undeniably great pitcher. His career ERA of 2.16 is 11th best all-time (he put up a 1.48 ERA in 1905, the year he won the pitcher's equivalent of the Triple Crown). He led the league in strikeouts six years in a row, including 349 in 1905, a modern-era record for more than 60 years and still the American League record for a left-hander. He threw 50 shutouts. He was the first major-leaguer to strike the side out on just nine pitches, doing so on July 1, 1902.

The Veterans Committee elected Waddell to the Hall of Fame in 1946.

9 Bash Brothers

At one point during the Haas family's ownership, the Oakland A's had a lot of legal firepower, but not necessarily a lot of baseball experience. GM Sandy Alderson, team president Roy Eisenhardt, and manager Tony La Russa, all held law degrees.

The A's gained a reputation for braininess, but Wally Haas remembered, "There were some moments early on when people were clearly trying to take advantage of us. Everyone thought,

'What do a bunch of lawyers know?' But by that point, baseball was more trading salaries than players."

That was right up Alderson's alley. A Dartmouth graduate who'd served in Vietnam with the Marine Corps and then earned a law degree at Harvard, Alderson energetically applied himself to learning advanced baseball statistics.

"We just went about learning the business of baseball, because when Billy Martin left, we were left to our own devices," Alderson said. "Roy and I were kind of new to the game, and this was about the time I got interested in Bill James and the Earl Weaver school of baseball. We began to approach things analytically. It was a gradual thing, but the first manifestation was drafting Mark McGwire instead of Shane Mack or Oddibe McDowell.

"Because I didn't have a scouting background, some means of analyzing players were a little more available to me than the traditional approach."

Others the A's pulled out of the draft: Jose Canseco, Terry Steinbach, and Walt Weiss, the foundations of one of the dominant teams of the late '80s and early '90s.

McGwire and Canseco became two of the great names in A's history, forever linked—but they were an unusual duo, polar-opposite personalities bound by their staggering ability to hit balls out of the park. McGwire, a quiet, red-headed first baseman, and Canseco, an outspoken and controversial outfielder, combined to hit more than 600 home runs while wearing green and gold, and they celebrated by smacking their forearms together after going deep.

Thus: the Bash Brothers. Canseco was the Rookie of the Year in 1986, McGwire in 1987, when he set a rookie record with 49 homers.

"It was definitely thrilling watching those guys hitting for the distance they did," outfielder Dave Parker said. "McGwire hit one in Oakland that hit the back wall (of the stadium) in left field, and that's when he was 6'5", 220. He was just strong."

The most memorable of the many homers the two hit was Canseco's blast into the upper deck at the Skydome in Toronto during the 1989 playoffs. The ball landed in the fifth level.

"The one Jose hit in Toronto, I was on deck. I was like, 'Woo, damn! Oh, man.' It's hard to impress me but that was in the top tier," Parker said. "It went very high and very far. It was eight rows from the back of the stadium."

"I remember Mike Flanagan gave up a homer to Rickey Henderson, and then he kind of threw me a cutter middle-in and I got my hands on it real quick and when I hit it, it's funny, I didn't think it would go that far," said Canseco. "I actually kind of missed it. But I got a lot backspin and that ballpark is known for giving up the long home runs and it went pretty far. That seat was painted [in recognition of Canseco's feat] until Manny Ramirez hit one up there a couple of times."

The previous season, Canseco had won MVP honors after becoming the first player in major-league history to record 40 homers and 40 stolen bases in one season, demonstrating his tremendous all-around talent.

"He did all that playing in a terrible park to hit in, with a lot of foul ground. That was pretty incredible," former teammate Don Baylor said. "Jose lived in the weight room, him and Mark. They were just specimens. They were hitting balls onto the road during spring training and I said, 'I think this might be my last year.'

"The guys were getting bigger and stronger. I never suspected anything then and I still don't really know what was going on."

What was happening, according to Canseco's statements and writings since he retired, was the use of performance enhancing substances. He confessed to his own use, and he implicated McGwire as well, permanently estranging the Bash Brothers.

"Canseco was juiced to the gills," closer Dennis Eckersley said. "I thought it was obvious there was something going on, but I was never sure what, exactly. I tried to keep my distance from Jose. Looking back, what an idiot I was. It's not like I ever said, 'Who cares what he's doing as long as he hits home runs?' But I knew there was something strange."

Canseco attended a reunion of the 1989 championship team at the Coliseum in 2014 and he said he regrets writing *Juiced,* though the book helped kick-start the movement to clean up the game.

"I don't think anyone doubted what I said was true. I think we all knew what was going on and I just came out with my story," he said. "I think I broke a code. When you step into a clubhouse, it says, 'What you see here, what you say here, stays here,' and that's the code I broke, the brotherhood, the family. I have a lot of regrets doing it, I really do."

Canseco was the center of attention in Oakland, and not always because of his power. He was young, charismatic, and handsome, as well as athletically gifted.

"Jose was an incredible five-tool player when he was younger," former owner Wally Haas said. "He could, and did, beat Rickey Henderson in a sprint. And he was truly a Latin Adonis, the only athlete I can remember in that 15 years we owned the team who could walk into a room and girls would scream like he was Elvis."

"Jose was like a rock star at that time," infielder Jamie Quirk said. "We'd have to go through the backdoor of hotels, through kitchens, up stairs, anything to avoid the lobby. The lobbies were packed with teenage girls because of Jose."

Alderson said Canseco brought the A's "a Q factor." The out-fielder also brought headaches. He was pulled over numerous times for speeding in expensive sports cars. (Canseco's best excuse: He told officers he was testing jet fuel in his Porsche.) He had public run-ins with his wife, Esther, and once rammed his car into hers during an argument. He was cited for having a loaded handgun under the seat of his car. And then there was the night he spent at Madonna's apartment in New York.

"Who knows what happened, but there was a picture on page 1 of the *New York Post* with Jose coming out of her apartment and wearing shredded jeans and a white leather jacket," traveling secretary Mickey Morabito said. "So we're on the bus that afternoon, ready to go to Yankee Stadium, and here comes Jose and he's wearing exactly the same outfit. Someone said, 'Jeez, Jose, the least you could have done was change.' At the game, fans were screaming at him about Madonna all night."

Few of Canseco's teammates minded the constant commotion, according to third baseman Carney Lansford, who said, "The media was so focused on him, it kept the pressure off us. It always seemed like Jose was doing something foolish—speeding and then saying he was testing rocket fuel, going out with Madonna. Everywhere we went, people were waiting for us, mostly to see Jose."

While Canseco embraced the trappings of fame, the details sometimes escaped him.

"I'd give him paychecks and he's such an airhead, he'd never cash them," Morabito said. "Accounting would call and tell me and I'd ask Jose and he'd say, 'Huh, I don't know where it is.'

"When they demolished Comiskey Park, they found one of his paychecks in a locker there. That's a true story."

"I was an entertaining player at least. I had fun," Canseco said. "I think people viewed me as so talented that I didn't fulfill what my legacy was supposed to be—I didn't work hard enough, I wasn't serious enough. But people who knew me understood how hard I worked.

"I ran with track stars at Miami. I trained eight to 10 hours a day. No one gives me credit for that. All people see is the wasted talent. Other guys were messing around, going out, and I wasn't like that. I promised my mother I would become the best player in the world, and I did that. Of course, I used chemicals, but I figured out a way to become the best in the world. I wasn't at clubs partying. I wasn't doing cocaine or marijuana. I wasn't dating. Madonna—that was short-lived. I wasn't drinking or anything."

Many see the great A's teams from 1988 to 1992 much like Canseco—unmet expectations, particularly after Oakland swept the 1989 World Series from the Giants, a series remembered far more for the massive earthquake that hit the region right before Game 3. The A's won 103 games in 1990 and swept Boston in the ALCS, so they went into the 1990 World Series as huge favorites. Instead, they dropped Game 1 7–0 and the Reds went on to sweep the A's, one of the most surprising outcomes in baseball history.

In 1992, the A's made it back to the ALCS but fell to eventual champion Toronto. Oakland wouldn't return to the ALCS again until 2006. Injuries hurt the club, especially a heel problem that kept McGwire out much of two seasons, and Canseco's production dipped as his focus appeared to shift. Canseco and Henderson became distractions, squabbling over contracts and reporting to spring training later every year. As the A's fortunes sank, such antics weren't tolerated as easily.

"Rickey and Jose were like dueling villain wrestlers out there at some point," Haas said. "Two superstars feeding off each other, but not in a positive way. If one wasn't showing up on time, the other one had to show up later.

"It's too bad what Jose did after he got his big contract—he only really cared about women and home runs, and his skills diminished."

Canseco's decline was disappointing to all, considering his talent.

"To me, he should have been a Hall of Fame player, no doubt," Baylor said.

"In hindsight, I'm frustrated and angry with Jose for the direction he chose to go," catcher Terry Steinbach said. "Those early years when he wanted to play, he was a phenomenal asset, but unfortunately, his interests changed and instead of being a huge asset, he became a major liability. A lot of stuff could get overlooked, but not when things are so far out of whack."

GM Alderson agreed and on August 31, 1992, he traded Canseco to Texas. This was Canseco, though, so there was nothing normal about it: He was dealt two hours before the deadline, right in the middle of a game. He had to be called out of the on-deck circle.

"Because it was the trading deadline, there were a lot of rumors," Steinbach said. "Jose made the comment when he saw his name in the lineup, 'Well, they can't trade me now!' We were all laughing when we saw Sandy in the runway because he never did that. We were like, 'Uh oh, something's going on.'"

"I think Jose was shocked," Eckersley said. "He thought they'd never trade him and he was caught off-guard. I think I saw a tear."

In the following days, Alderson was criticized heavily for the deal, which brought outfielder Ruben Sierra and pitchers Bobby Witt and Jeff Russell to Oakland. Sierra wound up being a headache too, and La Russa once famously referred to him as "the village idiot."

At least Haas got to put a long-standing disagreement with Texas owner George W. Bush to the test.

"I'd gotten to know George W. through our star players, Jose and Ruben," Haas said. "We would tell each other, 'I have the worst biggest star in the game,' and then tell their latest adventure. 'Jose crashed his car into his wife's car.' 'Ruben was wearing a gold piano around his neck.'

"So people said one of the reasons we made the trade was to see who was right. That wasn't the case—but we could both make a really strong case."

10 Winning Streak

Even with five playoff appearances in seven seasons, the top highlight of the Moneyball era came from August 13 to September 4, 2002, when the A's won an American League–record 20 consecutive games—baseball's longest winning streak in more than 70 years.

"It was the perfect storm the way the club was playing and the way the schedule set up," general manager Billy Beane said. "Through the bulk of it, you really felt we'd win all those games, and at the end, you could see the emotions carrying us through some games—and then we started to get lucky."

Especially extraordinary was the matter in which Oakland won games No. 18 (on a three-run homer by Miguel Tejada in the bottom of the ninth), No. 19 (a one-out single by Tejada in the bottom of the ninth) and, finally, record-setting No. 20.

In that one, the A's charged out to an 11-run lead after three innings before Kansas City staged an unlikely comeback. By the time Mike Sweeney hit a three-run homer in the eighth, the difference was one.

"We got up 11–0 and I remember thinking, 'Finally, we're going to win an easy one,'" Oakland manager Art Howe said. "The next thing you knew, things were rolling downhill. Incredible."

"After 11 runs, I don't think anyone was paying attention—at some point, we thought we had it all chalked up," Beane said.

Then pinch-hitter Luis Alicea tied the game in the ninth with an RBI single off Billy Koch.

"You could kind of see it was a sand castle getting taken away by the ocean, whittling down. You had a feeling it was going to slip away," first baseman Scott Hatteberg said. "I was in the batting cage, watching on a stupid little TV, going, 'Oh no. I can't believe it.' It's just a hollow feeling. When I got to the dugout, it was a real demoralized bench."

Hatteberg changed all that, providing one of the great celebrations in Oakland history with a one-out, pinch-hit homer off Jason Grimsley in the ninth.

"The last thing I was trying to do was hit a homer. Grimsley was on the mound, he had a heavy bowling-ball kind of sinker, and all you can do is try to see a ball up if he leaves one there," Hatteberg said. "I just wanted to hit one in the gap, have a man in scoring position. I got a pitch up, luckily, and I hit it pretty dang good."

The A's had a chance to run the streak to 21 in a row, but they had the day off the next day, then opened a series at Minnesota. And before the first game there, veteran David Justice called a meeting to applaud the team's accomplishment.

"Justice gave a team talk, very inspirational, 'I've been in the game a long, long time and what we just did was a special thing,' and then we went out and lost 6–0," starter Mark Mulder said with a chuckle. "David said, 'Fine, guys, I'm never giving another speech again.'"

"Twenty in a row, and he decides to have a team meeting," third baseman Eric Chavez said with a mock groan. "It jinxed the whole thing. He's one of my favorite guys all time, but he got a little ahead of himself."

"I have Dave's back on that one because I thought it was the perfect time to say something," ex-A's outfielder Eric Byrnes said. "The guy played in the playoffs every year, won the World Series, to have him stand up there and saying winning that 20th game was the best moment in his career, the most fun he'd had, that meant a lot to a young player like me.

"And, come on, we had to lose sometime."

11 Billyball

In 1980, Charlie Finley found yet another new manager—and he and Billy Martin, a former Kansas City A's player, were one of the most remarkable pairings ever. For one thing, Finley couldn't keep managers more than a year or two, and Martin was oft-fired. The A's were his fifth team, sixth, if you count his two stints with the Yankees; he'd been canned by New York owner George Steinbrenner four months earlier after getting into a fight that left a Minnesota marshmallow salesman with 16 stitches.

And like Finley, Martin was not well-loved by the commissioner; some thought that Finley hired his new manager as much to annoy Bowie Kuhn as anything. Even better, as far as Finley was concerned: The Yankees were still paying the bulk of Martin's salary.

"I liked working for Charlie," Martin said in *Billyball*. "He was the only owner who never bothered me. Can you believe it?"

Martin laid down the law immediately, according to starter Mike Norris.

"The first day of spring training, he had a meeting to let us know how he ran things," Norris said. "He told us that ballplayers are responsible for 50 percent of managers being fired and, he said, 'If you [mess with] me, I'll [mess with] you harder.'

"Half the room was rookies and the rest were second-year players and you could hear a pin drop, everyone was so scared, so I started to chuckle.

"Billy looked at me and said, 'Mr. Norris, do you find something funny? I want to see you after the meeting is over.' He'd been there for an hour, and I was in the doghouse.

"I went to his office and he said, 'Close the door.'

"I was thinking, 'I don't know if that's such a good idea,' but I did.

"He said, 'What the [heck] was funny?'

"I said, 'I looked around and everyone was scared to death.'

"He said, 'Weren't you scared?'

"And I said, 'No, sir, I wasn't.'

"He said, 'You weren't? Why not?'

"And I said, 'Well, because you said if we [mess] with you, you'll [mess] with us harder—and I'm not thinking about [messing] you around.'

"Billy said, 'That's a good answer.'"

Martin always had some appreciation for fellow hot-heads, or maybe it was just a soft spot for Norris, his best pitcher during his time in Oakland.

"The start of that season we were at Toronto and we lost in the 10th inning. I came into the clubhouse and annihilated the bathroom," Norris recalled. "All anyone could hear was *Boom! Bam! Boom! Bam!* because I took a bat in with me.

"I had a good snap for five minutes and when I came out, everyone was looking at me like, 'You're crazy.' But Billy was in the middle of the clubhouse and he said, 'Hey, pal, you did a good job tonight. You're the ace of my staff now.'

"I'll never forget the look on Matt Keough's face. He was like, 'Damn, is that how you get to be the ace of the staff around here?'"

Always an aggressive type, Martin used the team's speed as its primary weapon. Even the lumberers were let loose, particularly when it came to stealing home.

"It wasn't so much the steals of home, it was who stole them," former A's pitcher Keough said. "It was all the slow guys. It wasn't a matter of speed, it was a matter of catching them off guard.

"One time we had Mitchell Page at second and Wayne Gross at third and [Tigers pitching coach] Roger Craig walked out to the mound and told Jack Morris, 'Jack, do not wind up.'

"Jack threw out of the windup, Wayne Gross stole home and Paige nearly did, too, on the same pitch. Lance Parrish [the Tigers' catcher] went into the dugout and pulled the water cooler out of the wall, because you can't be slower than Wayne Gross."

"When a pitcher went into his windup, Billy had a theory that he put his weight on his back leg and that made it hard to react to the runner going from home," Rickey Henderson said. "We stole home easily until pitchers started going to the stretch all the time."

Twice in May 1980 the A's had two men steal home in the same game—once in the same inning (Henderson and Dwayne Murphy). During Martin's three-year tenure, the A's stole home 13 times, including seven times in 1980. In their previous 12 years in Oakland, they'd stolen home four times.

A local sportswriter, Ralph Wiley, called Martin's go-go style "Billyball."

"We'd have runners at first and third and whoever was at first—say, Wayne Gross—would shuffle off like they were trying to take a lead and fall down," second baseman Shooty Babitt said. "The guy at third would walk right in."

Martin taught his young team trick plays and squeeze plays. At one point, he even had a designated pinch hitter to squeeze bunt: Jeff Cox. One week, Cox squeezed home three runs.

Billyball helped the A's go from last place to second in 1980, and in 1981, a strike year, Oakland won one half of the division and went to the playoffs, beating the Royals in the first round and then falling to the Yankees in the ALCS.

Even in an ideal situation such as Oakland, Billy Martin continued to get into trouble. At a game in Minnesota, on April 25, 1980, he had to be held back from going after a fan who was throwing marshmallows at him, an unsubtle reminder of his brawl with the marshmallow salesman. The following year, Martin was suspended for a week after dumping handfuls of dirt on home-plate umpire Terry Cooney.

"It was interesting," Babitt said. "The most comical thing was watching Billy the day game after a night game to see how he reacted when he walked out and the sun hit his face. He was famous for closing the bar down. He had to have his coaching staff there to save him from fights.

"He and [catcher] Mike Heath got into it one day because Billy didn't like the pitches he was calling. Mike was so mad, he tore his jersey right in half in front of him. That's hard to do with nylon."

Martin often displayed his ire by turning over the postgame clubhouse meal, including once at Baltimore, where the players were particularly fond of the seafood option.

"We had a doubleheader, and we lost the second game, and it was humid and hot, just awful," Norris said. "Billy comes in and there are four tables, full of food, just lined up, and he kicked over every one of them and runs into the office.

"Rickey was still out on the field, and he was a guy who always went straight to the spread. So he comes in and he looks at everyone's face and he sees the food on the floor and he says, 'Is that [guy] crazy? Throwing away the food when I'm hungry?' It was the funniest thing in the world, and I know Billy heard him. You should have seen Rickey's face when he saw there was no food—hilarious.

"So the next time we're in Baltimore and Billy comes in, Rickey jumped on the table so Billy wouldn't knock it over. Billy just started laughing."

Martin was famous for run-ins with umpires, but according to longtime friend Mickey Morabito, that was misunderstood.

"Everyone thought the umpires hated him, he'd be out there screaming at them, kicking dust, but he'd also say at the same time, 'I'm only out here because George [Steinbrenner] wants me to be. I'm not really mad at you.' That's while he's screaming and throwing things," said Morabito, who has been the A's traveling secretary since Martin brought him over from the Yankees in 1980. "The next day, he'd say, 'Go tell those guys I'm not mad at them.' He didn't hold grudges."

Cooney threatened Martin with an assault charge after being showered by dirt. Then he called Morabito that winter.

"Terry had a luncheon in Fresno for charity and he said, 'I want Billy to come.' I said, 'But you wanted to sue him,'" Morabito recalled. "Cooney said, 'Tell him I'll send a limo.' So Billy went and they made total fun of their incident. Here it looks like they hate each other, and Billy's helping Cooney out with his event."

According to Morabito, when Martin was ejected, he'd head to the bar and check in with the coaches from there.

"He used to drink at the Holiday Inn by the Coliseum, and he'd go over there and call Clete Boyer on the phone," Morabito said.

That is, until umpire Ken Kaiser took note.

"Kaiser sees Boyer on the phone, grabs it and says, 'Billy, don't call anymore, you're out of the game,' and he pulls the phone out of the wall," Morabito said. "We sent Kaiser the bill."

Nearly the entire time he was with the A's, Martin's private life was complicated. As if his prodigious drinking wasn't enough, it was an open secret that he had an 18-year-old girlfriend living with him in the East Bay and another girlfriend in Los Angeles; at that point, neither knew about the other. He married the first in 1982, then, after his divorce, the second in 1988. One friend of Martin's said that wife No. 1 occasionally would spot future wife No. 2 seated near the dugout during telecasts and quiz Martin about her. He responded that she was Morabito's girlfriend.

In the meantime, the A's fine pitching staff was unraveling because of injuries, and Finley had sold the club to the Haas family of Levi Strauss fame. Even though the new owners gave him an extension, Martin's personal problems were weighing upon him, and with the starters down, the A's were going nowhere.

"When we all started getting hurt, I don't think he knew how to handle it," Keough said.

Near the end of the season, it became clear that he was trying to get fired: First, Martin demolished his office, doing more than $10,000 in damage.

"There was a fan in the manager's office and Billy went in there and he punched it," Norris said. "That's about the sickest thing he did. I thought, 'Damn, he could have lopped off his hand.'"

In late September, Martin was late for pregame warm-ups in Texas. When the players goofed off during batting practice, coach Jackie Moore, irate, ordered them off the field. Word of this got back to the new owners, who immediately gave the Yankees and Indians permission to speak to Martin.

The Yankees, who'd been circling for months, hired him again, for the third of his six stints with the team.

12 Rollie Fingers

Like another A's Hall of Fame closer, Rollie Fingers began his career as a starter.

Unlike Dennis Eckersley, Fingers wasn't all that great at starting. In fact, A's scout Art Lilly first signed Fingers as an outfielder on Christmas Eve in 1964.

Fingers was a left fielder at Upland (Calif.) High School and he was one of the top hitters in the nation for his American Legion team, batting .450 and being named the American Legion player of the year. The A's liked his 0.67 ERA for his Legion team, and though Fingers said he hit over .300 that first spring training with the organization, Oakland decided to move him to the mound full-time.

He was almost entirely a starter throughout his minor-league career, going 38–36 with a 2.84 ERA, but when the A's brought him up in 1969, he worked in both the rotation and the bullpen—and in Fingers' first big-league start, he threw a five-hit shutout at Minnesota. He made eight starts and 52 relief appearances, and the following year, he was Oakland's fourth starter.

It was becoming obvious by that point that Fingers fared better out of the bullpen, with an ERA under 3.00 there his first two seasons and over 4.50 as a starter. As a starter those years, he allowed 147 hits in 138⅔ innings but less than a hit per inning in relief, 106 in 128⅓ innings.

"I did give up a lot of hits as a starter," Fingers said in 2014. "I'd have two or three good starts and then give up a bunch of runs and move into the bullpen again. I'd pitch well there and then get more starts."

He made eight starts in 1971, but on May 29, Fingers worked three scoreless relief innings against Boston, and two days later, he worked 2⅓ scoreless innings and got the save at New York.

"Dick Williams said, 'From now on, you're my closer,'" Fingers recalled.

The role suited him, Fingers said. Many people associate the closer role with pressure, but he did not.

"It's just the mindset of a relief pitcher—you just have to maybe go three innings, and I knew I could pitch every day," he said. "I had decent command. I felt like I had more pressure on me during four days of waiting for a start than going into a game every day—I didn't even have to think about it."

In 1982, Fingers became the first man to record 300 saves; he finished with a then-record 341, but when he was closing, he often worked three innings at a time and piled up 100 to 120 innings a season, unheard of for the modern one-inning-only reliever.

"I don't think I could have pitched that way," Fingers said of today's reduced innings. "I needed a lot of work."

Fingers made the All-Star team every year from 1973 to 1976 with Oakland, and he was the World Series MVP in 1974. In 1981, with the Brewers, he received the Cy Young and MVP awards, the first relief pitcher ever to win both awards in the same year and one of only three (along with Eckersley and Willie Hernandez) ever to do so.

"As far as closers go, I'd put Rollie Fingers up against anybody," former A's outfielder George Hendrick said. "If you took your greatest closer ever and gave me Rollie Fingers, I'd have no complaints."

13 Unexpected Fun: 2012

Entering the 2012 season, no one expected anything of the Oakland A's. They'd gone 74–88 the previous year with a midseason managerial change, and they'd traded All-Star starters Gio Gonzalez and Trevor Cahill, as well as All-Star closer Andrew Bailey, over the winter. Another starter, Brett Anderson, was recovering from Tommy John surgery.

Then, on the first full day of spring training, starting third baseman Scott Sizemore blew out his knee. With no other everyday third basemen on Oakland's roster, the outlook for 2012 went from middling to poor.

One man believed from Day One, though, that the A's would surprise everyone: New outfielder Jonny Gomes arrived at camp and said that the young team had the talent to go to the playoffs and the bunch reminded him a lot of the 2008 Tampa Bay team he'd played for that went to the World Series, shocking baseball.

"If you don't set the goal and don't believe in it, it won't happen," Gomes said in late 2014. "If you're in the big leagues, you're a good player, and you've got a chance to shine. From there, it's just about getting everyone chain-linked in the right direction."

Gomes and veteran third baseman Brandon Inge, acquired in late April after his career had stalled out in Detroit, got the ball rolling, creating a relaxed clubhouse atmosphere in which the A's strange assortment of parts could mesh. Inge provided some big hits, too—including two grand slams in three days, one a walk-off shot vs. Toronto and the other against his former team, the Tigers.

Among Oakland's odds and ends: Outfielder Brandon Moss, signed to a minor-league contract before the season, wound up at first base; when first Sizemore and then Inge were injured, former catcher Josh Donaldson became the full-time third baseman; former first-base prospect Sean Doolittle joined the bullpen as a left-handed reliever; Cuban outfielder Yoenis Cespedes, in his first season in the U.S. after defecting, finished second in the Rookie of the Year voting; and finally given an everyday job, outfielder Josh Reddick hit 32 homers.

"There were a lot of unique stories in the clubhouse," Gomes said. "Moss, Donaldson, Doolittle, Reddick really stood out. The one thing they needed was the opportunity. Moss: boom. Reddick: boom. Donaldson: boom."

In mid-June, though, the A's appeared hopelessly out of it. They were nine games under .500, nine games behind division-leader Texas, and in last place in the AL West. They'd just been swept at Arizona, and to add a little extra insult, one-time Oakland All-Star Cahill beat them in that series.

That's when Moss, called up earlier in the month, began to show his muscle. He crushed four homers and drove in eight runs in Oakland's three-game sweep at Colorado. Still, by the end of the month, the A's were even further out of it; they won the final game of a four-game series at Texas to prevent getting swept, but they trailed Texas by a dozen games.

"I'll never forget [reliever] Brian Fuentes saying, 'Hey, now we're only 12 games back,' sort of making a joke of it," Moss said. "I was like, 'Hey, man, anything can happen.' The young guys were starting to do well. No one expected to win the division, except maybe Jonny, but you could feel the change. You could feel that everyone expected to win."

The next month, the A's made a national splash by sweeping the Yankees in a four-game series at Oakland, with Cespedes going 7-for-10 with two homers in the first three games and the A's getting two walk-off wins. That weekend, for the first time, Oakland moved into a tie for a wild-card spot.

Still, no one would have thought the A's would take the division crown from the front-running Rangers, who were coming off back-to-back AL pennants, especially when the A's lost three more starting pitchers: Bartolo Colon was suspended after a positive test for performance-ending substances; Brandon McCarthy was struck in the head by a line-drive and needed emergency brain surgery; and Anderson, back from Tommy John surgery, was sidelined by an oblique strain. Oakland's rotation down the stretch featured five rookies.

Yet there the A's were going into the final weekend, hosting Texas for three games and needing only one victory to clinch a wild-card spot.

"Going into that series, we were on the plane talking about the fact that we could still win the division," former Oakland third-baseman Donaldson recalled. "Then we win Friday night and we celebrate because we're in the wild-card game. Everyone's expectations were so low, no one thought anything was going to happen and all of a sudden we started winning and we were at an all-time high—it was a cool story, to win it at home on our field, celebrate with our fans, champagne pouring, it was just surreal.

"Saturday, we win again, and we're thinking, 'We can sweep them and win the division,'" and it seemed even more real. It felt like we'd taken away all of their momentum and we were using it on our side."

That final day of the 2012 season is among the most memorable in franchise history. Texas held an early 5–1 lead before Oakland scored six runs in the fourth inning; Coco Crisp contributed a two-out, two-run double to tie the game, then Rangers outfielder Josh Hamilton simply missed an easy fly ball by Cespedes that would have ended the inning. Instead, two more runs scored.

"Everyone called it Moneyball II, a perfect storm of positive things—we just started to play great down the stretch. It was incredible to see how everything came together," Anderson said. "And the way things ended up, with Hamilton dropping that fly ball—just crazy."

Oakland, picked to finish last in the AL West, spent one day all season in first place: that final day.

"I don't think anything can match that," Moss said. "That 2012 team—the intensity, the excitement of those last few months and that final weekend—it was magical."

The A's went on to play a taut series against the Tigers that went the distance and had some poignant moments, particularly Pat Neshek coming in to pitch Oakland out of a jam in his first appearance since the death of his infant son, Gehrig. The A's made some mistakes in dropping the first two games at Detroit, however, including a dropped fly ball by Crisp that proved costly in Game 2, and even more glaring, a wild pitch by Ryan Cook that catcher George Kottaras failed to block in the eighth inning, allowing the Tigers to tie the game.

In Game 3, the A's got a nice boost from Anderson, who returned from his oblique injury, still in pain, and went six scoreless innings for the victory at the Coliseum.

"That was probably the most fun, crazy atmosphere I've ever been a part of," Anderson said. "It was more like a college football game, the rally towels and everything. Being on the mound for that, that was really fun. I had the oblique and I hadn't worked in three weeks, but that game was something else."

Crisp and Cespedes made spectacular catches in that one, and in Game 4, the A's were down 3–1 in the ninth when they unbottled some of their regular-season walk-off voodoo. Seth Smith drilled a two-run game-tying single off closer Jose Valverde—and Crisp delivered a two-out game-winning single.

That tied the series, but Game 5 belonged to Justin Verlander, who allowed four hits and a walk in throwing a shutout. He'd given up only one run in seven innings in Game 1, and the following season's ALDS rematch with Oakland, he worked 15 more scoreless innings and recorded two more wins. Over the course of those two postseasons, Verlander allowed Oakland 13 hits and one run in 31 innings, striking out 43 and walking seven. He won the clinching game each year, a one-man wrecking crew.

"In 2012, Verlander had the biggest strike zone in America," Donaldson said. "I never saw a zone that big in Little League, and he's throwing 98 mph. But in 2013, he was the best I've ever seen him. He was hitting his target in every quadrant of the strike zone, you almost feel helpless, he's running it up there 98, 97, up in the zone, down in the zone, and then he's got the changeup. In 2012 I felt really bad afterward. In 2013, you've just got to tip your cap to the guy. He put his team on his back."

After the A's fell in Game 5 in 2012, the Coliseum fans stayed. They stood and cheered and cheered, and the Oakland players remained on the field and applauded their fans right back. The love-fest went on so long, even Tigers players praised the atmosphere.

"I think the fans appreciated the way we came back in that series, and the way we came back from last place during the season," Moss said. "We gave them something to cheer for—and they didn't want to stop cheering. I've never been part of anything like that. They were proud of us. We were proud of them. I have Detroit players still telling me how great our fans are."

"That was unbelievable. Things like that don't happen," Gomes said. "The crowd at the end, standing and cheering like that for so long, that should never be forgotten."

14 Tony La Russa

In 2014, Tony La Russa became just the third Athletics' manager inducted into the Baseball Hall of Fame, following Connie Mack and Dick Williams.

Because of his success with the Cardinals after leaving Oakland, as well as his first years of managing with the White Sox, La Russa chose to go into the Hall without a logo on his cap. A longtime Bay Area resident, however, La Russa forever will be linked to the Bash Brothers A's teams of the late 1980s—clubs that won three consecutive American League pennants and one championship.

"He was huge for us," former Oakland third baseman Carney Lansford said. "Tony kept us focused day in and day out. His intensity, how prepared he was. In all the years I played for him, I never saw him out-managed, with relievers, pinch hitters, always thinking ahead. He was very detail-oriented."

During his A's tenure, La Russa particularly became known for his use of the bullpen, modernizing the way relievers were used, with designated set-up men and one one-inning-only closer.

"It got to the point where no team ever said, 'Hey, let's get to their bullpen,'" Lansford said. "They might have been just as tough if not tougher than our starters, and our rotation was pretty darn good."

La Russa also had to contend with an unusual mix of personalities, including the occasionally high-maintenance duo of Jose Canseco and Rickey Henderson. Williams, who'd had his own dramas to deal with in managing the brawling A's of the early '70s, pointed out to La Russa early on that the egos might be an issue.

"I'd played for him and respected him, you talk about a mentor," La Russa said of Williams. "But he told me, 'You know, it's a very impressive club, but it's going to be a circus there. And it's not going to be a baseball circus.'"

When La Russa's A's swept the Mariners later that year, Williams told La Russa he'd been wrong in his assessment. "That Bash Brothers stuff kind of hid the true nature of our club," La Russa said. "We made all the routine plays, we played hard every day. The team leadership was excellent."

La Russa set the tone, though, the A's players said—even Canseco, who could be a handful.

"You have to put all these moving, talented parts together," Canseco said. "There were a lot of characters, attitudes, personalities, egos, superstars, entertainers. You have to know how to oil that wheel and move the chess pieces to win the game. And he did it well.

"We had a good relationship. To be honest, he was like my second father, in baseball. It was good—he was strict when he needed to be, lax when he needed to be. He demanded, 'Never come late to the ballpark,' and 'Be ready when the game starts.' So he didn't ask a lot but you were definitely prepared to play when you got there, prepared to play properly."

Mike Gallego, the A's former second baseman and the team's longtime third-base coach, said he learned an enormous amount just sitting near La Russa on the bench.

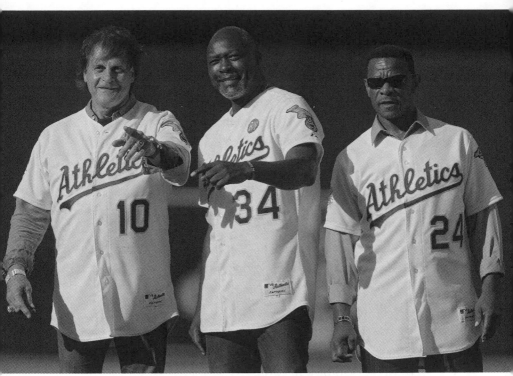

Tony La Russa, Dave Stewart, and Ricky Henderson hang out at the 25ᵗʰ anniversary celebration of the A's 1989 World Series championship on July 19, 2014. (Brian Bahr)

"He was definitely the adult of the group," Gallego said. "He disciplined us in a way to let us know how things would be run on this ship and after that, he pretty much let us police ourselves and in the end, we didn't want to disappoint him. We respected him so much, we wanted to impress him."

La Russa always blamed himself for the fact that the enormously talented A's teams won just one title during his time in Oakland, the 1989 "Earthquake" World Series against the Giants.

His players beg to differ.

"Every single one of his players felt the same way. I felt I could have done something better, you ask Dennis Eckersley, he thinks he could have done something better, you ask Mark McGwire, he thinks he could have done something better," Gallego said. "All we cared about was winning for the organization and doing our part.

"And as far as Tony, there was no doubt he was pitches—innings—ahead of other managers, other teams."

La Russa, hired to be Arizona's chief baseball officer in 2014, finished his managing career with 2,728 wins, third all time behind Mack and John McGraw.

The Second of Three: 1973

There were no significant lengthy holdouts before the 1973 season, though catcher Dave Duncan, who had knocked heads with Finley, refused to sign. He was traded with center fielder George Hendrick for catcher Ray Fosse and infielder Jack Heidemann.

Fosse, the A's longtime broadcaster, was coming from a perennial loser, the Indians, to the league's most talented team.

"Standing around the batting cage, seeing almost a lackadaisical attitude after coming over from Cleveland, I was upset," Fosse recalled with a laugh. "Here it was a year after winning the World Series, and I was like, 'Lightning is not going to strike twice.'

"So I asked Dick Green, 'What is it over here with these players, they seem like they're going through the motions.' And he said, 'We're ready. We're going to win the division, we're going to play someone from the East and we're going to the World Series.' They just had a tremendous amount of confidence. And sure enough, it turned out that way."

As Green promised, the A's took care of business, winning 94 games and claiming the West by six games; taking 20 of 27 games in August was the real key, as was Reggie Jackson's excellent season. The team also had three 20-game winners: Catfish Hunter, Ken Holtzman, and Vida Blue.

In the ALCS against Baltimore, the A's got phenomenal work from Holtzman (three hits and one run in 11 innings of work) and Hunter (three earned runs in 16⅔ innings) to edge Baltimore three games to two. Oakland hit .200 in the series, the Orioles .211, and Hunter threw a shutout in the finale.

In September, A's outfielder Billy North had sprained his ankle, knocking him out of the playoffs. Owner Charlie Finley wanted to replace him on the roster with infielder Manny Trillo and for the ALCS, the Orioles agreed, even though Trillo hadn't been with the A's on August 31, the deadline for postseason eligibility.

Mets manager Yogi Berra, however, would not let Oakland use Trillo for the World Series and Finley was furious. PR man Bob Fulton wound up in the crossfire.

"I was down on the field, getting ready for the first pitch when Charlie told me, 'We've got to get the crowd behind us. We're only going to be playing with 23 men on the roster because they won't allow Trillo. I want that announced to the crowd.'

"Johnny Johnson from the commissioner's office said, 'We're not going to have any announcement. The World Series doesn't belong to Charlie Finley, it belongs to Major League Baseball, and we control the announcements.'"

Finley asked Fulton to do an end-around and make an announcement to the media, instead.

"Then he called me in the second inning and said, 'What was their reaction?' And I told him, 'There were some pencils tossed in the air, some laughs, maybe, but that's it,'" Fulton said. "So Charlie said, 'Take it to [PA announcer] Roy Steele and have him announce it to the crowd. Screw the commissioner.'

"I said, 'Okay, Charlie,' and typed up the announcement and gave it to Roy. I said, 'Roy, you don't know where this announcement came from, you just got it somehow,' and I got out of the press box. Sure enough, it got the crowd yelling and screaming.

"Later, the guys in the press box said, 'Hey, Bob! Where'd you go? Some guy from the commissioner's office is looking for you.'"

The A's won the game 2–1 behind Holtzman, who also doubled and scored.

Finley wasn't done showing his displeasure, ignoring a long-standing rule about making changes to the lights only at the top of an inning.

"In the seventh inning, it's getting a little dark, so Finley has the lights turned on in the bottom of the inning," Fulton said. "Yogi goes nuts. Finley got fined for the lights and for the [Game 1] announcement."

The A's owner was spotted flipping peanut shells at commissioner Bowie Kuhn that evening.

Oakland lost Game 2 in extra innings, and Finley blamed second baseman Mike Andrews' defense; he was so furious, he tried to have Andrews sidelined the rest of the series with a bogus medical report. The A's players revolted, however, and after a 3–2 Oakland victory in Game 3, Andrews returned for Game 4 and manager Dick Williams used him to pinch hit, despite Finley's orders not to play him. Oakland fell 6–1 in that one.

Though Vida Blue pitched well in Game 5, the A's lost 2–0 and the defending champs suddenly faced elimination. Jackson—who was greeted by a sign at the Coliseum that read "Reggie Jackson, LVP (Least Valuable Player)"—told reporters that he'd thought he wouldn't feel any pressure, but, he said, "I feel it now and I'll respond to it."

He was 5-for-21 in the series to that point, but Jackson hadn't homered and he'd driven in just two runs. He'd also struck out six times.

In Game 6, Jackson hit a two-out double to drive in Oakland's first run. Then, with two outs in the third, he duplicated the earlier effort. He also singled in the eighth, dashed to third when the ball was dropped, and scored on a fly ball. The A's won 3–1.

In the finale, Campy Campaneris hit a two-run homer in the third, and Jackson added a two-run shot of his own, a blast to right center that sent him leaping and jumping around the bases. He also made two sensational catches—and later in the game, he had to chase down a fan who'd come onto the field and snatched his glove.

The A's won 5–2 and Jackson's bodyguard carried him off the field as the team celebrated in the middle of the diamond. Finley thanked Williams after the game, then announced that the manager wouldn't be coming back. Jackson took the mic, said he was sad to see Williams depart—and for the first time, he revealed a death threat that had been made against him.

Jackson was named the series MVP—and the man who'd longed so much to be in that position said he would have voted for A's shortstop Campaneris, who was deeply disappointed he didn't get the honor.

16 Jimmie Foxx

Jimmie Foxx impressed even at the age of 16. That's when former A's star Frank "Home Run" Baker discovered Foxx playing in Maryland and convinced him to drop out of high school to play minor-league baseball.

In 1925, Foxx made his debut with the A's at the age of 17, and by 20 he was an everyday player. In 1929, he hit 33 homers, the first of 12 consecutive seasons with 30-plus homers—including

58 in 1932. He was named the American League MVP that year and the next.

The great 1929–30 A's title teams were a cantankerous bunch, but Foxx was quite the opposite, a muscular first baseman who often was referred to as a gentle giant. He did instill great fear in the opposition—and a mixture of awe and humor in Yankee pitcher Lefty Gomez, who got off numerous one-liners about his biggest nemesis, including the following attributed quips:

"Jimmie Foxx wasn't signed. He was trapped."

"He has muscles in his hair."

"One day, my glasses fogged up when I was pitching, but when I cleaned them and looked at the plate and saw Foxx clearly, the sight of him terrified me so much I never wore them again."

Pitching to Foxx was easy, Gomez said: "I just throw him my best pitch and then run to back up third."

Once, when catcher Bill Dickey came out to ask Gomez what he planned to throw to Foxx, Gomez told him he'd kind of been hoping Foxx would just get bored and go home.

Ted Williams, Foxx's teammate in Boston, called Foxx the best hitter he'd ever seen besides Joe DiMaggio, and said that Foxx hit line drives that "sounded like gun fire…a hell of a lot louder than mine."

Not surprisingly, one of Foxx's nicknames was "The Beast." The other, of course, was "Double X."

Asked how the family's name had taken on an extra X, Foxx once said he had no idea. "But that was the way my grandfather handed it down to us," he said, "so I guess it belongs there."

Foxx nearly won the Triple Crown in 1932, when his 58 homers established a record for right-handed hitters that stood until Mark McGwire's 70 in 1998. Foxx also drove in 169 runs and he hit .364, second in the league.

In 1933, Foxx did claim the Triple Crown, hitting .356 with 48 homers and 163 RBIs. Three years later, he was gone, joining

Mickey Cochrane, Lefty Grove, and Al Simmons in Connie Mack's second massive dynasty sell-off. The Philadelphia Athletics never would see first place again.

Mack parted with Foxx and three others in return for $300,000. Foxx spent the next six and a half seasons in Boston, where he won another MVP in 1938.

Foxx worked as a minor-league coach and manager after he retired in 1946, and in 1952, he was the manager of the Fort Wayne Daisies of the All-American Girls Professional Baseball League. Though his club lost to the Rockford Peaches in the playoffs, Foxx is widely believed to be the inspiration for Tom Hanks' character, Rockford manager Jimmy Dugan, in *A League of Their Own*.

In 20 seasons, Foxx hit 534 homers, second only to Babe Ruth at the time he retired. He recorded 13 seasons with 100 or more RBIs, and finished with 1,922. He had a lifetime average of .325. In 18 World Series games, he hit .344. In his final season, with the Phillies, the 37-year-old even pitched in nine games and had an ERA of 1.59.

Foxx was inducted into the Hall of Fame in 1951 and he died in 1967.

According to author Robert P. Broadwater, two years after Foxx's death, he was still on Lefty Gomez's mind. When Apollo 11 landed on the moon, Gomez cracked, "When Neil Armstrong first set foot on the moon, he and all the space scientists were puzzled by an unidentifiable white object. I knew immediately what it was. That was a home-run ball hit off me in 1933 by Jimmie Foxx."

17 Eck

The A's didn't initially realize what they had with then-starter Dennis Eckersley when they acquired him from the Cubs in early April 1987. There was no spot for him in the rotation and he appeared on the down side of his career—32 years old and coming off a 6–11 season.

"Tony La Russa didn't know what to do with him," A's coach Rene Lachemann said.

Unbeknownst to the A's, however, Eckersley had kicked a serious drinking problem. He was focused and in shape.

"I was just out of rehab, and nobody knew that," Eckersley said. "At that point in my life, after what I'd just been through, the biggest thing wasn't pitching. I had a different perspective."

With no set role, Eckersley said, "I did everything. I set up, did a couple of long relief jobs. I was caddying for Moose Haas and Joaquin Andujar, because they never knew if they were going to start game to game. It was horrible. I didn't know if I'd throw one inning or five innings. I wasn't thrilled about it, but I knew I had to prove myself."

Eckersley showed perfect control and that he was physically sound and when closer Jay Howell began to have some arm trouble, Eckersley wound up pitching later in games.

"It's a wonder how things work out sometimes," equipment manager Steve Vucinich said.

Eckersley wasn't sold on bullpen life, however.

"At the end of the season, Tony asked me what I wanted to do next year, and I said, 'Start.' That's how stupid I was," Eckersley said with a laugh. "But we got Bob Welch that winter and Jay left,

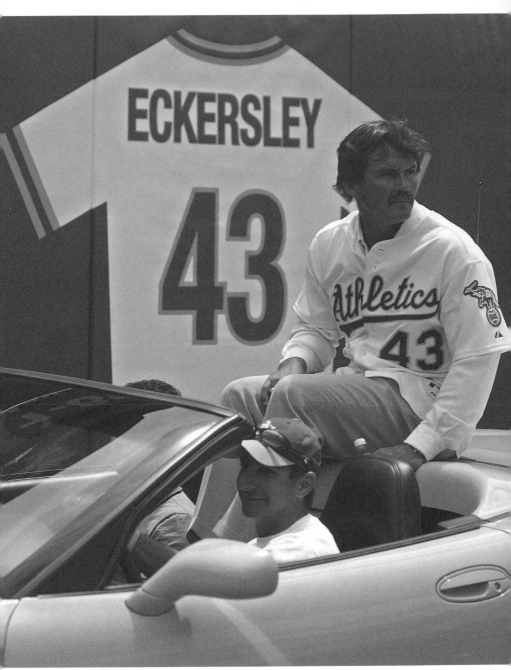

Dennis Eckersley is driven past his retired jersey in right field. (Ben Margot/AP Photo)

and that was that. I was like, 'Okay,' sigh. Little did I know I'd have so much success with it."

Eckersley also credits Welch with helping his frame of mind. After Welch's death in 2014, Eckersley said they had a special bond, as recovering alcoholics, and Welch's book, *Five O'Clock Comes Early*, was significant for Eckersley.

"At that time, I just started my recovery. I was sober for a year when I met him," Eckersley said. "He came at the right time in my life. Looking back, he was brave to write that book, man. He touched a lot of people, helped a lot of people. He leaves his mark with that book."

"Eck" went from 16 saves in 1987 to 45 the next year, when he finished second in the Cy Young voting and was named the series MVP when the A's beat Boston in the ALCS.

In 1990, Eckersley allowed five earned runs—five—all year, and had an ERA of 0.61. Over the course of 114 games in 1989–90, he walked seven batters, total—one of them intentionally. In 1990, he recorded more saves (48) than baserunners allowed (45), which is extraordinary.

In 1992, he took both the Cy Young and the MVP awards after saving 51 games and putting up a 1.91 ERA; he was the first player in history to have recorded a 20-win season and a 50-save season in his career. He also threw a no-hitter with Cleveland in 1977.

"I knew he had it the whole time," catcher Ray Fosse told reporters after the game. "The only thing I had to remind him was to tuck his shoulder in."

Eckersley always has heaped credit on Fosse, who'd played for two Oakland championship teams and who has worked as an A's broadcaster for nearly 30 years, for helping steer him through that 1977 feat.

"Catching Eck's no-hitter and then calling his 300th save so many years later is one of the thrills of my career," Fosse said.

Over the course of the decade, Eckersley amassed 390 saves, and he was one of the dominant pitchers of the era, known for his steely glare and his emphatic finger points and fist pumps after nailing things down. His success changed the way teams used closers; he worked almost exclusively in the ninth, the trend ever since.

Like many of the A's stars over the years, Eckersley is from the Bay Area, born in Oakland and raised in Fremont. On January 6, 2004, he was elected to the Hall of Fame, and the following year, the A's retired his No. 43.

"When he was in, the game was over, like clockwork," Lachemann said. "We knew if we had the lead in the ninth, we would win the ballgame, and the teams on the other side knew they were done."

18 Catfish Hunter

The A's had done well with their amateur signings even before the major-league draft came along. Under Charles Finley—who did much of his own scouting—the team signed Joe Rudi, Dave Duncan, Paul Lindblad, John "Blue Moon" Odom, and two future Hall of Famers, pitchers Roland Glen "Rollie" Fingers and James Augustus "Catfish" Hunter.

Most teams were leery of Hunter, who'd lost a toe in a hunting accident during his senior year of high school in North Carolina. He still had shotgun pellets in his foot. That didn't sway Finley, however, who gave the right hander a $75,000 bonus even though Hunter couldn't pitch at all in 1964. Finley paid for a trip to the

Mayo Clinic for an operation, and by 1965, Hunter was in the big leagues, age 19.

Finley's team had an ace to build around in their new home in Oakland. And the Oakland A's gained national attention for the first time just a month into the 1968 season when Hunter pitched a perfect game against the Twins on May 8 at the Coliseum.

Hunter struck out 11 of the 27 men he faced, including Harmon Killebrew three times and pinch-hitter Rich Reese to end the game. Hunter also recorded three hits and drove in three of his team's four runs with a pair of singles.

Rudi had just been recalled from the minors that day, he said, "So obviously, I was scared to death. I had two or three half-tough plays and I was so nervous."

Equipment manager Steve Vucinich, then a ballboy, said he was stationed down the line, and he was too scared to go in and even use the bathroom because he didn't want to disrupt anything.

It was the first regular-season perfect game by an American League pitcher in 46 years, and just the seventh in modern baseball history.

Hall of Famer Joe DiMaggio, in his first season as an A's vice president and coach, called Hunter's performance "a masterpiece."

Even Finley was impressed. He gave Hunter a $5,000 bonus.

Club broadcaster Ray Fosse was traded to the A's from Cleveland in 1973 and, he said, "Catfish Hunter was the first pitcher I caught. Can you imagine losing 90 to 100 games with Cleveland and going from that to warming up Catfish Hunter? He didn't break a sweat. That was 15 of the easiest outs of my life. I was like, 'You've got to be kidding me.' Like going from catching Little League pitchers to Cy Young. The control, the mastery. And I'd just showed up and he never shook off.

"After three, four starts I said, 'Catfish, you never shake me off. Why?' And he said, 'Your job is to tell me what to throw and where to throw it, and I'm going to do it.' And sure enough, the only time he'd shake me off is when he was trying to mess with the hitters."

Hunter was a major cog in the A's 1972–74 championship teams, but he and Finley battled often about Hunter's salary and the impasse between the two wound up shaping baseball's future and hastening the end of the A's dynasty.

Always looking for a way to save a buck, the A's owner had violated the terms of Hunter's 1974 contract. Half of the deal was supposed to be set aside as an annuity, but because that would not qualify as a tax-deductible expense, Finley decided to make a lump-sum payment of $50,000 instead. Hunter contested this action by going to the players' union.

"I was sitting in the office during the ALCS," said A's PR man Bob Fulton, "and the secretary brings in a telegram from Marvin Miller of the union declaring Catfish a free agent because Finley broke the terms. I found Finley at the pool at the Edgewater Hotel and he gets Miller on the phone and said, 'What's going on?'

"Then he held a big press conference to say, 'Catfish is staying until the conclusion of the season,' and Charlie went to war. It was the only time in history that Major League Baseball and Finley were on the same page. They were hoping the arbitrator would say he either had to pay the annuity or he didn't and that would be the end of it, but the arbitrator said 'Mr. Hunter is a free agent.'

"The A's got nothing for a Hall of Famer. Finley lost him over pocket change."

Hunter was baseball's first superstar free agent. After the season, he signed a then-astronomical $3.5 million deal with the Yankees.

"Finley didn't want to pay the taxes and it hit the fan," A's starter Blue Moon Odom said. "I have nothing bad to say about Charlie, but if we'd had another owner, we would have been better off as far as going to the bank. We always had to fight just for a few thousand."

The next year, Andy Messersmith and Dave McNally began the wave of free agency for real; they did not sign deals for 1975 and elected free agency after that season. Following their lead would be Oakland's best and brightest, but it was Catfish Hunter who got the ball rolling.

Hunter was immensely popular with his teammates, and they were crushed when he died of ALS (amyotrophic lateral sclerosis, Lou Gehrig's disease) in 1999, age 53. Fosse recalled the streets being lined in every direction for Hunter's funeral procession in North Carolina. "Everyone loved Catfish," he said.

"He looked out for me," outfielder George Hendrick said. "I love him to this day and I'll love him until the day I die. I played hard for everyone but when Catfish was on the mound, I was even more intent on doing whatever it took to win the game. Playing behind him, he was one of the most comfortable pitchers I've played behind; he worked fast, attacked the strike zone. You were always on your toes."

"Umpires would get behind the plate, see Catfish, and tell me, 'Today's going to be a great game, an hour and a half and we'll be out of here,'" Fosse said.

Hunter had a remarkable winning percentage, going 224–166 in his 15 seasons, and he was a member of five championship teams, including two in New York. In 1987, he was inducted into the Hall of Fame, and in 1991, the A's retired his jersey number, 27, the first number the franchise had so honored in 50 years.

19 Grow A Handlebar Mustache

For most of the 20th century, major-league players were clean-shaven, with few exceptions. Teams even had rules forbidding mustaches and beards.

Then came the 1970s, and Charlie Finley's Oakland A's. Reggie Jackson started it all, according to his teammates, when the outfielder showed up to spring training with a mustache in 1972.

The rest of the A's hated it and tried to get Jackson to part with it, but according to reliever Rollie Fingers, "Reggie wouldn't shave, so Catfish [Hunter] and Darold Knowles and I were in the bullpen one day and decided, 'Let's start growing mustaches.' That way, Dick Williams would get upset and say, 'You all have to shave them off,' and that would mean that Reggie had to shave his."

That plan backfired. The unpredictable Finley, instead of blowing his top, loved the idea. He announced plans for "Mustache Day" at the Oakland Coliseum, and promised $300 to every player who participated by growing one.

"For $300," quipped pitcher Ken Holtzman, "I'd grow hair on my feet."

The A's were winning with their new look, and, Fingers said, "Ballplayers are the most superstitious animals who ever lived. A lot of guys kept their mustaches and we kept winning and then we won the World Series. We became known as 'The Mustache Gang' and we won again the next year and the next year."

Fingers' Snidely Whiplash–style whiskers were the most recognizable of all.

"I grew mine as a handlebar just to be different," he said. "When I let it grow, it got kind of long, and I said, 'What the heck,

I'll twirl it up to see what it looks like.' I got more and more press, so I said, 'Okay,' and kept going and going.

"I've had it since 1972," Fingers said 42 years later. "I came close to shaving it off toward the end of the season—I lost both heads of a doubleheader against the Twins. I was real close, but I thought, 'Nah.'"

Not everyone wanted to participate.

"There were three of us who chose not to do it," Sal Bando said. "Me and Mike Hegan and Larry Brown. Charlie called us together and said in so many words, 'Grow the mustache.' I just didn't want to do it. I didn't think it looked good. I was right, it didn't look that good. But it became a trademark."

Bando thought that there was a plus—a big plus—in some cases, however.

"Of all the people that had them, Rollie Fingers went from being an ugly ballplayer to at least decent looking," Bando said with a chuckle. "He was ugly, trust me."

Finley selected Father's Day, June 18, for "Mustache Day," and every fan with a mustache was allowed free admission. The club brought in California native "Frenchy" Bordagaray as the honorary chairman: The former Brooklyn Dodgers outfielder had shocked baseball 37 years earlier by showing up during the spring with a mustache. He was forced to shave it off, and that, Bordagaray claimed, led to a hitting slump.

A four-sport star at Fresno State, Bordagaray is known for one of baseball's best quotes. Asked about his penalty for spitting at an umpire, Bordagaray responded, "It was more than I expectorated." That was Finley's kind of guy.

Finley came through on the bonuses, and the next year, Fingers hoped to add another mustache bonus in his contract. Finley, amused, agreed, and in a press release, he announced, "Rollie not only got a substantial increase in salary, but his 1973 contract also includes a year's supply of the very best mustache wax available. In fact, this is what held up the final signing. I wanted to give Rollie $75 for the mustache wax and he wanted $125 for it." They settled on $100.

Facial hair became a staple of many of the A's successful teams all the way into the 21st century, when Josh Reddick's shaggy beard and Derek Norris' caveman look, complete with mullet, were standouts for the 2013–14 playoff clubs.

"Heck, nowadays it looks like guys have come out of the backwoods," Fingers said. "I grew a beard one winter and no one recognized me because my mustache just blended into it."

Like Fingers, Dallas Braden, he of the 19th perfect game in history, featured a handlebar mustache—on the side of his right index finger.

"It's not an homage to Rollie Fingers, much as I'd love to say it was," Braden said. "I met a girl in Tacoma with a ton of artwork, and asked her if I could check it out. It was so cool, I still remember it—she had an angel and devil, very elaborate. She turned around, and I said, 'Great stuff,' and she said, 'I'm sorry, I didn't get your name,' and she had her index finger sticking out—with a handlebar mustache on it.

"I thought, 'That's the dumbest, greatest tattoo I will ever get.' I remember thinking, 'That's the finger that will be sticking out of my glove, maybe it will distract hitters.'"

When Braden filmed a commercial with Fingers the next year, he got the Hall of Famer's input on the tattoo version, and, Braden said, "Rollie was very appreciative. He loved it."

The Fingers-style mustache is the epitome of the A's style to many, including Braden.

"I'm a fan," he said. "The handlebar mustache represents the green and gold just like elephants, white shoes, and Afros. The A's have always been about ridiculous facial hair, it's an ode to the players of the past and Charlie Finley. There is a lot of room to express yourself in that clubhouse, and Oakland embraces it.

"If you don't think of handlebar mustaches and reach out to twirl the ends of your non-existent imaginary mustache, you need to re-check your fanhood."

Fingers provides handy tips for those who'd like to emulate his fabulous 'stache:

"First, you have got to have pretty decent facial hair—if you don't have a good amount, especially over your lip, it's not going to work. I doubt very much that Sonny Gray could do this.

"Second, it will take three months of full growth once you let the ends grow. You've got to let it get an inch long before you can start twirling it and training it with wax.

"The wax to use: Pinaud Clubman, clear. Then, when it dries, you don't see the wax."

Or, if you're considering the look for yourself and don't want to have to mess with mustache wax, you, too, can go the Braden route and just hold up your tattoo of a handlebar mustache above your lip.

20 Dallas Braden's Perfect Game

He didn't know the count on the final batter of the game on May 9, 2010, and Dallas Braden's confusion helped him complete the 19th perfect game in major-league history.

Braden had retired 26 in a row on that day at the Coliseum, and he threw a 2–1 fastball to Tampa Bay's Gabe Kapler.

Home-plate umpire Jim Wolf "screwed it up," Braden said four years later, chuckling a little. "It was a 2–1 count and Landon Powell calls a fastball outside, and I was like, 'Absolutely, let's do it.' It was a hell of a pitch. I thought it was a strike, but Jim must have called it a ball because it was 3–1. I didn't know that—in my mind, it was 2–2. Landon calls a changeup next pitch, and I'm thinking, 'No, Landon, fastball! It's 2–2!' So I shook him off, and I'm going to beat him inside with a fastball because I'm thinking it's 2–2."

Kapler tapped the fastball to shortstop, Cliff Pennington picked it up and threw to first, setting off an on-field celebration. Braden was enveloped by teammates, including Powell.

"I just let Dallas work," the A's catcher said. "He was magical."

Braden and Powell had worked together for years in the minors and knew each other well. Braden said he shook Powell off just twice the entire game. It might have fallen apart at the last moment, though, had Braden known the correct count.

"I was in a dream. I'd thought it was 2–2. I would have thrown the changeup otherwise," Braden said. "I've talked to Kapler since then—and he was sitting soft, so the fastball tied him up.

"It wasn't until after the end of the game when I heard the radio highlights, and Ken Korach said, '3–1 fastball,' and I was like, 'Wow, did Korach screw up!' That was the first I'd heard about it. Because when I threw it and got the groundball and everyone went nuts, no one was saying, 'Hey, by the way, it was 3–1.'

"The fact I had no idea what the count was speaks volumes about how tuned out I was to what was going on in the moment."

The reason Braden was so out of touch? It was Mother's Day, always the most difficult day of the year for the left-hander, who lost his mother, Jodie Atwood, to melanoma when he was a teenager. There never was any doubt in Braden's mind that his mother was looking out for him that day in May.

"That's the kind of woman my mother was. She very easily and all the time put aside how she was feeling to make sure I was okay—and I processed that on that day," Braden said, "Ever since she died, I've had to think, 'Yeah, Mother's Day sucks, but I've got to put that aside, I have 24 other guys depending on me when I'm on the field. I have to put personal demons aside.'

"I was tapping into my mother's spirit, the way she battled, that day. Because that's the only reason I even got out of bed in the morning. I can still remember her going through chemo, spitting up blood, and not even thinking of herself, just worried about her boy, hoping I didn't notice. So there's no way I'm not going to go out and battle, what she went through was much harder."

Braden's beloved grandmother, Peggy Lindsey, was in the crowd at the Coliseum. She had raised him after his mother died, and when she climbed down from the stands and was helped onto the field to embrace her grandson, there were few dry eyes in the place. It was one of the most touching scenes in the history of the franchise.

"My thought process after the last out was, 'Oh my God, this is happening.' I looked up to Section 209, and it was the first day of a deal I had with the A's where I sponsored seats in the section and tickets were $2.09," said Braden, who is from nearby Stockton, area code 209. "I immediately thought, 'My grandmother is here and just witnessed this. It's not something I have to go home and tell her about—she experienced this, too.'

"My grandmother saw everything from when I started playing at four years old to my debut to that day. That was a special moment. If you weren't there, you don't understand."

Braden, so out of it he didn't know the count, also ran to embrace...first baseman Daric Barton when the final out was recorded. He was following the throw from Pennington to Barton and kept going, with Powell racing to catch up to him.

"I always give him a hard time about that," Powell said. "You're supposed to hug your catcher first, and he hugged Barton. I was yelling, 'Turn around, turn around, I'm right here!'"

Told that Randy Johnson had given his catcher a $10,000 watch for catching his perfect game, Braden laughed and recalled that Powell had once said that Braden wouldn't even buy him a

Braden vs. A-Rod

Right after Dallas Braden's Mother's Day perfect game, his grand-mother, Peggy Lindsey, raised some eyebrows in an impromptu press conference.

"Stick it, A-Rod," Lindsey said.

The backstory: The previous month, Braden had a spat with Alex Rodriguez, the less-than-popular Yankees third baseman, when Rodriguez retreated to first base after a foul ball—and took a short cut across the pitcher's mound.

Starting pitcher Braden let Rodriguez have it, shouting, "Get off my [expletive] mound!"

After the game, Braden, irate, said that Rodriguez had broken an unwritten rule of the sport. "If he wants to run across the pitcher's mound, tell him to go do laps in the bullpen," Braden said. "This one? This one is mine."

Rodriguez told New York reporters he "thought it was pretty funny, actually."

As for the "rule," he added. "I've never quite heard that, especially from a guy who has a handful of wins in his career."

It was on. The two traded barbs over the next few weeks until Braden's May 10 perfecto. "Uncle!" Rodriguez declared. "Good for him."

More than four years after the incident, Braden, now retired and a studio analyst for ESPN, still feels strongly he was in the right, as numerous other players and former players had said at the time. And he made no apologies for his grandmother's feisty comments.

"I've always had such a respect for the game and the people who play it," Braden said. "We've all traveled a long road to get there, and some have more bumps than others. You need to show everyone respect.

"So for my grandmother to be there for our shining moment and to basically throw up the middle finger to ARod—well, that speaks volumes, like, 'Yeah, keep running your mouth, pal. This moment you can't buy with any of your $200 million contracts.'

"I take things like basic baseball etiquette very seriously. There's a time and place for antics, and yes, they're becoming more commonplace in our sport—the celebrations for strikeouts, it's almost like the NBA. But when you're out there, you have people depending on you to act a certain way every day. You couldn't respect me for a minute if I didn't behave professionally.

"And you understand who you play for. I know the Oakland fan base. I understand the Oakland fans. I come from that demographic, I am that demographic, blue collar, you don't accept insults from anyone. This is our home. You're the visitor."

Beyond that, there are practical matters that make messing with the mound a no-no.

"I've got my landing hole. I've got my pivot spot. He ran between me and the pitching rubber—you do the math, that's way too [expletive] close," Braden said. "Let's put it this way: If he'd had a dog-shock collar on, he'd still be spasming right now."

The day after the incident, Yankees second baseman Robinson Cano came to the ballpark with "Get Off My Mound" T-shirts. That made Braden laugh—but he asked MLB to halt production of the shirts because he didn't believe it was right to pit two union members against each other for monetary gain.

"I didn't want to put myself over another player in the game," Braden said. "That's kind of what had started the whole thing in the first place, really."

Gatorade on the golf course. Powell, who is now the baseball coach at North Greenville (S.C.) University, has numerous mementos of the game, though; among other things, the A's presented him his glove in a glass case, and Braden signed Powell's game-worn jersey. Powell considers the game the highlight of his career.

"There were times before that I'd think, 'How cool would that be to be part of a no-hitter?'" Powell said, "and I'd realize, 'I don't have a chance to do that, I'm a backup catcher.' I never thought it would happen, but that day felt like it was scripted. It was storybook, the odds of me being in there and a guy throwing 87 mph who's a contact pitcher throwing a perfect game? It was like winning the lottery."

Powell said he felt something unusual was going on all day— and he cites two oddities from the game. Early on, he and home plate umpire Jim Wolf inadvertently tossed balls to each other from 20 feet away, not realizing the other was doing so—and the balls collided in midair. They laughed and thought nothing of it until several innings later, when Wolf and Braden, who was on the mound, did the same exact thing, the balls again colliding.

"There was something in the air," Powell said. "It was a special day."

Braden retired from baseball before the 2014 season, but he said he is constantly reminded of his perfect game.

"What's great is getting to recount memories of my mother every day, because every day someone comes up to me and tells me where they were when it happened—or more often, where they weren't, because it was Mother's Day," he said. "People stopped to watch or listen to the end of the game, and then got yelled at by their wife or mother because they were 45 minutes late to the barbecue or getting back from the hardware store.

"Some people say they got home late to find their family crying because they'd seen it, too, and seen me and my grandma.

"That day was my mother's doing. Because there is no way I do that without my mother inspiring me."

21 And the Third of Three: 1974

A week before spring training in 1974, it was unclear who would helm the team, with Dick Williams seemingly still a possibility—despite both resigning and getting fired, even as he remained under contract to Oakland.

Owner Charlie Finley, never predictable, suddenly re-hired Alvin Dark—the same man he'd fired, re-hired, and fired again during one 24-hour period in 1967.

Many of the players never took to Dark because he was seen as Finley's lackey. He followed the owner's suggestions to the letter, and he even listened when Finley barked orders from the stands. It wasn't subtle.

"At Texas one time, I was getting ready to hit and Charlie was sitting next to the dugout and said, 'Pinch hit for him,'" A's catcher Ray Fosse said. "Alvin put someone in for me.

"In Game 2 of the playoffs, Alvin told me and Gene Tenace he wanted both of us to warm up because he didn't know who was going to start. Of course there was talk that Charlie was controlling the lineup, and that's what Alvin was basically saying.

"I found out later that the coaching staff and Alvin wanted me to start and I hit a three-run home run to help beat the Orioles. In the postgame press conference, Finley came in and said, 'That's my boy!' I said, 'If I'm your boy, why didn't you want me to catch?' I couldn't believe I said it. I was kind of joking. But that was the feeling I got."

At one point during 1974, team captain Sal Bando groused that Dark "couldn't manage a meat market." (He came around on Dark the following year.)

The other major event that winter: Second baseman Dick Green, in his annual ritual, announced his retirement and then changed his mind.

Reveling in their usual turmoil, the A's went 90–72 in 1974. It was their worst mark in four years, but they still won the AL West by five games and they faced Baltimore again in the ALCS. The Orioles took Game 1, before phenomenal performances by starters Ken Holtzman, Vida Blue, and Catfish Hunter sent Oakland to the World Series for the third consecutive season.

The 1974 World Series might not be the most memorable Oakland played—it was over in five games, with the A's taking the title again. But it stands out for a couple of reasons. Off the field, the news about Hunter's contract snafu had just broken—it would lead to his departure as a free agent—and then Blue Moon Odom and Fingers got into a big brouhaha before Game 1.

On the field, the notables were Green and Holtzman.

In Game 1, Holtzman doubled in the fifth and wound up scoring on a squeeze bunt by Campy Campaneris, and the A's won that game 3–2. He homered for the A's first run in Game 4.

"When I joined the A's, I'd spent seven years in the National League, so I knew how to hit. I had a bat," Holtzman said. "What was strange was that I hit that well [in the World Series] after not batting for an entire year—and then hit all those doubles and the home run. Let's face it, if you step up in a World Series game and you're facing a great pitcher and hit a double, that's luck."

Holtzman is all over the TV highlights of the series, but he's eclipsed by Green and his numerous dazzling plays—some of the finest defensive work in World Series history, especially the second baseman's two great stops in Game 3, a one-run A's win, and his dive to start a game-ending double play in Game 4.

"If you asked any member of the team who was the MVP against the Dodgers, they would say Dick Green," Holtzman said, "and I think I had more hits than he did. But he made six or seven unbelievable plays to keep games from getting out of hand. We wouldn't have won the championship without him."

Green had opted to return for one last year in 1974, but he didn't get the raise he wanted the following spring, and Finley placed him on waivers when Green wouldn't sign, ending his career.

The A's did little wrong in the 1974 Series, but their biggest mistake was widely publicized because of its ties to Finley's wacky ideas.

In Game 2, Oakland's lone loss, the A's scored twice in the ninth to cut L.A.'s lead to 3–2, when, with one out, Herb Washington, Finley's designated pinch runner, went to first base for Joe Rudi.

He was promptly picked off by Dodgers reliever Mike Marshall, killing the rally, and afterward, the A's players blamed Finley.

The Dodgers had a goat of their own in the series: Bill Buckner, the man who in 1986 would make one of the most famous flubs in World Series history.

Throughout the 1974 series, Buckner insisted that the A's, particularly Green, were just lucky, and he called Hunter "overrated." A's fans threw garbage at him in left field in response.

Then, with the Dodgers trailing by a run in Game 5 and facing elimination in the eighth, Buckner ripped a single to center and he tried to make it to third when the ball got by Billy North. Reggie Jackson made a perfect throw to Green, who fired to third to get Buckner. The Dodgers were cooked, with Series MVP Rollie Fingers pitching a perfect ninth.

Rudi hit the game-winning blow in Game 5, a solo homer off Marshall in the seventh inning, and though the A's hadn't hit much at all that series, North said he had an inkling Rudi would get the job done when Marshall came in. Rudi's game awareness made the difference.

"I was standing right on the side by the backstop, and I said, 'We're going to win this game, but I don't know how, because this guy can get you out, Mike Marshall,'" North said. "And the thing was, Joe noticed Marshall didn't throw any warmup pitches. So he said, 'The first pitch he's going to throw me is a fastball,' and I'm standing right there and the first pitch he threw was a fastball and Joe hit it out of the park. I said, 'There it is.'

"I tell you, Joe Rudi was more observant, and Mike Marshall was arrogant. That's the kind of thing that makes champions. Joe Rudi said, 'Bam,' and there it is."

Crown in hand, the A's still had personality clashes on full display. Finley and Reggie Jackson were on the outs much of the year. So after the A's wrapped up their third straight title, PR man Bob Fulton figured Jackson would stick it to Finley somehow.

"We're up 3–1 against the Dodgers and baseball puts out a postgame edict: No alcohol is to be visible on the platform," Fulton recalled. "There's a memo, 'No champagne on the podium,' so I make sure everyone knows, put a copy of the memo in their lockers. And Charlie tells me before the ceremony, 'I don't want Reggie on the platform, I want Sal and Joe Rudi there.'

"In the middle of the postgame presentation, here comes Reggie. He shakes up a bottle of champagne and he pours it on [commissioner] Bowie Kuhn's head."

Fearful for his job, Fulton went to find Finley to explain. "I said, 'I don't know what happened, everyone knew about the alcohol edict. And Charlie, I have no control over Reggie.'

"Charlie smiled and said, 'Bob, I told Reggie to do that.'"

22 The Big Three

From 2000 to 2003, the A's went to the playoffs every year. The main reason, despite what you might read or see elsewhere: the Big Three.

In 2002, the year Michael Lewis highlighted in the book *Moneyball,* the A's had a high on-base percentage, a stat featured heavily in Lewis' book, but they finished in the middle of the pack in runs scored—while they led the league in ERA. Mark Mulder, Tim Hudson, and Barry Zito combined for 57 wins and Zito earned the Cy Young.

"It was as much if not more the Big Three than it was *Moneyball*," one-time A's outfielder Eric Byrnes said. "That was a philosophy, but you still have to have pitching and the one thing Oakland had was pitching.

"Zito, Mulder, and Hudson, when they were at the top of their game and pushing each other every single night, it was fun to watch the competition. I don't think any of them would admit it, but I think they wanted to upstage each other."

General manager Billy Beane pointed out that the three starters fit the *Moneyball* ideal as low-risk collegians. Hudson, in particular, was a bargain, lasting until the sixth round of the draft because of his small stature, while Zito was knocked by some teams because he didn't throw hard. Beane often has joked that drafting the three pitchers made him look smarter, and there's no doubt they drove the A's success: During their time in Oakland, the Big Three went a combined 275–144, and they made seven All-Star appearances.

"That was obviously a unique situation," Hudson said. "I think a lot of GMs around baseball would give their right arm for that. My time in Oakland, pretty much any time any of us was mentioned, we were all grouped together. That was kind of our identity, which was great."

They were often compared to the original Big Three, Atlanta's John Smoltz, Tom Glavine, and Greg Maddux, though the Braves developed only Glavine.

"I thought people make a little bit too much of a big deal about that," Mulder said. "You look at what the guys in Atlanta did, we can't even compare to that. I do think it made us better, being compared to them, though. I can laugh about it. [Former A's reliever] Jason Isringhausen would see something on TV and go, 'Big Three this, Big Three that!'"

"After 2001, it was really the Big Three," Zito said. "We had that energy. I thought it was flattering to be included in that group."

The three came up within a year of each other, and though lumped together, they have distinct personalities. Small-framed but fearless Hudson; thoughtful and unusual Zito, who initially drew attention for wearing outlandish clothes and carrying pink pillows and scented candles with him on the road; and Mulder, known by teammates as "the golden child" for his supreme confidence and his all-around athletic ability.

"You could tell they were something special," former A's first baseman Jason Giambi said. "Huddy was such a bulldog. I loved the way he competed, the way he threw the ball, he was incredible. Zito was always zany, but he had such great stuff and it was so fun to watch him develop. We rode him about the pink pillows. Mulder came up and he was the anchor. Every night, we felt we had a chance to win."

"Zito is exactly how he's described; very eccentric, basically on his own planet," said Byrnes, a close friend of the left-hander. "He's a very hard worker and pitching is an art for him. He was so dedicated to his craft—I've never seen anyone care so much. That was the biggest misconception about Barry, that he was loopy or flaky. That's the last thing he was.

"Mulder was just doing what he does. He's 6'6" and left-handed and the most physically gifted of the three. He was going to get outs, he was so talented, he'd just go at guys. Huddy for me is the little engine that could, the ringleader. The Alabama gun-slinger, he got by on straight grit. He was going to put it all out there, he was cutthroat. You want him on your side in a fight, and don't ever play poker with him. He took an entire paycheck from me once."

Early on, Hudson gained a reputation for gutsiness after stare-downs with stars such as Nomar Garciaparra and Barry Bonds and big wins against Pedro Martinez and Randy Johnson, when both were at their peak.

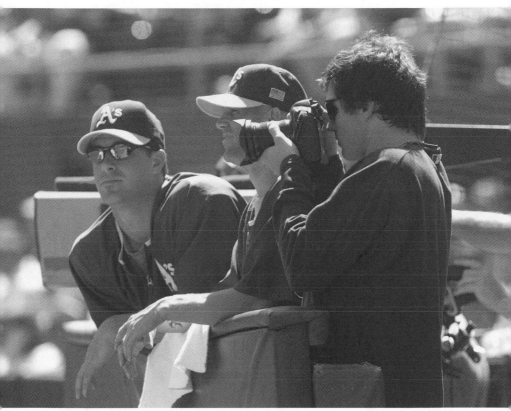

Barry Zito borrows a photographer's camera before a 2004 game as Tim Hudson (center) and Mark Mulder (left) look on. (Don Smith)

Hudson's August 19, 1999, start at Fenway Park vs. Martinez stood out for Rick Peterson, then the A's pitching coach.

"I took him to the corner of the clubhouse to explain, 'There's no place like this, but if you can keep your focus, you're not facing Pedro, you're facing the Boston lineup,'" Peterson said. "Timmy was looking at me with this cool Clint Eastwood squint and he said, 'Rick, I'm pitching against Pedro Martinez at Fenway Park in the pennant race. That's what I've waited for my whole life.'"

Zito displayed equal poise during big games, according to Peterson, who recalled a conversation with the rookie before his

Game 4 start in the 2000 division series, with the A's facing elimination. Peterson was trying to chit-chat with Zito to make sure he was relaxed when, Peterson said, "I realized he hadn't heard a word. Barry's looking at the 360-degree panorama of Yankee Stadium and he said, 'Rick, this is the real Yankee Stadium. This is the playoffs.'"

Zito then took off his jacket and cheerfully told outfielder Matt Stairs how much fun the game would be.

"Art Howe was filling out the lineup card and he said, 'How's the kid?'" Peterson said. "I said, 'Better than you and I are.'"

Former first baseman Scott Hatteberg recalled Mulder's famously quick outings—which included three sub-two-hour games against Chicago's Mark Buehrle in 2003.

"I'll never forget Mulder saying on Fireworks night that he was going to finish so early everyone would have to wait in the stands for an hour before it was dark enough for fireworks—and he did it, and he did it more than once," Hatteberg said.

The trio was split up after the 2004 season, when in a stunning three-day span, Beane traded Hudson to Atlanta and Mulder to St. Louis. After the 2006 season, the Giants signed Zito to a $126 million deal, then the richest ever for a pitcher; he was with the Giants for championships in 2010 and 2012, while Hudson was a member of the Giants' 2014 title team.

23 Campy Plays All Nine

One of the first amateurs signed in the Charlie Finley era was a skinny, speedy Cuban named Dagoberto "Bert" Campaneris. He was 19, and a catcher, when the A's gave him a contract for $500 in March 1961 (the same month the Cuban government abolished professional baseball). He was one of the final Cuban players to come to the United States before 1962's Cuban Missile Crisis.

Campaneris played all over the diamond in the minors. He was a shortstop when he came up on July 23, 1964, summoned urgently from Birmingham to Minneapolis, and once there, he made a huge splash.

"Campy broke into the big leagues in a special way," said A's broadcaster Monte Moore, who called Campaneris one of his all-time favorite people. "It was in Minnesota and he was called up because Wayne Causey had separated his shoulder in a night game. Campy was shipped up from Birmingham, traveled all night—and he didn't speak English, so they put a note on his shirt that said where he was supposed to go. He barely got there in time.

"The A's were playing against Jim Kaat, who was one of the best in baseball that year, and Campy's first time up, he hit a home run. And then he got another hit his next time up. And the third time, he hits another home run.

"Here's this little, 5'9" guy, he weighs maybe 150 pounds and this is his major-league debut. The team was getting requests from all over the country saying, 'Who is this guy?' So they had an interpreter after the game, and someone asked, 'How does it feel to hit a home run off Jim Kaat?' He said, 'I don't know…. Who is Jim Kaat?'"

The 22-year-old was so small, the equipment manager initially refused to give him a uniform, according to some accounts.

To go along with his single and two homers in his remarkable debut, Campaneris made a terrific running catch.

Versatility was one Campaneris' primary traits. Ambidextrous, he'd pitched both left-handed and right-handed in the minors, and on September 8, 1965, as a promotional stunt against the Angels, he became the first major-leaguer to play all nine positions in one game. He went 1-for-3 with a walk, a strikeout, and a stolen base, and made five putouts. He also gave up a hit, two walks, and a run while pitching the eighth inning of the A's 13-inning, 5–3 loss, and he struck out Bobby Knoop, one of the five men he faced.

His night was cut short, however, when, while playing catcher in the ninth, he was knocked unconscious blocking home plate to record the final out of the inning. Campaneris was able to start only once in the next 17 games.

"Campy was cold-cocked," said Rene Lachemann, who took over at catcher. "Ed Kirkpatrick knocked him silly when he took him out at home. Campy was such a slim guy, he didn't even fit into the catcher's gear, but people forget, he'd signed as a catcher."

Campy made it back full-time on September 25 against Boston—the same night that Satchel Paige, the A's starting pitcher, made his final big-league appearance.

24 Lefty Grove

Many believe Lefty Grove, who pitched for Connie Mack's A's dynasty of the late 1920s and early '30s, is the greatest pitcher of all time, or at least the best left-hander ever.

Even modern sabermetricians debate this, because not only did Grove lead the majors in ERA a record nine times and strike-outs seven years in a row, but he also led the league in Wins Above Replacement (WAR) eight times, tied with his idol, Walter Johnson, for most ever, and Johnson pitched in the dead-ball era. Until Clayton Kershaw (151 over his first seven seasons) emerged, Grove had the best ERA-plus, 148 over 17 seasons, among all left-handers in major-league history. Author Donald Honig said that Grove "was Babe Ruth on the mound."

There is little dispute that Lefty Grove had the best three-year stretch of all-time, winning 79 games and losing just 15 from 1929 to 1931. In fact, he was the very first American League Most Valuable Player in 1931, when he was 31–4 with a 2.06 ERA.

The son of a coal miner, Grove left school after eighth grade to work in the mines, but he lasted only two weeks before laboring in a glass factory instead. He played baseball on Sundays, and one day, he threw a no-hitter against one of the top amateur teams in Maryland, leading to a job in pro baseball. And when he was traded from that Martinsburg, West Virginia, team to the minor-league Orioles it was for another player—plus the cost of some outfield refurbishments. "I was the only player ever traded for a fence," Grove said.

Grove finished with 300 wins on the nose, and that's despite not playing in the major leagues until he was 25, thanks to the fact that Baltimore refused to sell his contract until 1925. Mack paid $100,600 for Grove, a record at the time.

Grove threw hard, almost entirely fastballs in the early part of his big-league career. Babe Ruth is said to asked, "What's that guy got up his arm, a machine gun?" and several humorists are attributed with this gem: "Lefty Grove could throw a lamb chop past a wolf."

Tall for the day, at nearly 6'3", Grove was described as "a straight line with ears on it," by writer Westbrook Pegler. He also was known for his prickly disposition, and Mack said that no one gave him more difficulty. Grove frequently smashed up the clubhouse and tore off his uniform during temperamental outbursts, and he had a well-deserved reputation for hitting batters.

He was once asked if he had any funny baseball stories. "I never saw anything funny about the game," Grove replied.

Grove helped the A's to three consecutive World Series appearances, including titles in 1929 and 1930, but when the A's attendance dipped 100,000 in 1933, Mack sold Mickey Cochrane to Detroit for $100,000 and Grove, Rube Walberg, and Max Bishop to Boston for two players and $125,000.

Retiring after 300 wins wasn't part of Grove's plan: When he won No. 300 in 1941, he was asked if he'd hang it up and he said, "They'll have to cut the uniform off me. I'm going out for another 300. They couldn't be any harder to get than the first 300."

Injuries, though, cut short that season, and Grove never pitched again. He mused that had he made it to the majors earlier, he'd have reached 400 wins—and as author Jim Kaplan notes, Grove had 411 victories when his minor-league numbers are factored in. His Orioles, in particular, were a high-level club considered on a par with many big-league teams.

Interviewed by Maury Allen in 1969, at the age of 69, Grove was asked about the great hitters he'd faced during his career. "Dammit," he snapped. "There isn't a man playing the game [now] I couldn't strike out."

Robert Moses "Lefty" Grove was inducted into the Hall of Fame in 1947, and he died in 1975.

25 The Jeter Flip

Billy Beane often says the A's best team of the past 20 years was the 2001 club, which featured Jason Giambi, Johnny Damon, Jermaine Dye, and the Big Three, among others.

And yet Derek Jeter knocked that star-studded Oakland team out of the postseason pretty much by himself.

That year, the A's jumped ahead of the defending world champs by taking the first two games of the American League Division Series at Yankee Stadium.

Game 3 turned out to be a classic duel, with Mike Mussina and Barry Zito both sensational at the Coliseum. Zito allowed only two hits, but one was Jorge Posada's solo homer. In the bottom of the seventh, though, the A's had a great shot to tie it, when Jeremy Giambi hit a two-out single and Terrence Long followed with a double to right.

That's when Jeter turned in one of the great plays in postseason history.

Right fielder Shane Spencer overthrew both cutoff men, and as the ball rolled near the first-base line, Jeter suddenly appeared in a spot not usually patrolled by shortstops. He picked it up and, from foul ground, flipped it backhanded to Posada at the plate.

Giambi, who went in standing up, was called out.

Afterward, manager Art Howe and A's third-base coach Ron Washington both suggested Giambi would have been safe had he slid, which is what on-deck batter Ramon Hernandez had been signaling for him to do.

Some, however, argued that Giambi appeared to be safe on the replay and that he had made the right decision.

"I talked to my brother and I was like, 'What were you thinking?'" A's slugger Jason Giambi said. "But when I looked at the play, I saw how it transpired. Jeremy saw the ball being thrown in and he knew there'd be a play at the plate and he saw Posada standing there, so he was thinking he had to barrel Posada over. But he didn't see the overthrow until he saw Posada leave the plate to get the flip.

"So Jeremy thinks Jorgie is leaving the plate and he's halfway between either running him over or sliding. So he tried to reach the plate as fast as he could, but Posada comes back and tags him on the back of the leg.

"I really don't think Jorgie did tag him. It was from behind. But if Jeremy does slide, he might be more out. The way Jorgie went down and had his glove out, he would have gone straight into it."

Said general manager Billy Beane: "In fairness to Jeremy, there's this perception that if he'd slid, he would have been safe—I don't think so. And if he'd scored, there's an assumption we would have won, but they had Mariano Rivera available for a couple of innings.

"Baseball purists would say he should have slid, but he's in a no-win situation. That was a great play by the Yankees, even now you look at it and it was amazing. Jeremy has been unfairly criticized; maybe that was the best way he could have gone in."

There were no disagreements about Jeter's remarkable play.

"I had probably the best seat in the house to watch that play unfold, at ground-level at the end of the dugout," pitching coach Rick Peterson said. "My eyes went to the ball, they went to Giambi and when the ball came out of Spencer's hand, I saw the whole thing right in front of me and I knew he'd overshot everyone.

"Jeter realized immediately, and he started running with the flight of the ball. He was 30 or 40 feet in front of Giambi, running in the same direction. I'm watching them running neck and neck and then Jeter gets the ball 20 feet up the line and makes the flip. I couldn't see well enough to see if he beat the play or was tagged, but the ball got there at the same time.

"What incredible instincts Jeter has. The overshot was very clear to him right away and that he was the only one who could run after it."

"First of all, for Jeter to even be there—we were like, 'What the hell is he doing?'" Jason Giambi said.

Damon, who like Jason Giambi went on to play with Jeter in New York, said, "He had no business being there, I've told him that. And I still think Jeremy was safe."

"I wish we'd had instant replay," Howe said. "I'd like to know if he was out or not—it looks like his foot is on the plate as he's getting tagged. Replay would have clarified the whole thing."

Jeter said 13 years later that bench coach Don Zimmer had had the idea of backing up such throws, and that Jeter had practiced it during spring training. It was so unusual to see a shortstop in that spot, though, that many were skeptical about any previous drills—but former A's infielder Randy Velarde, who was with the Yankees that season, said that he spotted Jeter working on that exact play that February in Florida.

"What's crazy is that Jeter was doing that during spring training," Velarde said. "I said, 'What's going on with that?' and then he does it during the playoffs. I absolutely saw him doing that during the spring."

Jeter laughed off any skepticism, saying, "I was where I was supposed to be. I'm there as the third cutoff man, but I'm not there to throw home."

Jeter added that if Spencer had thrown the ball to second baseman Alfonso Soriano or first baseman Tino Martinez, "then Giambi would have been out by 15 feet. So my job is, if there's no play at the plate, I would cut it off and throw it to third. Throwing home was something sort of improvised. I was in the place I was supposed to be, but the end result was not what was supposed to happen."

In the wake of the Yankees' win, George Vecsey of the *New York Times* composed an ode titled, "Slide, Jeremy, Slide."

It concluded:

Slide, Jeremy, slide, and in the long and official replay of time, you will always be safe.

Slide, Jeremy, slide. Relocate the center of the baseball universe to the East Bay or the Pacific Rim or the Arizona moonscape.

Slide, Jeremy, slide. Change the world. Get down, man.

In such a close game, Howe wanted to keep Giambi's bat in the lineup for the later innings, but he'd planned to pinch run for him if he'd made it into scoring position. Some of the A's thought Howe should have done so immediately, with speedy Eric Byrnes available.

"We were all on the bench and we knew that Mariano was down there warming up and we needed to score a run," Jason Giambi said. "We had 'Third Degree' Byrnes on the bench, and Jeremy had a quad injury. I remember thinking, 'We need Byrnes in there to maybe steal a bag.'"

"We were all in the dugout saying, 'Pinch run, pinch run,'" third baseman Eric Chavez recalled. "Players second-guess a lot. But to me, Jeremy was safe. It's just that if it's Byrnes, he's definitely safe. But we still would have had to score off Mariano. Who knows if we would have?"

The Yankees went on to win the series three games to two.

"It was best-of-five and up until that point, no team had been down 2–0 and come back and won after losing two at home, so it was a big game for us, and a big play during that game," Jeter said. "You could say it turned it around."

26 Dick Williams

Even before taking the Oakland A's to two championships, Dick Williams had done notable work with Boston—in 1967, his first year as the Red Sox's manager, the "Impossible Dream" team won the American League pennant, Boston's first since 1945.

Injuries and personality clashes led to Williams' ouster late in the 1969 season, however, and Charlie Finley hired him to manage the A's in 1971. Finley had employed 10 managers in the previous decade, so Williams knew going in that security wasn't in the job description.

Williams was known as a no-nonsense manager in Boston, and he continued in that vein even with the free-wheeling A's. He exerted his authority early in his tenure after telling the team off on the bus one day after it was discovered that someone (widely believed to be Catfish Hunter) had stolen a megaphone from the airplane. The contraband megaphone quickly appeared after Williams' tirade.

Rollie Fingers recalled that Williams was very clever about keeping the team on its toes.

"In 1972 we went into Kansas City after losing three in a row, and we played Friday night and got our butts beat," Fingers said, "Afterwards, it was going around that there was going to be a bed check.

"I had friends in Kansas City who'd driven down to see me from St. Louis, and I told them that there was going to be a bed check at midnight, so I'd have to be in my room then and would sneak out and meet them later. But I was in my room at midnight, and there's no knock on the door. I waited until 12:15 and there was no knock by then, so I just left, and I came back about 2:00 AM."

Ken Holtzman, Fingers' roommate, was still watching TV and he said there'd never been a bed check.

"No one ever came by," Fingers said. "I thought, 'Perfect, no fine!'

"The next day, Williams called a meeting and read off the names of seven or eight guys and said, 'You all get a $200 fine for not being in your room at midnight.' Everyone was looking around, because we knew there was no bed check. So we all wondered how he knew."

Williams, crafty fellow, realized that the team hotel had only one elevator, so at midnight, he asked the elevator operator if he'd be there the rest of the evening.

"The guy said he was," Fingers said. "So Dick gave him a baseball, and he said, 'Everyone who comes in after I do, have them sign this ball.' And there were eight names right there on the ball."

His teams were loaded with talent, of course, but it took a special manager to handle the brawling band of A's players—and to put up with constant interference from Finley. After three seasons of Finley's orders—including instructions not to play Mike Andrews in the 1973 World Series after Finley's controversial attempt to have Andrews declared unfit to play failed—Williams just couldn't take it anymore, despite three division titles and two world championships.

"It was a number of things," Williams said. "The Mike Andrews incident was a big factor. Finley firing Mike didn't set too well with me. And your time was never your own. As soon as I got up the runway from the dugout, the phone would be ringing, with Charlie saying, 'If you did it this way, we'd win,' or 'You did this, so we lost.'

"He wanted to control everything. We had a house guest one Sunday and we were just getting ready to have dinner when Charlie called and he wants to talk baseball. I said, 'I can't talk right now, we have a guest.' Charlie said, 'What's more important, your guest or the owner of the ballclub you work for?' And I said, 'Charlie, right now, it's my houseguest.' I was the first manager he ever had last more than a year and a half."

The A's players respected Williams and enjoyed playing for him. Several tried to get him to change his mind.

"I loved playing for Dick Williams. He fit in perfectly with that team," Holtzman said. "He would do anything to win, but if you went all out, he didn't have any problems with you. I felt he was a very good tactician and he knew the game very well. He was always straight up with me, brutally honest. If you were bad, he'd say, 'You're horse[bleep], now get out of here.' I like that, no B.S. He didn't mince words. And look at those teams, great teams, 100 wins, and the entire team was a bunch of characters."

After the A's won the title in 1973, both Finley and Williams made it clear that Williams wouldn't return in 1974, despite a recent contract extension.

With everyone in baseball aware that the Yankees wanted Williams, Finley tried to pull off a trade, but he asked for either outfielder Bobby Murcer or catcher Thurman Munson. The Yankees offered $150,000 in cash and lesser players. No deal was reached. (In 1976, Finley did trade a manager, sending Chuck Tanner to Pittsburgh for catcher Manny Sanguillen and cash. Tanner went on to win the 1979 World Series with the Pirates.)

The Yankees went ahead and signed Williams, though he was still under contract to Oakland, so AL president Joe Cronin voided the deal and New York hired Bill Virdon instead.

Williams went on to manage the Angels, the Expos, and, most notably, the Padres, leading San Diego to the NL pennant in 1984. He finished his career with the Mariners, was elected to the Hall of Fame in 2007, and inducted in 2008. Williams died in 2011 at the age of 82.

He and Bill McKechnie are the only managers to lead three different franchises to the World Series. Seven times, his teams won 90 or more games.

And though he might not have shown it, even Finley appreciated him.

"Dick Williams is the best manager I've ever had," Finley said. "I ought to know. I've fired enough of them."

27 Travel Overseas With The A's

In both 2008 and 2012, the A's opened their season in Tokyo, playing two big-league games and two exhibition games against Japanese teams each time. And in 2018, Oakland is on the shortlist for more international travel, potentially a trip to Australia.

Several hundred A's fans flew to Japan for the games in 2008 and 2012. Major League Baseball put together travel packages for the event, although many fans opted to make their own way there. Americans living in Tokyo showed up for the series, too, so there was plenty of green and gold.

For A's fans of Japanese descent, the games in Tokyo were especially meaningful.

"For me, it was special because my mom is from Japan," said longtime A's fan Carrie Olejnik. "I'd never seen baseball there, and it was a bucket-list thing, a special splurge. I take one road trip a year and I'd absolutely recommend it. Japan was the ultimate, the coolest thing."

Among the top highlights for A's fans and even the Oakland players was seeing the differences between the American and Japanese teams (which, among other nifty things, double up on batting cages for batting practice) and of course the unique fan environment. Japanese fans have elaborate chants for their teams and they wave flags throughout the games; there is beer in the stands of course, but it's delivered by women with pony kegs strapped to their backs. Sake is for sale, and so are bento boxes with sushi and other Japanese specialties.

"The exhibitions were trippy with the cheering sections, kind of orchestrated, playing in a huge dome," Olejnik said. "It was so bizarre but so great!"

Such trips don't necessarily have to break the bank, with some smart planning.

"I found a really small, nice hotel just a short subway ride away for $90 a night, so even though you think of Tokyo as expensive, it worked for us," Olejnik said.

The A's appreciated having friendly faces in the crowds, and, Olejnik said, "I'd told most of the coaches and players at spring training that I'd be there in Japan, so before the first exhibition I went down near the field and waved and they were like, 'You made it!'"

"It was neat to see A's fans there, faces we recognized and wearing our colors, people who know you and who can identify with you," A's manager Bob Melvin said. "That's when you know someone is a die-hard fan, when they show up in Japan."

And there was another plus for the world travelers.

"I also met a lot of people, fans from the Bay Area but also fans who live in Japan I'd gotten to know corresponding on Facebook," Olejnik said. "I definitely made some friends."

The A's also traveled outside the U.S. for a spring exhibition in Hermosillo, Mexico, in 2001. The team's front office and management is all in favor of international trips; along with the fact that the A's do well financially (they were guaranteed sellouts for two home dates for each Japan series), the club feels that the players benefit, too.

"It brought guys together even before the season started," said Melvin, whose 2012 team won the AL West title on the final day of the season. "For us, it wasn't just a business trip. The players got a lot out of it. I'm sure the fans did too. It's ideal; check box: foreign city, learn and enjoy the culture, watch baseball."

28 Yoenis Cespedes' Journey

Oakland general manager Billy Beane shocked baseball on February 13, 2012, when he outmaneuvered many richer teams to sign Cuban outfielder Yoenis Cespedes to a four-year, $36 million deal.

Cespedes went on to help the underdog A's win the American League West that year, Oakland's first playoff appearance since 2006. The team also went to the postseason in 2013 and in 2014—although Cespedes unexpectedly was traded to Boston on July 31,

2014, for Boston ace Jon Lester and former A's outfielder Jonny Gomes.

During Cespedes' two and a half seasons with Oakland, the team's record with him in the lineup was a remarkable 228–131. He was an All-Star in 2014, he won the Home Run Derby during the 2013 and 2014 All-Star weekends, and Cespedes was the runner up to Mike Trout for the 2012 AL Rookie of the Year award.

As amazing as Cespedes' rookie season was, it's even more impressive in retrospect, because he was dealing with a huge amount of personal anxiety. In a special report on July 15, 2013, the *San Francisco Chronicle* detailed Cespedes' harrowing escape from Cuba in 2011, as well as his family's dangerous journey from the Dominican Republic in 2012 to try to join him in the United States.

While the A's were beginning their stirring run to chase down the Rangers and win the title on the last day of the season, Cespedes was frantically worried about his family, including his mother, Estela Milanes. In August, the 10 Cubans, including an infant, had been abandoned on a small uninhabited islet in the Caribbean for two days with no food. A cousin caught and cooked an iguana, another a seagull, but no one could stomach either—and family members told the *Chronicle* that they began to lose hope.

For those three days, Cespedes had no idea what had happened to his family. His teammates didn't realize anything was amiss and Cespedes kept playing through it all, unable to discuss it with anyone apart from coach Ariel Prieto.

On the third morning, a yacht appeared and the group was taken to the island nation of Turks and Caicos, where they planned to establish residency and apply to immigrate to the U.S. But on October 2—the final weekend of the baseball season, with the A's engaged in their battle with Texas—Cespedes' family was taken into custody in a raid and detained as illegal immigrants.

Again, Oakland's star was consumed with worry at an important juncture, but he hit .316 in the A's five-game division series loss to Detroit.

Most of Cespedes' family members were held for the next 103 days, but once they were released, they quickly escaped to the U.S., with Cespedes making arrangements through contacts in Miami. They were reunited in March 2013, and Milanes, a former Olympic softball player, was there for Cespedes' All-Star week heroics in 2013 and '14, and his terrific postseason in 2013, when he hit .381 vs. Detroit.

On June 10, 2014, at Anaheim, Cespedes added to his legend when he uncorked one of the greatest throws of all time. With the game tied 1–1 in the eighth inning and Howie Kendrick at first base with one, Trout hit a drive toward the corner in left that Cespedes couldn't handle cleanly, a potentially costly error.

And yet, Cespedes picked up the ball, and with seemingly zero chance to throw out Kendrick, he made a high, arcing rocket of a throw right into catcher Derek Norris' glove. Astonishingly, Kendrick was out, and out of nowhere.

"When I saw the play initially, I was ticked off because Cespy picked up his head and kicked the ball into the corner," Oakland first baseman Brandon Moss said. "Cespy is the only guy who could turn the worst play of the year into hands down the best play of the year. We were joking with him afterwards, 'Did you kick the ball to the wall so you could throw him out?'

"He's got a cannon. I can believe he threw it that far. But Norris didn't even have to move—he literally just dropped the tag on Howie. Howie was like, 'What the heck just happened?'"

Even the opposing manager was floored. "Just an incredible throw from that distance, that angle, everything," Mike Scioscia said. "That was a special play."

29 The White Elephant

Right from the start, the ever-colorful A's embraced an unusual identity, spinning an insult into a time-honored tradition when, in 1902, New York Giants manager John McGraw told the press that Benjamin Shibe had "bought himself a white elephant."

The phrase "white elephant" usually indicates that something is more trouble that it is worth, a term from Thailand, where albino elephants were prized, but extremely expensive to maintain. Calculating kings could ruin troublesome courtiers with such a gift; the white elephants were considered holy, so could not even be used as work animals. Useless but pricey, that was the implication.

McGraw is likely to have known of an incident in 1884, when showman P.T. Barnum sent a representative to Burma to purchase a white elephant for a staggering $75,000—but when the elephant showed up, it was pink and splotchy, and competitors hammered Barnum for unfulfilled expectations. Barnum stopped showing the expensive but inadequate elephant in exhibitions, while a rival circus owner whitewashed a gray elephant and drew big crowds for showings in…Philadelphia.

McGraw's insult popularized the term, and "white elephant" sales became all the rage for shoppers to exchange unwanted items.

In something of a franchise-long trend, Mack embraced the quirk rather than taking offense. He turned the gibe into an asset by placing the white elephant logo on the A's uniforms and pennants.

Even now, the Oakland Athletics wear elephant patches on their sleeves. And their costumed mascot, Stomper, is, of course, an elephant. Stomper is gray, rather than white—which sort of makes sense. A mascot paying tribute to the "useless" white elephant probably shouldn't be perfect.

The alternate nickname proved popular with fans and sports-writers. As provided by the Philadelphia Athletics Historical Society, an excerpt from the 1909 game program reads: "The Athletics battled a way through dark and dismal times when they started back in 1901 and until that magic White Elephant title appeared to brighten things up, it was rough going for the Americans. But once seizing on that title as a suitable nickname, things began to look better and gradually the Athletics in leaps and bounds went to the top of the American League with that White Elephant flag flying in their teeth, an emblem of success and glory.

"The White Elephant cry was quickly grasped by every true-born rooter as the war shout, and in many a sensational game since, the old blue and white elephant flag which graced the side arm of the big flag pole at Twenty-ninth Street and Columbia Avenue has waved triumphantly over the opposition.... White Elephants may come and go, but it's doubtful if any circus promoter ever possessed the kind of animal which brought them in the same amount of revenue as the one the Athletics have in captivity."

30 Bob Melvin

Were you to program in the ideal characteristics for an Oakland A's manager in the current age, you couldn't do better than Bob Melvin.

Melvin, who took over the team in the middle of the 2011 season at the age of 50, is from the Bay Area—he grew up in Menlo Park rooting for the A's and Giants, he attended UC Berkeley, and he played for the Giants. His local ties are immensely important to him, and Melvin understands and appreciates the Oakland fans and the A's traditions.

And in each of his first three full seasons with Oakland, Melvin has taken the team to the playoffs—including a wildly unexpected run to the 2012 division crown, won in thrilling fashion on the final day of the regular season.

"Shoot, there were so many facets to that season but the main thing to me is that the last month and a half is as exciting as anything I've ever been a part of," said Melvin, who was named AL Manager of the Year after the season ended. "Not just because of how we were playing, but reigniting the fan base. The team bonded with the fans, and it became a very powerful and rewarding experience."

"That 2012 team had so few expectations, and I remember at the start of the season, Melvin said, 'We don't listen to anyone else's expectations, no one can tell us we're not supposed to win,'" team broadcaster Ray Fosse said. "He believed in those players, and you listen to what they say—they'd take a bullet for him, they'd run through a wall for him."

Despite his abundant success with Oakland, including two division titles and a 325–260 record in three-plus years, Melvin doesn't have the simplest job around. The A's employ numerous platoons, which can be a landmine for a manager.

"Let's not take lightly how hard it is to manage platoons—one is hard enough, we had as many as six sometimes, and he's had to keep everyone on the same page," former A's outfielder and platoon regular Jonny Gomes said. "He is completely respectful of everyone involved—he is basically at your bedside when you wake up to make sure you aren't ambushed about not playing that day or the next day or later in the week. Bob Melvin's communication skills are second to none."

Another added degree of difficulty: Oakland's roster turns over rapidly because the team doesn't spend much compared to most other contenders. Among other things, Melvin has had to change closers numerous times—and three have wound up as All-Stars in the process: Ryan Cook, Grant Balfour, and Sean Doolittle.

Many of the A's better players during Melvin's tenure were overlooked elsewhere, castoffs or bit players who have thrived in Oakland and who credit Melvin for that.

"I don't mean any disrespect to anyone else who has helped me in my career, but I can truly say that Bob Melvin has had everything to do with how I've played, 100 percent, because I believed he had total confidence in me," said former A's outfielder Brandon Moss, who hit 76 homers in three seasons with Oakland after struggling with a string of other clubs. "Bob is honest and straight up with you, he doesn't talk down to you, you know he has your back.

"I know a lot of people think that managers don't have that much to do with team success anymore, the front office makes the moves and the manager carries out their wishes, but to me, Bob Melvin is the No. 1 reason we've been where we are the last three years."

It's no secret that A's general manager Billy Beane can be tough on his managers—it's detailed in *Moneyball,* the book and the movie—but he and Melvin have turned out to be an excellent combo.

Fosse played for an A's manager, Dick Williams, who also worked for a bigger-than-life figure in owner Charlie Finley, and Fosse sees definite similarities.

"Dick kept us in line and we never knew what he had to deal with otherwise, and Bob is exceptional when it comes to keeping the team together," Fosse said. "Dick's a Hall of Famer and on a day-to-day basis, I'd absolutely compare him with Bob.

"It would be nice to see what Bob could do with a $152 million payroll, but with the challenges involved, I don't think I've seen anyone better besides Dick. When Bob Melvin is given the authority and autonomy to run a team the way he wants to, I don't think there *is* anyone better."

31 Stewart vs. Clemens

Like Hall of Famer Dennis Eckersley, starter Dave Stewart was a scrapheap steal for Oakland, which picked him up in 1986 after he'd been released by the Phillies.

In each of the next four seasons, Stewart won 20 games or more. No pitcher has come close to that feat since.

"It's not going to ever happen again. It could, but I just don't see it. Not in consecutive seasons," Stewart said.

Oakland third baseman Carney Lansford credited former A's pitcher Joaquin Andujar with helping start Stewart's run.

"Andujar popped off and told our starting pitchers that none of them would ever win 20 games, they didn't know how," Lansford said with a laugh. "And Stew looked at him and said, 'Is that right?'

"So I tip my cap to Joaquin—I didn't know what it did to Dave, but four straight years after that, he won 20 games."

Stewart was the best pitcher in the game during that stretch, though he didn't win the Cy Young in any of those seasons—a miscarriage of justice, many believe.

"I think Stew is one of the most underrated pitchers of all time," catcher Terry Steinbach said. "To go four years in a row winning 20 games, he's not talked about enough. He was our go-to guy. If we had a losing streak, it pretty much ended."

In another parallel with Eckersley, Stewart's role was unsettled initially. He didn't become a full-time starter until Tony La Russa's first game as manager.

"Tony called me and said, 'I'm joining the team in Boston and the good news is that you're going to be starting for me in Boston. The bad news is that it's going to be a nationally televised game and you're going to be pitching against Roger Clemens,'" Stewart

Dave Stewart pitches against the Red Sox in Fenway in Game 1 of the 1990 American League Championship Series. (Bill Waugh/ AP Photo)

recalled. "I said, 'Actually, that's all good news. I'm looking forward to it.'"

Stewart beat the Red Sox for his first victory with Oakland, and La Russa's. He wasn't done with Clemens, either. Stewart became known for dominating the Boston star, going 8–0 with a 1.80 ERA in their matchups.

"After that, it didn't matter—if Roger Clemens saw Dave Stewart was pitching against him, Clemens was done," said Wally Haas, son of team owner Walter Haas.

"Stew had a chip on his shoulder to beat the best. He felt dissed," Eckersley said. "When it came to Roger, it really energized Stew—he always pitched his best against Roger."

Stewart's first 20-win season came in 1987, but Clemens, who also won 20 that season, received the Cy Young Award.

"I know for a fact he took it personal, pitching against Roger," Lansford said. "He was really upset the first year he won 20 games, he didn't win the Cy Young. And he told me, in my living room in Northeastern Oregon, 'That guy will never beat me. Never.' And he never did.

"Oh my gosh, he got in Roger's head. The Boston Red Sox couldn't beat him, and they knew it and we knew it, too."

Stewart said he had an edge because he was six years older than Clemens and he was just happy to have a starting job again. He felt no pressure, while Clemens always had huge expectations and was trying not to make a single mistake. Stewart's success rate against Clemens was such that La Russa started altering the rotation to make sure that Stewart would oppose Clemens.

"The intimidation factor set in," Stewart said. "I was beating him regularly during the season and the postseason and it started to have a psychological effect on him. I always knew I was going to pitch well against them—the Sox were easy, in my opinion. At no point, did I think they would score more runs than Roger would give up."

The most famous showdown between the two came in the 1990 American League Championship Series. With Boston trailing 3–0 in the series and down 1–0 in the second inning at the Coliseum, Clemens began jawing at home-plate umpire Terry Cooney and he was ejected, then he bumped an umpire while protesting. He appeared unhinged.

"Cooney takes a lot of heat for it, but I remember Cooney being really patient," Steinbach said. "In a nutshell, it was total frustration coming to a head, 80 years since they'd won a World Series, and Clemens was supposed to be the guy. They put so much on him as a savior, he'd reached a breaking point. And Stew's success against him was so lopsided, that added to it."

"That was a big meltdown," Stewart said. "He had a history of getting away with that kind of stuff, and he cussed the umpire out three different times—he was asking to come out of that game. It's unbelievable how much he melted down, after only one run."

Stewart, who also threw a no-hitter vs. Toronto during that 1990 season, was named the ALCS MVP after beating Boston twice and putting up a 1.13 ERA. He won another ALCS MVP award in 1993, while pitching for the Blue Jays.

After his playing career, Stewart worked in the front office for several teams, including the A's, and as a pitching coach before becoming an agent—he represented Eric Chavez when the third baseman signed the biggest contract in Oakland history, a $66 million deal in 2004.

On September 25, 2014, Stewart was named the general manager of the Arizona Diamondbacks, reporting to an old friend—La Russa, now the DBacks' team president.

32 Sit with the Zany Right-Field Crowd

For all the knocks the Oakland Coliseum takes, the stadium boasts one of the best—and most inviting—fan experiences in pro sports.

If you really want to know what it's like to be a hardcore A's fan, sit in the right-field bleachers. It's a crazy bunch, but in a good way. They came up with Bacon Tuesdays—and wound up with an opposing player celebrating it with them in the parking lot. They've had outfielders from other teams send them food, and A's right fielder Josh Reddick contributed a wrestling championship belt.

They're a blast, and they'd love you to stop by.

"For anyone considering it, just do it," said Benjamin Christensen, an Oakland fan who rose to prominence as part of MLB's Fan Cave. "Just introduce yourself to the people there—we're very welcoming. You'll have the most fun you've ever had. There's always something going on."

"Try once or twice, and if you love it, do it again and again," Balfour Rage creator Will MacNeil said. "We've met a lot of people, become a family—we do stuff in the off-season, go bowling."

Tony Cogley, who started the right-field bleacher crew in 1998 when the left-field drummers created too much demand for seats on that side, has some practical advice. "If you sit out there, you need to know you're going to be doing more than just watching the game," he said. "It's hectic, it's loud. People complain, 'They're playing drums for nine innings, they're standing the whole time.'

"But it's great for people who are all in and want to roll along and take part, go along with all our superstitions."

Wear green and gold, maybe bring a witty sign—and a love of pork products is a plus. That's how the section started up its friendship with Royals outfielder Jeff Francoeur, who sent pizzas to the stands along with $100 wrapped around a baseball with instructions to use it for bacon or beer. Francoeur and Reddick both showed up to mingle with fans at the third annual Bacon Tuesday just outside the Coliseum.

Angels outfielder Torii Hunter sent the section $300 worth of Popeyes chicken one night after years of pleading. "We started chanting, 'We want food,' at him one day, 'How many millions of dollars do you have?'" Cogley said. "We even went to Anaheim to heckle him. He laughed; he's great."

Angels outfielder Josh Hamilton—whose error with Texas helped give Oakland the AL West title on the final day of the 2012 season—good-naturedly accepted a Butterfinger bar presented by the right-field crew and took a bite out of it.

"Everyone has been very cool," MacNeil said. "Josh Reddick is by far the best. He was a little upset about Francoeur and Bacon Tuesday at first, but when he gave us the championship belt, he wrote on the back, 'I'm taking Title Thursday.' He knows we have his back."

They also have the best view in the park some nights when Reddick, a Gold Glove winner in 2012, makes one of his home run–robbing plays.

"We give him a lot of love," MacNeil said. "A lot of those catches, any other outfielder would not have made."

"They're huge for me—not only for me, but the whole team," Reddick said. "Monday, Tuesday nights against the Astros, they're there. They've helped me tremendously through some rough patches. I can't help but laugh at them even if things aren't going great. They've been so supportive, it's unbelievable."

There aren't brawls, as there might be in the famous Black Hole during Raiders games at the same venue, but there is some head-banging, for this is the birthplace of Balfour Rage, the whirling arms, spinning hair tribute to former A's closer Grant Balfour.

"It was at a random game against Minnesota in 2011, and Balfour came out to Metallica's 'One,' and I said, 'Let's pretend we're in a moshpit," said MacNeil. "My buddies started doing it, and then it sort of took on a life of its own until finally the whole stadium was doing it during the playoffs. It was amazing to see. It was a thrill."

Down the stretch in 2014, the same bunch came up with the "I believe in Stephen Vogt," chant, which became so popular that it even was heard in other stadiums when the A's catcher/first baseman came to the plate.

The Coliseum is known for fun crowds; the Wave started there during the 1981 ALCS, and in the early 2000s, the drummers in left field were featured in team ad campaigns—then gained even more attention when opponents started complaining about them. Yankees owner George Steinbrenner successfully pressured Major League Baseball to have the drums silenced whenever a pitcher was on the mound or in his delivery.

"Basically," drummer Ben Rosenberg told the *San Francisco Chronicle* at the time, "Steinbrenner's flipped his lid."

Christensen said that there are reasons mass fan interaction has taken off in the Coliseum.

"The way the Coliseum is laid out helps. You can get from one section to another very easily. Other places, there are all these exclusive areas you can't go through," he said. "And it's a blue-collar town, everyone knows everyone, the atmosphere is very friendly, generation after generation, so many years. It's a younger demographic, especially in the left-field and right-field bleachers, and we don't see baseball as one-dimensional or slow-paced—we see it as something that is personally enriching."

33 Gibson's Homer

Hall of Famer Dennis Eckersley seldom failed, but he's forever linked to one of the most famous moments in World Series history. On the wrong side.

On October 15, 1988, Game 1 of the World Series between the A's and the Dodgers, Eckersley took over with a 4–3 lead in the ninth. With two outs, he walked pinch-hitter Mike Davis on a 3–1 pitch, something that surprised everyone. He'd walked only 11 men during the season.

"Eck didn't walk anyone. No one. It was shocking," Oakland third baseman Carney Lansford said.

The Dodgers also did the unexpected: As the packed stadium erupted, outfielder Kirk Gibson, supposedly out of action because of severe leg injuries, hobbled to the plate.

"I'm thinking, 'Wait a minute, he's limping, he hasn't played, he can't even run—but this man is dangerous because he's got such fast hands, he's really strong, ridiculously strong,'" Oakland outfielder Jose Canseco said. "'I've seen him hit balls over the roof in Tiger Stadium.'"

In his only at-bat of the series, Gibson put up a battle. He fouled off four of the first five pitches he faced, and with a 2–2 count, Davis stole second and Eckersley's slider just missed, running the count full. Manager Tony La Russa didn't consider walking Gibson, because he represented the tying run.

Then Gibson remembered the scouting report, which warned that Eckersley liked to throw backdoor sliders 3–2.

That's what Gibson got, and he wristed the pitch into the bleachers in right to give the Dodgers a 5–4 victory.

Eckersley's immediate reaction: "'Check his bat, somebody check his bat.'

"The scouting report was 'Do not throw him breaking balls. Don't even think about it,'" Eckersley said. "Isn't that awful? But I got tired of throwing him fastballs."

"That was probably the only pitch Gibson could hit, a breaking ball," Oakland outfielder Dave Parker said. "With his legs as bad as they were, he couldn't have hit a fastball out. But he kept fouling off fastballs and Eck threw him a slider and he hit it out. I almost smiled. I knew it would happen.

"That ended the series. Because there was no way in hell anyone thought the Dodgers could beat us, and that gave them the momentum."

Los Angeles went on to take the Series four games to one, with Orel Hershiser winning two games. Not everyone felt that Gibson's blow made the difference, however.

"People say the Gibson thing killed us, but we just didn't hit," coach Rene Lachemann said. "The Dodgers got the hits; every time they put the hit and run on, it worked, and Hershiser pitched a shutout. It was not that one ballgame."

"When Gibson hit it, I remember Dennis looking at me at third base with a look like, 'I can't believe this happened.' I shrugged my shoulders like 'It's one game,' and I meant it," Lansford said. "We wouldn't have been in the World Series if not for Dennis. That's not what cost us the World Series. We never got it going at the plate, and I was one of those guys who wasn't hitting. The Gibson home run was minuscule."

Reporters will always remember the grace that Eckersley showed after one of the worst nights of his career. He patiently answered questions as long as they kept coming, staying at his locker for more than half an hour.

"I was like, 'Hey, man, if you can take all the good things, suck it up and take what's coming.' I'm surprised I realized that so quickly. It was almost instinctive, but I'm really proud of that, 20 years later," Eckersley said. "I realized how good I had it to be there with my whole life turned around.

"What if that had happened at Fenway Park? I would be like Bill Buckner. But when we got back to Oakland, they gave me a standing ovation there. That was great."

His feelings about Gibson aren't warm, though.

"It's not like sour grapes; I don't like the guy anyway, and I never did," Eckersley said. "He always seemed like a jerk, and now I've got to be linked with him the rest of my life? We do interviews about it and I have to sit there listening to him say, 'Oh, I could barely walk out of the dugout.' Seeing it hundreds of times…. So finally, when someone asked again, I said, 'Well, I'm in the Hall of Fame and he's not.' I had to laugh a little, but I did feel better. I've got to have something."

Over time, the Gibson homer has taken on so much significance that many people think it actually decided things, as if it happened in the Dodgers' final at-bat of the series.

Said A's DH Don Baylor: "I went to a celebration of the 100 greatest moments in the history of Los Angeles sports. My winning the MVP in Anaheim was 56th and I thought, 'At least I made the top 100,' you know, with Kareem Abdul-Jabbar and all those Lakers titles, and a lot of Heisman winners. But even with Jabbar and Jerry West and UCLA and USC, the number one thing was Kirk Gibson's home run.

"I guess that was the turning point of the series. It was his only at-bat. I see it all the time and you'd think it was the game winner in Game 7. And it was so Hollywood."

Dave Stewart started for Oakland, he felt he should have stayed in the game, and he told La Russa so.

"I talked to Tony and I said I didn't think Eck should ever have been in there, based on my performance over the course of the year," Stewart said. "I wasn't in agreement when he took me out of the game. Who knows what would have happened if he'd left me in? But psychologically, the best reliever in baseball, with the numbers Eck had, to lose in the ninth in that fashion, that was fateful. Anybody else can say what they want, but that single blow changed the complexion of what was going to take place."

Canseco was the man who watched the ball sail over his head, and he felt the A's hopes going with it.

"As he released the pitch, I'm playing him where he can do the only damage to us, in the gap," Canseco said. "As soon as he hits it, I take one step back, fly ball, I'm going to get back and glove it somehow. But when I take a step back, I'm like, 'Holy [expletive], it's like 7–10 rows back. This did not just happen. That's incredible.' You've got to give Gibson a lot of credit. To me, that was an incredible script, you couldn't write a better one. I was shocked and amazed at the same time that he actually did it. And you see the momentum shift. He strikes out or pops out, okay, they expected us to win, now we've got them on the run. But one swing of the bat changed things completely.

"Now they believed they could beat us. And they did."

34 Moneyball

Michael Lewis' best-selling book *Moneyball,* published in 2003, was a fascinating look at the A's inner workings that helped to revolutionize the way major-league teams, and many other pro sports franchises, operate. And in 2011, *Moneyball,* despite being at heart a business book, was developed into a major motion picture with Hollywood-star Brad Pitt playing A's general manager Billy Beane.

The book detailed Beane's desire to avoid drafting players, well, like himself: players who "look" good to scouts—well built, "good face"—whose flaws might be spotted using more advanced statistical analysis. Beane never latched on as an everyday player in the big leagues, and he wanted to make sure that the A's found talent based on something more than surface appearances. Sabermetrics, as first popularized by ground-breaking baseball analyst Bill James, were the answer.

The book was immensely popular and influential, but it was controversial in some baseball circles. Beane's critics slammed him for "discovering" on-base percentage as a tool to find talent, which Beane never even remotely suggested. Some longtime execs resented the book's conclusion that Beane had figured out a better business model for baseball. A perceived indifference toward scouting operations and some slights toward various A's personnel, including manager Art Howe, were condemned.

"At no point did I ever think it would be a big public debate. That was a little bit of a surprise," Beane said. "I don't think we were ever saying. 'This was a new way to do things,' we were just trying to do some things people had written about for years, like Bill James. The situation we were in, we were the perfect Petri dish.

"There's a perception that this is some sort of template of how to run an organization, which isn't the case. And there's an idea that we think we created on-base percentage, which, believe me, Branch Rickey was looking at a long time ago."

Other common complaints: There is little mention in the book of the A's Big Three starters, Tim Hudson, Mark Mulder and Barry Zito, or shortstop Miguel Tejada—who was the American League MVP in 2002. All had far more to do with the team's success that year than did some of the more minor contributors highlighted by Lewis.

And then there's this: The A's did not win a championship that year, and they have not advanced past the ALCS in Beane's term as GM. As Angels manager Mike Scioscia noted, Lewis could have written a similar book about Anaheim's numerous cast-offs and unique bit players that same year—and at the end of the book, the team would win the 2002 World Series.

One common misconception that amuses Beane: Many people believe the A's GM wrote the book, including Hall of Fame second baseman and former national broadcaster Joe Morgan, who continued to assert that despite repeated corrections.

"I always say, if I could write that well, I would be in St. Bart's right now, writing my next book," Beane said.

Beane has been in continual demand as a public speaker since the book's publication, and he has a strong following in the business world because of the book. Several organizations, notably Boston and Toronto, followed the *Moneyball* trend even before the book's publication—Boston tried to hire Beane after the 2002 season, while the Blue Jays made Beane's protégé J.P. Ricciardi their GM in 2001, and the Dodgers hired assistant GM Paul DePodesta in 2004, then A's assistant GM Farhan Zaidi for the same position after the 2014 season.

The Red Sox became a hot-bed of *Moneyball*-school analysts and executives after failing to land Beane, and most teams now employ statisticians trained in advanced metrics, many of them Ivy League products.

"Billy is pioneering, whether people want to say so or not," said former Oakland first baseman Scott Hatteberg, who now works in the A's front office. "Whether you believe it or not, all of sports has changed since then, taken a hard turn toward metrics and advanced statistics."

Lewis' book also detailed the A's 2002 draft, now known as "the Moneyball draft." After the 2001 season, the A's did not retain expensive free agents Jason Giambi, Johnny Damon, and Jason Isringhausen, so the team wound up with a record seven picks in the first and supplemental rounds in 2002. That translated into

Billy Beane and Brad Pitt at the Oakland premier of Moneyball, *a benefit with the Oakland Children's Hospital and Research Center in Oakland and Stand Up to Cancer.* (Eric Charbonneau/Invision/AP Images)

several future major-leaguers, including outfielder Nick Swisher, starter Joe Blanton, and third baseman Mark Teahen. Jeremy Brown, best known from the book as "the fat catcher," also had a brief call-up.

"I didn't know when I was drafted what *Moneyball* was, but that is pretty much my style of play," said Swisher, a high on-base percentage hitter. "I fit the mold at the plate. I wasn't drafted out of high school and I might not be the most talented guy or have 17 tools, but I walk a lot—and maybe that's why I'm here."

Hatteberg was profiled in *Moneyball* as one of Beane's creative pickups, a catcher the A's converted to first base in order to take advantage of his good strike-zone discipline.

"It's kind of like here's a guy who roamed yard sales, and I was one of those finds," Hatteberg said of the depiction of Beane. "I'm such a big fan of how he put value on things other teams didn't."

Initially, Hatteberg was tabbed to star in the movie version, as were Howe, pitching coach Rick Peterson, and other figures. "When they said it would be a movie, I thought maybe an after-school special with William Shatner playing Billy," Hatteberg said. "Originally, we were supposed to play ourselves—hours before filming started, they pulled the plug, but Stephen Soderbergh had this whole vision of us playing ourselves, so thank goodness that didn't happen."

The project eventually wound up at Pitt's production company, with Bennett Miller directing and Oscar-winner Philip Seymour Hoffman portraying Howe. The movie depicted Beane and DePodesta (Jonah Hill's "Peter Brand" character) building the 2002 team with an unusual collection of parts, including Hatteberg.

The film took a number of liberties with the facts, but it perfectly captures Beane's creative spirit and his desire to buck conventional thinking, willing to innovate in an environment in which change was not always welcome. Pitt, in particular, is terrific in portraying Beane's go-for-broke, shake-it-up leadership. The highlight of the film, Oakland's record 20-game winning streak, is handled beautifully—stirring and exultant.

Moneyball, which had a premiere at the Paramount Theater in downtown Oakland, earned more than $110 million and received six Academy Award nominations.

Unlike most sports movies, there's no championship at the conclusion, though there is a mention that the Red Sox went on to use the A's methods in winning Boston's first World Series in 86 years.

"It would have been cool if we'd actually won," former A's third baseman Eric Chavez said. "Then it would be a really interesting movie."

Former Oakland outfielder Eric Byrnes has no such reservations. "Say what you will about *Moneyball,*" he said, "but how many world champions have they made a major motion picture about?"

35 Captain Sal Bando

Sal Bando was the undisputed leader of the A's 1970s dynasty, a central figure in team history whose influence is still felt.

Yet despite helping Oakland to three titles in a row, Bando remains underrated, the most prominent A's player from that era not voted into the Hall of Fame and a man never given enough credit for his solid defense.

"Sal was the captain, obviously, and the glue that kept the team together," outfielder George Hendrick said. "When Sal spoke, it was gospel to all of us. Very quiet, great sense of humor—but everyone in the clubhouse knew he was the man.

"He was the one that nobody would mess with. Everyone knew not to, even Reggie Jackson.

"A lot of other third basemen were talked about more and in the spotlight then—they got more of the acclaim, but Sal Bando kept winning championships. That tells you a lot about the guy."

Bando hit five homers in ALCS play, and he was durable, playing in all 162 games three times. His 162-game average in his 11 seasons with the A's: 21 homers and 88 RBIs.

After his playing career, Bando became the Brewers general manager, and in that role was a mentor to Bob Melvin. He hired Melvin as a scout, and eventually Melvin worked his way up to bench coach under manager Phil Garner.

So when Melvin became the A's manager in 2011, he chose No. 6 for his jersey number—which is what Bando wore.

"I was lucky enough to have him take an interest in me in Milwaukee and recommend me for my first bench-coach job," Melvin said. "Sal took good care of me."

And growing up in the Bay Area, Melvin's favorite player was…Sal Bando.

"He was Captain Sal. He led the team," Melvin said. "Those clubs had so many unique personalities, guys didn't always get along and there were some fights in the clubhouse—so someone had to make sure everyone is united on the field, make sure they were all together, and that was Sal. You look at the production and clutch hits, too—that has captain written all over it."

A's broadcaster Ray Fosse saw that in person as an Oakland catcher from 1973 to 1975.

"He was the captain for a reason," Fosse said. "He was very well respected, he handled things so well. A great man. A great person. If guys were out of line, Captain Sal stepped forward.

"Reggie Jackson put up the great numbers, Catfish Hunter was a great pitcher, Rollie Fingers did a great job out of the bullpen—but when it came down to one guy who took care of business, it was Captain Sal."

36 Bill King

Hall of Fame announcers worked the airwaves in Oakland, along with notable characters like Jimmy Piersall and the UC Berkeley college crew, but one A's broadcaster stands out above all others.

Bill King, the multi-sport play-by-play genius, was the A's radio man for 25 years, until his death in 2005. King, who also did Warriors and Raiders broadcasts, is recognized as one of the best radio announcers in NBA history and numerous times he has appeared on the short list for the Baseball Hall of Fame's Ford C. Frick Award.

"Bill was the best all-around broadcaster ever," former A's TV announcer Moore said. "He could do all sports. And he had that great dry wit about him."

An erudite Renaissance man who enjoyed fine dining, opera, ballet, history, and sailing, King was also earthy and unconventional, known for bizarre eating habits, wearing sandals in all weather, berating officials and umpires, and driving an old beater that stood out next to the players' expensive cars.

"He had a succession of junkers, two-toned things that looked out of the demolition derby, until his attorney took him to a used car lot and made him buy a Camry," A's radio man Ken Korach said. "He forced Bill to buy it because he was tired of seeing him driving cars with the floorboards missing."

King had a rule about never purchasing a car for more than $200, according to equipment manager Steve Vucinich, who recalled his shock when he saw King driving a 1955 Chevy in the early '80s. Once, when the team was on a road trip, the battery was stolen out of King's car, so, Vucinich said, "After that, before every road trip, he'd take the battery out and put it in his trunk, and every time we got back, we'd see him in the parking lot, hauling the battery out of the trunk and reinstalling it."

For 10 seasons, Korach was King's radio partner and he saw a lot of strange food combinations, including King's pressbox favorite: popcorn mixed with onions, tomatoes, and nacho cheese.

"Bill also liked to eat pats of butter, straight," Korach said. "Sometimes he'd make a peanut butter and jelly sandwich, wrap it up and put it in his briefcase. We used to kid about him being a medical miracle, but he said it's not that he ate junk, he just ate everything."

King was also a connoisseur of expensive restaurants, too, though. "He really savored the dining experience and good conversation," A's travel secretary Mickey Morabito said. "He was such a great storyteller, you wouldn't realize how long you were there. Bill could go to the very best restaurants, then get a breakfast burrito in some dump the next morning.

"He could put on a tux and go to the symphony, or sit at the pool in a Speedo and flip-flops with a wrap on his head. I've never seen a guy who could be so different in his tastes and in his attire. He just didn't care what people thought."

Former A's catcher Ray Fosse, who worked with King for many years, said he felt lucky to break into broadcasting sitting between King and Lon Simmons. King's vocabulary astonished Fosse.

"I remember he was saying something so perfectly, so well, it was like it had been scripted—I looked to see if he was reading it, and he was looking at the field, just talking," Fosse said. "That's how his mind worked, how he went about his business. I remember he once told my wife, Carol, 'If Ray learns a word a day, he'll be fine,' but I was more on the simple side. Lon was erudite, but I remember one day Bill said something and even Lon looked at me like, 'Well, I don't know, either.' And whatever Billy was throwing out, the words were appropriate for the situation. He was a master of the English language, and so quick. Bill was just brilliant."

Bay Area natives were spoiled to have King working basically year-round.

"Bill King was my man," former A's starter Mike Norris said. "He was eccentric, he had that raggedy car and he dressed like he had no money, but he was the best. To hear him describe things, it was like being there. Basketball, he was the best. You could see it as he was saying it.

"That head had a lot of information. He's one man who could pretty much say he'd seen it all."

Korach idolized King, whose "Holy Toledo" catchphrase now adorns the A's radio booth, and he detailed King's eccentricities and brilliance in a book called *Holy Toledo, Lessons from Bill King, Renaissance Man of the Mic,* published by Wellstone Books. It's a fascinating look at the man many believe to be the greatest all-around sports announcer in history.

"To me, it was just a thrill to be next to him," Korach said. "Bill was always able to rise to the occasion in the big moments. He just had so much energy and passion."

Korach has campaigned annually for King to receive the Frick award; the Hall of Fame recently divided the award into three-year candidacy cycles, King is next eligible in the fall of 2016.

37 Finley's Gimmicks

One of owner Charlie Finley's most high-profile stunts in the 1970s was his proposal to use orange baseballs. Like the A's brightly colored uniforms, Finley believed the orange balls would show up better on TV. (He also suggested using green bats at one point.) He thought the Day-Glo balls would be easier for fans to see—and might increase scoring, because the hitters should see the ball better, especially coming out of a green background. Finley enthusiastically promoted the idea, juggling the orange balls at a press conference and waving a bright orange glove over his head.

Commissioner Bowie Kuhn refused to consider the idea, but on March 29, 1973, the A's used the orange balls in an 11–5 exhibition loss to the Indians. Fan reaction was generally positive, but the players weren't sold.

"The orange baseball, it was colorful, but the leather was too slick because of the dye," pitcher Blue Moon Odom said. "You couldn't grip it, you couldn't control it. I thought the color was okay, for the fans, I thought it would be a nice color."

Catcher Ray Fosse said, "The material was so slippery the pitchers couldn't grip the balls. You couldn't put enough rosin on your hands."

Later, though, there was another, better batch of balls, according to Fosse. The problems had been resolved, but too late for Finley's brainchild to catch on.

"Because of the better cowhide leather that used, they were manufactured well enough that they could have been introduced," Fosse said. "The slipperiness was gone. When I saw them, I went 'Wow!'"

A's broadcaster Monte Moore remembered that Finley, always a fan of branding, wanted to give the phosphorescent color a specific name: "Alert Orange," in honor of the Air Force.

"The ones they used against Cleveland in Yuma were orange with white stitches and the players said they couldn't pick up the spin of the ball," Moore said. "So then he used an orange ball with green stitching.

"There was only one spring training game where those were used, and the complaint was that they were endangering players who couldn't see the ball. The day they were used, George Hendrick hit three home runs, so he saw them pretty well."

Hendrick, now a special advisor with the Rays, copped to liking the balls when asked about them in 2014.

"I had gotten traded to Cleveland and we came into Mesa and Catfish Hunter was pitching, and I hit two or three home runs off him with the orange baseballs," Hendrick recalled. "They asked me about the orange baseballs, and just to spite Finley, I said, 'I hate it.'"

Finley, who always kept an eye on his wallet, didn't like losing baseballs during batting practice or when they were fouled off, and he was especially protective of his specially ordered orange balls, recalled equipment manager Steve Vucinich, who said, "Because Charlie was so stingy, the baseballs were guarded more than anything."

Obsessed with speeding up the game and boosting offense, Finley had another nutty scheme, first unveiled in a spring game on March 6, 1971: three balls would constitute a walk and two strikes a strikeout.

"That didn't go very far, either...about as far as the orange baseballs," Moore said.

The A's beat the Brewers 13–9—and 19 walks were issued.

"I remember that game," Odom said with a groan. "The umpires didn't like it, and definitely the pitchers didn't like it. We'd rather have ball five."

The same rules were in effect in a game against the Indians, and again, there were 19 walks. The third and final game was against the Angels, who'd initially refused to participate but were told that Kuhn had approved the idea (erroneously, according to Ron Bergman's book, *Mustache Gang*. The Angels were simply shown a press release put out by the A's).

The Beatles Play K.C.

Owner Charlie Finley's relationship with Kansas City went south quickly, but while his club was there, he did something that many still thank him for: Finley brought the Beatles to town in 1964 after being impressed with their concert in San Francisco.

"I was covering that concert at the Cow Palace for AP, dictating my story over the phone," reporter Ron Bergman recalled, "when this man burst in in a suit, saying he's the owner of the Kansas City A's. He said, 'I'm going to have these young guys at my ballpark. These young men are the greatest!'"

It was not a scheduled stop on the Beatles' tour, but Finley promised Kansas City he'd bring the group to Municipal Stadium, anyway. He contacted Beatles manager Brian Epstein and told him he'd make them an offer "they couldn't refuse," a total of $150,000—at the time, the highest fee ever paid for a single performance.

Epstein asked the band if they'd like to play there on September 17, which had been scheduled as a day off, and John Lennon responded, "We'll do whatever you want, Brian." The Beatles added the date to their schedule, and they augmented their standard set list with "Kansas City/Hey Hey Hey."

The front of the tickets for that night read: "Charles O. Finley is pleased to present...for the enjoyment of Beatles fans in mid-America, 'The Beatles' in person." And the back of the tickets for the event featured a photo of Finley—wearing a Beatles-style wig and pointing to a photo of Beatles drummer Ringo Starr.

Finley lost about $50,000 on the concert, with more than 7,000 tickets going unsold. According to Bergman, the money from ticket sales went to charity.

That third three-ball, two-strike game resulted in 16 bases on balls, and Kuhn called a halt to the experiment, citing excessive walks.

"His crazy ideas went on and on and on like anything," manager Dick Williams said.

Here's another one: Finley proposed red and blue bases—and he used gold bases for the home opener in 1970. The Rules Committee immediately banned them.

Even though some of his suggestions were way out there, Finley never stopped trying to promote baseball and bring in more fans. And several of his ideas were adopted and were successful.

Finley requested that the 1972 World Series games be held at night for a bigger television audience and greater revenue. Not only did that go into effect, it's been standard for World Series games for decades. He also advocated evening start times during the week to enable working people to see the games and early afternoon starts on Sundays to accommodate churchgoers—common scheduling these days.

The A's owner was one of the primary campaigners for the designated hitter and he pushed the American League to adopt it. (It wasn't a new idea—former A's manager Connie Mack had mentioned it as a possibility all the way back in 1906.)

"I can't think of anything more boring than to see a pitcher come up, when the average pitcher can't hit my grandmother," Finley said.

Always the contrarian, Finley didn't actually wind up voting for the rule before it went into effect in 1973 and his no vote nearly killed the DH, according to fellow owner Calvin Griffith. Finley was protesting, upset because he had wanted his notion of a designated runner added at the same time and the other owners rejected the proposal.

That brainstorm of Finley's called for a runner to stand just outside the batter's box when a slow-footed batter was up, and at the crack of the bat or on ball four, the runner would take off. He'd function as the runner for that hitter for the rest of the game.

Another of Finley's innovations eventually caught on, but not until after he was gone: Major League Baseball adopted interleague play in 1997. Finley had suggested interleague games 32 years earlier, saying in the *Sporting News* that, without interleague play, "baseball fans are getting only half the show."

Promotional nights were nothing new for Finley, who came up with some doozies back in the Kansas City days, trying to drum up attendance. He had "Farmers' Night," complete with greased pigs. Foreshadowing "Mustache Day" was "Bald Headed Day." There were pretty ball girls down the lines nightly, and there was also the very popular Hot Pants Night.

"On Hot Pants Night, there was a riot on the field," third baseman Sal Bando recalled. "It was a doubleheader and in between games, guys judged the girl with the best hot pants. But there were so many women on the field, they had trouble starting the second game."

Finley always was fond of fireworks, too, and he wanted to use them regularly when the team moved.

"I guess the craziest thing early on in Oakland was that Finley wanted to shoot off fireworks whenever we hit a home run, but there was a city ordinance against it and they told Finley he couldn't," said Bando, who was the team captain. "Charlie got really mad and he called me up to the office and said, 'They're not going to do this to me,' and he whips out a box of sparklers and says, 'If we hit a home run, pass them out to the guys and they'll go to home plate with lit sparklers.'

"I called a team meeting to tell everyone and I said, 'There's no way we can do this.' That was probably the first time ever where a team hoped it didn't hit a home run. We didn't hit one, and that was the end of it."

Moore, the A's broadcaster, said that Finley's desire to shorten games was briefly on display, too.

"Charlie always complained that the game was too long when the team was in Kansas City," Moore said. "I don't know where he got the idea that it was too long because pitchers were fiddling with the ball, but that's what he thought, and he thought that the 20 second rule before they deliver the ball wasn't being enforced.

"So he installed a clock on the left-field light tower that was 15-by-15 and everyone in the park could see it start to count down, 20, 19, 18, as the pitcher held the ball. A game or two was all that lasted before the commissioner ordered it taken down."

Said Finley at the time, "Every other game has a clock. Why not baseball?"

Other Finley gimmicks that turned up at Municipal Stadium included Harvey, a mechanical rabbit with a basket between his ears. At the press of the umpire's foot, Harvey sprang up from behind home plate to deliver balls as the organist played "Here Comes Peter Cottontail." Eventually, a player, unamused, took a bat to Harvey.

"All the rookies had to stand outside and pass out Charlie O. rabbit feet and bats," catcher Rene Lachemann said. "One day, I gave a dozen bats away to one guy and said, 'The hell with it.'"

There was also a device dubbed "Little Blowhard" that blew dirt off home plate. Some umpires liked to startle unsuspecting batters with a quick blast of compressed air as they settled into the box.

38 Origins

In 1901, the American League was established—and the Philadelphia Athletics were back on the scene for at least the fourth, maybe the fifth time.

In an effort to rival the National League, Charles Comiskey and Ban Johnson banded together some teams in the Midwest, Comiskey founded the White Stockings in Chicago—and in Philadelphia, former Pittsburgh Pirates catcher Connie Mack was offered 25 percent of the stock to co-own the team with Philadelphia sportswriters Sam Jones and Frank Hough.

Benjamin Shibe, who ran a sporting-goods firm with Al Reach, was the primary shareholder, holding 50 percent of the club.

Shibe had invented the machinery to produce standardized baseballs, and in 1909, he earned a patent on the first cork-centered baseball, while a family member came up with the double-seam baseball. Comiskey and Johnson convinced Shibe to come aboard by making the A.J. Reach and Co. baseball the league's official ball.

According to the Philadelphia Athletics Historical Society, Reach, a former star second baseman for a previous iteration of the team, was the first official pro baseball player—the Philadelphia Athletics paid him $25 a week in 1865. (There are other claimants to the title of first pro player, including Lipman Pike, "the Iron Batter," who played for the Athletics in 1866 and is best known for hitting six homers in a game that had a final score of 67–25.)

Reach owned a cigar shop during his playing days, but near the end of his career, he realized there was an increased need for equipment because of baseball's booming popularity. Shibe, a leather expert who made whips, joined his venture, a store on South Eighth Street in Philadelphia. A.G. Spalding later bought the men out.

In 1883, Reach established the National League's Phillies, calling them that because, he said, "It tells you who we are and where we are from." Because Reach owned the Phillies, Shibe decided to pursue a similar opportunity when the American League arrived on the scene.

There wasn't much discussion about the new team's name. Mack went with something familiar, just as Comiskey had in Chicago. There was a Philadelphia Athletics team in the National League in 1876 that was expelled for failing to finish out its schedule; there was an American Association team that played from 1882 to 1890; plus a Players League/American Association team fielded in 1890–91. Reach's Athletics team was in the National Association (1871–75), but that was not recognized as a major league.

John Thorn, Major League Baseball's official historian, noted that the first professional championship, in 1871, was won by the Athletics. In keeping with the future A's teams, there was a colorful character involved, one-time Civil War soldier Nate Berkenstock, who came out of the stands to save the day.

The Athletics played the Chicago White Stockings in Brooklyn—Chicago's ballpark had burned down earlier that month in the Great Chicago Fire. Philadelphia center fielder Count Sensenderfer left with an injury, so Berkenstock, 40 and long retired, was called out of the crowd to play right field. Philadelphia won 4–1, and though Berkenstock went 0-for-4 with three strikeouts, "he made a running catch to end the game," Thorn said.

Even before that, there was the Athletic Club of Philadelphia, an amateur team formed in 1860. The name was a common one for gentlemen's sporting clubs, and was the precursor to every future Athletics team.

All of the Philadelphia Athletics teams bore a simple 'A' in script lettering on their jerseys, and as a result the nickname "the A's" has been used interchangeably with "Athletics" throughout the history of the franchise. The shorter name proved popular in headlines, too, but only once has the team officially been called "the A's"—Charlie Finley insisted on the designation in the 1970s and '80s.

Mack, again hearkening back to the olden days, always pronounced his club's name in the style of the 1800s, using the four-syllable "Ath-uh-let-ics." He also called the players "Ath-uh-leets," rather than Athletics or A's.

39 Do The Wave

Some love it, some hate it—the worldwide phenomenon that began at the Coliseum.

During the 1981 ALCS between the A's and the Yankees, professional cheerleader Krazy George Henderson introduced the Wave, pounding his ever-present drum and getting stadium sections to rise in sequence on October 15.

"That was cool, it really was," starter Mike Norris said. "The first time I saw it, it was even better because I'd never seen that many people there. And here's a wave, all the way around, and with people in every damn seat. It was thunderous, almost. You could feel it, physically. And Krazy George, all crazy-lookin'. He was just a character."

The Wave looks simple—stand up when it reaches your section, whoosh your arms over your heard, sit down—but it requires a willing crowd, someone to get things rolling and a degree of synchronicity. Without mass participation, The Wave is just kind of…lame, and its popularity has ebbed and flowed over the years.

Keys to doing the Wave and doing it well: "Number one, fans in the stands—have the place full is real important," said Krazy George, noting that it took a sellout at the ALCS to really do it properly—his earlier attempts at minor-league hockey games didn't work as well. "The shape of the stadium helps, too—if it's a real oval, it's special, because you see it coming. Flat-sided stadiums, horseshoes, it has to slow up or jump. With an oval, you get a nice swoop around.

"The timing is crucial—if you don't do it when there is some excitement, it won't start. I see people trying to start the Wave after their team has given up two touchdowns in a minute and a half— that's not going to work. There's a philosophy to it, you want be able to transfer the energy of the crowd, let the fans feel like they're involved, they've created something, added a little bit extra to the event. At the Coliseum, I liked to start one after the A's scored a run or two, had some runners on base and less than two outs—you don't want to start one just when the third out is made."

The University of Washington long has attempted to claim credit for the first Wave, but the Huskies crowd performed their rise and fall on October 31, 1981. The ALCS game was two weeks earlier, and televised, thoroughly debunking such an idea.

Broadcaster Joe Garagiola was one of the TV announcers for that series, and he told the *Dallas Morning News*, "I remember during the game that all of a sudden the fans started getting up and then sitting down…. Our producer, Don Ohlmeyer, was trying to get the cameraman to catch the Wave, but he was always one section behind. He kept pounding on [the cameraman] saying, 'Get it! Get that thing!'

"I had never seen anything like it. It was super."

Krazy George says it took several attempts that night in 1981— only three sections at a time could hear his instructions, and the other sections didn't catch on right away. Finally, he got the Wave circling the stadium, but it came to a halt at the original section because that section just stood and applauded the effort, so excited were they to have started it. George told that section to start it again, and the next time it got back to them to keep it going.

The Wave raced around the Coliseum five times.

"It was spectacular," Krazy George said 33 years later, crediting the A's former owners for helping kick-start things. "I really think the Haas family were so visionary when it came to the fan experience, trying to find out what might entertain them, get them participating. The Haases really set the tone for everything."

During the Los Angeles Olympics in 1984, the phenomenon took off, especially in the soccer venues, and Mexican fans took the Wave back home. When the World Cup took place in Mexico two years later, the Wave was televised internationally and suddenly, it was worldwide.

In most countries, it's still called the Mexican Wave, though it all started at the Coliseum, with Krazy George.

"I like to say I'm the man who made the whole world stand up and cheer," he said. "That was my heyday, at the Coliseum. What an atmosphere."

40 Wild-Card Drama

With the addition of the second wild-card team, all postseason clubs desperately want to avoid that one-game playoff game, a crapshoot if ever there was one.

For the A's in 2014, though, the wild-card game appeared to set up just as they wanted. General manager Billy Beane had acquired All-Star starter Jon Lester precisely for such an occasion. And Oakland had Lester on the mound with a three-run lead, 7–3, after seven innings at Kansas City.

Cue the craziness.

Lester, one of the great postseason pitchers of all time, gave up three runs in the eighth, and the Royals tied it up in the ninth against All-Star closer Sean Doolittle. Former A's outfielder Josh Willingham provided a pinch-hit dunk single, pinch-runner Jarrod Dyson went to second on a sacrifice bunt and stole third, and he scored on a sacrifice fly by Nori Aoki.

Oakland took the lead again in the 12th on a pinch-hit RBI single by Alberto Callaspo, but Kansas City came back in the bottom of the inning against one of the A's most reliable relievers, Dan Otero. Eric Hosmer tripled to left and scored on Christian Colon's single past third, and with two outs, Colon stole second—the Royals' seventh steal of the game and their sixth since catcher Geovany Soto left with a thumb injury incurred on a play at the plate in the bottom of the first.

And Salvador Perez ended it, with a two-out, two-strike single off starter Jason Hammel, Oakland's sixth pitcher of the game.

It was a brutal loss for the A's, who have won only one potential series-clinching game in 14 tries in the Billy Beane era. Adding to the frustration, Oakland had loaded the bases in the top of the ninth and did not score.

"We had a few chances," former Oakland outfielder Jonny Gomes said. "More than a few."

"Our offense had been dismal—and we put up seven runs and we end up losing, that was frustrating," ex-A's third baseman Josh Donaldson said. "I can't remember scoring seven runs and losing, not with our bullpen and starters and how great they were. It definitely stung. But luck isn't always on your side—that ball down the third-base line by Colon, I was like, 'What is going on?' In my mind, whoever gets past that game is going all the way."

And the Royals did make it to the World Series, falling in seven games to the Giants—losing really only because of one man, World Series MVP Madison Bumgarner. K.C. had the tying run at third with two outs in the bottom of the ninth in Game 7, but the Royals couldn't quite continue their fantasy season.

The wild-card game was an instant classic. And many of the A's players said afterward that the game was a treat to play in, despite the outcome. It was the first postseason game at Kansas City in 29 years, and the capacity crowd was overjoyed throughout, the atmosphere electric.

"A game like that is like a Game 7, it had that level of excitement," Oakland outfielder Josh Reddick said. "You knew whichever team came out of it would carry the momentum, and they won eight in a row, that was kind of fun to see. They made a heck of a run, you couldn't help but root for them. What a great game. It was fantastic.

"I felt bad because Brandon Moss had such a great game, it was like, 'Okay, Moss is getting back, this is what we need,' and then it just didn't work out. But it was a great game to be a part of, that team just seemed destined—that Hosmer triple on a ball two feet off the plate? Come on."

Moss, who'd received a cortisone shot for a hip injury before the series, hit two homers, and, he said two months later, "I've never played in a game that fun, that was No. 1. We score seven runs, they score eight—unless it's a game you just give away, which we didn't, you can't feel bad. We played our best, they played their best. Even though we lost, that game was a blast."

The A's announced after the game that Soto and Coco Crisp, who'd left the game with a hamstring injury, would not have been available had the team advanced to the division series. DH/first baseman Adam Dunn, still wearing his full uniform more than an hour after the game, though he hadn't played, indicated he was retiring from baseball, despite being 38 homers shy of 500.

It was the final game in an Oakland uniform for Lester, Lowrie, Callaspo, Gomes, and Gregerson, all free agents. And in December, in a shocker of a move, the A's traded Donaldson, an All-Star who'd helped Oakland to three consecutive postseason appearances, to Toronto, then dealt Moss, another All-Star, to Cleveland and Norris, still another All-Star, to the Padres..

41 Jason Giambi

Dating back to Rube Waddell more than 100 years ago, free spirits always have felt at home with the A's, and in the 1990s, one of them just happened to be Oakland's best player.

Meet Jason Giambi, the MVP with the gold thong.

Giambi, who came up in 1995, cultivated a shaggy, party-hearty persona with the A's, and yes, he did have a gold thong hanging up in his locker, a good luck charm of sorts.

"I don't know if Jason ever actually wore it—I never saw him wear it, but to be honest, it wouldn't shock me if he wore it a lot of the time," longtime A's third baseman Eric Chavez said. "There was that one article with him on the cover of *Sports Illustrated*, his hair all hanging down, in a cut-off shirt, and a picture inside with someone feeding him grapes—that's Jason."

"I'm pretty sure G wore that thing, because there sure was enough talk about it," former A's outfielder Eric Byrnes said. "His thing was 'Party like a Rock Star, Hit like an All-Star,' that was his motto, that's who he was.

"I remember asking him what he was thinking about when he was at the plate and he said, 'I want to feel sexy,' and that was not a joke, he meant it."

Jason Giambi is picked up by Frank Menechino after the A's 3–0 victory over the Rangers on Sunday, October 1, 2000, gave them the American League West title. (Ben Margot/ AP Photo)

That approach paid off: Giambi hit 43 homers and drove in 137 runs in 2000, winning MVP honors, and in seven-plus seasons with Oakland, he recorded 198 home runs, 715 RBIs, and a .300 average.

And for all his man-about-town image, Giambi was focused when it came to his job.

"I think people overestimated whatever he might be doing away from the park, everyone thought he was out partying all night, going to WWE events all the time, thought he was a loose cannon, but we never really saw that," former A's ace Barry Zito said. "He was conscientious, very professional, very classy—he'd step up and get guys riled up if needed, but he wasn't this super loud, obnoxious guy or anything.

"He was just around, shooting the breeze, he was comfortable in his own skin and that did carry over—when I got called up, I was like, 'These dudes are a bunch of freaks.' It was like a free-for-all."

"There were a couple of bolts loose in that head, but we all loved him," Chavez said. "Everyone does, I've never heard anyone say a bad word about him. Jason had more influence on me than anyone in the game—the way he treated people, even when he was making a big name for himself, he was just such a gentleman and baseball players don't have that reputation. He treated me with so much respect when I was just a rookie, and back then rookies were supposed to get crushed. Jason would say, 'Hey, I put on the uniform and the shoes the same way you do.' I always appreciated that, he was like my older brother."

Kind, a little outrageous, and one a heck of a player—that's Giambi's legacy in Oakland. He's often credited with setting a friendly, fun tone for the A's clubhouse for the next decade or more.

"The mindset was: whatever works, keep throwing the hits out there," one-time A's infielder Randy Velarde said. "And he did. Jason could hit. He was always getting on base, always driving in runs. What a bunch of characters, and he was the leader. It was fun playing the game with that knucklehead, he was a kid at heart. The gold thong, that was him, he was just something."

42 Herb Washington

A's owner Charlie Finley loved innovation—or as some might say, gimmicks.

He was a primary force behind the implementation of the designated hitter, but Finley didn't want to stop there, he also wanted to add a "designated runner." That notion never gained traction, so Finley incorporated the idea on his own, using sprinters Allan "the Panamanian Express" Lewis (a Finley nickname) and "Hurricane" Herb Washington to dash around the basepaths—and do little else.

The plan was not terribly successful, former A's manager Dick Williams recalled, saying, "We had a player, Allan Lewis, I don't even know if he owned a glove. I put him in one day, and he started to steal when the batter hit a pop-up. He kept running, and the third-base coach said, 'Go back! Go back!'.... So he cut across the mound. The whole thing was kind of idiotic."

A's catcher Ray Fosse said, "The funniest thing was that when Herb Washington's Topps baseball card came out, there was the bat on his shoulder, but he never hit once.

"He was a sprinter, and it was kind of a joke initially. When he got to second base, we'd say, 'Turn, Herbie!' Because when you're a sprinter, you run straight. Early, there were some wide turns. It was fun to watch him run, but basically, you're playing with a 24-man roster."

Washington said that he got a lot of flak from his teammates for being one-dimensional, but he had such a polished track resume, it bounced off him. "There were still guys who questioned the choice of having a specialized runner, and my contention then as well as today is that the runner can work on certain teams if you have a pretty set roster," Washington said in 2014. "If you can get a guy who can change the game, it's worth it to you. It certainly was for us."

Finley cold-called Washington, then working in television but fielding offers from football teams, to try to lure him to the A's in 1974.

"His first words were, 'This is Mr. Finley, the owner of the world champion Oakland A's.' And my response was, 'Hello Mr. Finley, Herb Washington, the world's fastest human,'" Washington remembered. "I said, 'You know I haven't played baseball in years. You want to talk football or track, okay.' And he says, 'No, I want you to steal bases.'

"We get to the point of talking about a contact, and I said, 'The first year, I want a no-cut clause,' and Mr. Finley said something to the effect that there are only a couple of guys on the team with a no-cut: Reggie Jackson, Catfish Hunter, and Vida Blue. He says to me, 'Do you think you're as good as those guys?' And I said, 'No, but last time I checked, none of them had world records in track and field either.'

"So we come to an impasse, because he won't give it to me. We conclude the interview, and I'm in the outer office and he buzzes his secretary to get me. I go back and he says, 'Do you play poker?' I said, 'I play a hand or two.' He said, 'I just folded.' He says, 'But, you have to grow a mustache by Opening Day and I'll give you another $2,500.'"

Though Washington always resented the suggestion that he didn't know much about baseball, he said he did have to learn the pitchers and some of the finer points of the game.

"I knew how to slide, but it was easier for me to go headfirst," said Washington, who worked with noted base-stealer Maury Wills on baserunning during the spring. "I was a track guy, everything for me was straight ahead. It's the quickest line from point A to B."

"He didn't even have a glove!" said outfielder Billy North with a chuckle. "Herb didn't know how to slide, how to stop. You don't know how to slide, you're going to cut yourself, his strawberries would be long, long. You can't put a patch on that.

"He ran the bases at 90 degree angles. But I'm telling you, he scored some runs on some cheap hits. He won some games for us. I don't care what they say, our 25th man did more than any other 25th man in the game. You talk about running, that's a whole different ballgame right there, baby."

Washington's best-known moment came in Game 2 of the World Series against the Dodgers. He pinch-ran for Joe Rudi, who'd delivered a two-run single to cut L.A.'s lead to 3–2 in the ninth—and Washington was picked off.

"Because of his speed, any type of hit and he's going to score," Rudi said. "He'd just never seen Mike Marshall before, and Marshall had a tricky move to first. He gave him a couple of slow things, slow things, and then boom, picked him off. Sal Bando was pretty hot."

Washington still claims it was a balk by Marshall, and the memory rankles.

"I would have much rather been thrown out by a few yards than picked off in the series," he said. "Picked off is dramatic in baseball. But I had a chance to talk to Finley that night, and he said, 'Keep your head up, and you're going to play tomorrow.' That helped."

In Game 3, Washington was so tentative, it was noticeable. "The next day he got sent in, and he had one of those Little League leads, maybe even had a foot on the bag because he didn't want to get picked off again," Fosse said. "It was kind of funny."

Washington doesn't dispute that, but he said it wouldn't have mattered. "I could be more cautious, especially with the speed I had," he said.

There was no dispute about that. "He was incredibly fast," Rudi said. "And we had some pretty fast people—Billy North, Blue Moon Odom, they challenged him to a couple of races, and he ended up running backwards over the last part of the race. Amazing."

"If someone ever beat me in a footrace, how long do you think I would have been here under Finley?" Washington said with a laugh. "I wouldn't have finished the race and got back to the dugout, my stuff would have been packed."

43 Make an A's Mix Tape

The Yankees have "New York, New York," and the Red Sox "Sweet Caroline," but apart from that, few teams are as closely associated with one song as the A's are with their post-win standard, Kool and the Gang's "Celebration."

That song is the starting point for any A's-themed music mix—the team has played it after team victories since an 11-game winning streak to start the 1981 season, thanks to baseball's first-ever in-house DJ, Roger Inman. "Celebration" is such a staple, it even blared out at the Tokyo Dome when the A's played there in 2008 and 2012.

"'Celebration' is obviously the most important one," A's closer Sean Doolittle said. "But they also play 'Zorba the Greek' every chance they get every night, and it's good, it gets stuck in my head every time."

So throw that stadium-organ staple into your mix, too, and make sure to add "U Can't Touch This" and "Too Legit to Quit" by one-time clubhouse employee and assistant to the owner Stanley Burrell, aka MC Hammer, whose first record was funded by A's players Mike Davis and Dwayne Murphy. Hammer's hits remain in the regular rotation at the Coliseum, and "U Can't Touch This" was Dave Stewart's music of choice when the great A's right-hander took the field in the 1990s.

In 2014, Josh Reddick made headlines for his choice of walkup music: the '80s pop-ballad "Careless Whisper," with its sexy-sax solo. Reddick's unusual choice wound up getting him into the pages of *Rolling Stone,* and the A's even tried to get George Michael to make an appearance at the Coliseum.

The crowd loved it, and so did the bullpen. The relievers were spotted grooving along to the song every time Reddick came to the plate.

"No one knew it was coming, and it was amazing—everyone was like, 'Whoa, that is awesome!' " Doolittle said. "Reddick got a few hits, so [he] kept it, and everyone was excited about it, it started so spontaneously. And it was cool, like everything else our crowd latches on to. They were bringing little saxes to the game.'"

Doolittle said the bullpen also enjoyed Nick Punto's late-season selection of Taylor Swift's "Shake It Off," so he'd recommend that for any A's compilation.

Doolittle, like many closers, has Metallica belting out for his entrance. He uses "For Whom the Bell Tolls," and Grant Balfour, another All-Star A's closer, used Metallica's "One." You may choose one, or heck, both.

Then there's former reliever Jerry Blevins, who told the A's sound-system folks that he didn't throw hard enough to go onto the field with Metallica—so instead, they played the band's "Sanitarium" when he came off the field *after* a successful appearance.

A's Hall of Famer Dennis Eckersley was one of the first closers to emerge to hard-charging guitar strains: George Thorogood's "Bad to the Bone."

Blevins and Coco Crisp take credit for coming up with the team's anthem in 2012, and it was accompanied by a full dance routine: The Bernie Lean, inspired by the movie *Weekend at Bernies II*. There are actually two versions, both must-haves. The original and the inspiration for the A's choreography, was ISA's 2010 "Moving Like Bernie." There's also "Bernie Lean" by ATM and IMD; members of the A's appear in the official music video.

Over the years, Oakland has had some notable walkup music, including John Jaha stepping to the plate with Black Sabbath's "Crazy Train," and at the other end of the musical spectrum, Josh Willingham's selection, '80s ballad "Your Love," by the appropriately named The Outfield.

Tower of Power, which originated in Oakland, is a staple at the Coliseum, and these tracks get extra credit for including the town's name: "Oakland Stroke" and "Oakland Zone." Another local band, Huey Lewis and the News, performed their first-ever stadium national anthem at an A's game; that rendition is still occasionally used before games.

The song most specifically tailored for the team? "They Are the Oakland A's," by the Baseball Project, a band that includes Mike Mills and Peter Buck of R.E.M. Billy Beane and Dallas Braden both get shout-outs in the song.

Members of Berkeley-based bestselling punk band Green Day are A's fans—and the A's even held a Green Day Fireworks night in 2013. "Know Your Enemy" is a popular choice at the Coliseum.

And speaking of punk bands, feel free to throw on anything by GM Beane's favorite band, the Clash—maybe "Should I Stay or Should I Go," to commemorate his decision not to go to Boston after initially taking the Red Sox's GM job in late 2002.

44 Second Mack Dynasty

After an absence of 14 years following the sell-off of the first A's dynasty, Philadelphia made it back to the World Series in 1929 with a team considered among the best of all time.

The 1929 A's featured four future Hall of Famers—pitcher Lefty Grove, young first baseman Jimmie Foxx, outfielder Al Simmons, and cantankerous catcher Mickey Cochrane. The A's plowed over the rest of the league, taking a 10-game lead by June. They completed the season 104–46, a full 18 games ahead of the Murderer's Row Yankees, whose 1927 club is considered the tops of all time.

Grove had the league's best ERA (2.81) and won the strikeout crown. Simmons topped Babe Ruth for the RBI title, with 157, and he batted .365 with 34 home runs. Foxx, who'd shuffled around in search of a position, finally landed at first base and hit .354 with 33 homers, 118 RBIs, and 123 runs, and he led the league in on-base percentage. Cochrane, back at catcher after some brief attempts to put Foxx there, hit .331 with 95 RBIs and 113 runs.

The A's had other notable contributors that year, most notably George Earnshaw, who was 24–8, and Eddie Rommel, whose 2.85 ERA was second only to Grove's.

The Yankees, with Ruth and Lou Gehrig, did out-homer the A's that year, but Philadelphia was tops in the league in pitching and defense. The contributions from the mound were no surprise: One of Connie Mack's top skills throughout his lengthy career was finding and nurturing pitching talent.

He'd also found some overlooked offensive talent in Simmons, who scared away other teams because of his unorthodox left-handed hitting style—he took a big step toward third when he started his swing.

"Have you always hit like that?" Mack reportedly asked.

"It's the only way I know," Simmons replied.

"Then keep doing it, son," Mack responded.

Simmons hit well over .300 in each of his first 11 seasons and he drove in more than 100 runs in each of those years.

Mack liked Gordon Stanley "Mickey" Cochrane so much, he shelled out $50,000 to buy the 21-year-old's contract in 1925. Cochrane was a tremendous athlete, a five-sport star at Boston University—he played baseball, basketball, and football, he ran track and he boxed. He was the quarterback and captain of the football team, and his 53-yard field goal in 1921 was the school record for more than 60 years.

Cochrane hit third, Simmons fourth, and Foxx—one of the greatest right-handed power hitters of all time—fifth. Talk about a murderous row.

Every bit as important as their skill was the Athletics' attitude. This was a tough, focused team, driven by several men, Grove, Simmons, and Cochrane, who were known for their hot tempers. Simmons, whose real name was Aloysius Harry Szymanski (his new last name was the result of seeing a billboard for a hardware company), was a sworn enemy to those on the mound.

"Pitchers," he groused. "I wanted them dead."

Cochrane was known as "Black Mike" for his moods, but he was a tremendous team leader and an off-field hero: In 1923, he rescued a boy who'd fallen through pond ice while skating, and in 1932, he helped save dozens of people from a burning apartment building, single-handedly rescuing three women and two men, according to author Robert P. Broadwater. Cochrane also served in the Navy during World War II.

Mack, who had assembled this tremendous collection, was back in the spotlight after more than a decade—and the 1929

World Series is best known for Mack's most unusual move in his 50 years of managing.

He had the American League's best pitching staff with Grove, Earnshaw, and Rube Walberg. So his Game 1 starter against the Cubs was a shocker: Howard Ehmke, a 35-year-old junkballer who'd won only seven games during that storied Philadelphia season. He was the seventh-best man on the staff, and he hadn't pitched in nearly a month. Even his teammates were startled when they saw him warming up.

Ehmke threw a complete game and struck out 13 batters, a record at the time, as the A's won 3–1. It was Ehmke's greatest game ever—and the last that he won in the big leagues.

Though many baseball analysts and historians believe that the decision was typically crafty of Mack (using a right-handed side-armer against the Cubs' heavily right-handed hitting lineup), the Athletics manager always claimed that the move was purely a hunch.

Legend has it that Mack told Ehmke late in the season that he'd made his last appearance for the team, but the right-hander pleaded for a chance to throw in the World Series, saying, "Mr. Mack, there is one good game left in this old arm. I'd like to prove it."

So Mack sent Ehmke out to scout the Cubs from the stands in the final weeks of the season. "Learn all you can about their hitters. Say nothing to anybody," Mack told him. "You are my opening pitcher for the World Series."

Up until that point, Ehmke had been known for several things: He'd won 20 games with Boston in 1923, and he'd nearly become the first man in major-league history to record back-to-back no-hitters; only a controversial scoring decision on a groundball single to start the second prevented him from going into the record books. Ehmke also had allowed the first of Babe Ruth's record 60 home runs in 1927.

The 1929 World Series featured the famed "Mack Attack," as the A's came back from an eight-run deficit by scoring 10 runs in the seventh inning of Game 4. Philadelphia sent 15 men to the plate in the inning, and Chicago's Hack Wilson lost Mule Haas' fly ball in the sun for a three-run inside-the-park home run. Instead of evening the series, the Cubs fell 10–8, and the A's took their fourth title in franchise history, winning Game 5 by a score of 3–2. Haas hit a two-run homer and Bing Miller a walk-off double after a double by Simmons and an intentional walk to Foxx.

The following year, the A's won their final title in Philadelphia, beating the Cardinals in a six-game series. Grove and Earnshaw each won two games, with Simmons and Cochrane hitting two homers apiece and Foxx a game-winning shot in Game 5. "He hit it so hard, I couldn't feel sorry for myself," Cardinals pitcher Burleigh Grimes said.

The A's won 107 games during the regular season in 1931, the most in franchise history, and they accomplished the feat when the regular season was just154 games. They lost the World Series in a rematch with the Cardinals, though, falling in seven games—two of them won by Grimes.

Scrappy St. Louis essentially won with speedy base-running and well-placed singles and bloops, leading Mack to say as he watched, "Goodness gracious, can't anyone catch these things?" Pepper Martin went 12-for-24 and stole five bases, one of the Series' all-time great individual performances.

Over the three-year span from 1929 to 1931, Philadelphia had won 313 regular season games, three pennants and two titles. It was a remarkable stretch—and one that would not be approached by another A's team for 40 years.

45 Campy Suspended

Six weeks before the 1972 American League Championship Series, the A's and Billy Martin's Detroit Tigers had tangled in an ugly 15-minute brawl. Three Tigers had been ejected as a result.

Tensions ran high from the start, therefore, when the teams met in October. The first game was an exciting one: Detroit took a 2–1 lead in the 11th on Al Kaline's homer off Rollie Fingers, but Oakland won it in the bottom of the inning when Gonzalo Marquez smacked a pinch-hit single to drive in one run and Kaline's throw to third skipped away, allowing Gene Tenace to score.

Game 2 went to Oakland 5–0, and with three hits, two runs, and two stolen bases, A's shortstop Campy Campaneris was a major factor. So when he came up in the seventh, Campaneris was expecting reliever Lerrin LaGrow to throw inside. LaGrow did more than that: He drilled a pitch off the speedster's ankle, spinning Campaneris all the way around.

Enraged, Campaneris got up and, with an overhand motion, flung his bat at the mound, over LaGrow's head. That brought Martin and the rest of the Tigers onto the field; restrained by two umpires, Martin screamed at Campaneris to come fight him, and he yelled similar things at the Oakland dugout.

The A's, to a man, believed that Martin had instructed LaGrow throw at Campaneris' legs, but they didn't want to risk injuries or more suspensions by venturing onto the field; it was obvious Campaneris would be slapped with some sort of punishment.

Martin, who was from nearby Berkeley and had starred for the Oakland Oaks, ripped the A's for refusing to fight and he called Campaneris' actions "gutless."

"Lerrin LaGrow, the pitcher, threw at his legs—because Campy could run," A's manager Dick Williams said. "He wanted to hit him. Billy Martin did a wise thing: He wanted Campy out of the game. With an injury, so be it. He got more than he bargained for."

American League president Joe Cronin said that Campaneris would have to sit out the remainder of the series. A's owner Charlie Finley announced that Campaneris' ankle injury was too severe for him to play, anyway, which might have been the case.

Campaneris told reporters that he wasn't aiming for LaGrow, he was only trying to scare him. If he'd meant to hit the pitcher, Campaneris said, he would have flung the bat sidearm. And Campaneris believed, like the rest of the A's, that Martin had deliberately targeted him.

Things only got crazier. Before the A's departed for Detroit, there was a bomb scare on the team plane, delaying them by more than an hour. When the A's worked out on the field on the off-day, there were 50 policemen on hand. And when the Tigers came back from a 3–1 deficit in the 10th to win Game 4, it was mayhem, Tigers fans ran onto the field and began to rampage, according to equipment manager Steve Vucinich.

Vucinich and other A's employees had to stand on the bench, wielding bats, to keep the club's property safe, while two police offers were sent to the bullpen to escort coach Vern Hoscheit through the unruly masses and back to the clubhouse.

Tempers continued to flare on both sides. Finley consistently defended Campaneris, and though his request to allow the shortstop to sit on the bench for the finale was denied, he still flew Campaneris back from Oakland to attend the game. He also detailed for reporters the details of each of Martin's well-publicized fights over the years, prompting Martin to call Finley "a born liar" before Game 5.

Game 5, the finale, was just as nutty, especially after the A's took a one-run lead. The crowd, unruly throughout, grew more troublesome. Someone threw a smoke bomb at Ken Holtzman when he warmed up in the eighth. George Hendrick, playing center, was hit by numerous objects: an ice cube, a bottle, a rock, and at one point, a beer can that landed in his glove.

"Someone put a pinhole in it and shook it up," Hendrick said. "They threw it and it bounced up in my glove and there it was, spraying everywhere."

When Vida Blue induced a fly ball from Tony Taylor for the final out, Hendrick made the catch and was slammed in the back by another bottle.

Things weren't much cooler in the clubhouse. Even as the champagne was flowing, Blue made a choking motion at Blue Moon Odom, right in front of the media, and asked, "Why can't you starters finish what you begin?" Odom flew at Blue and had to be pulled back by teammates; while he was pushed back against the wall and sobbing, according to reports, Blue came over and apologized.

"I pitched four shutout innings and I came into the locker room and joking, I said to John, 'Nice going, you choked.' And he came after me," said Blue, who considers Odom to be like a family member. "It did get the headlines, but that was the extent of that."

Odom said that he'd told Williams he'd be okay, he could stay in the game, but Williams went with Blue.

"At the end of the game—I guess Vida didn't mean it, but what he said was that I choked. And that was around all the sportswriters," Odom recalled 35 years later. "I went off on him. I shook the locker and I said, 'Don't ever do that again.' In 14 innings in that series, I hadn't given up anything. I was a pressure pitcher with Oakland, I could come through. I wouldn't have choked."

46 Out of the First Round: 2006

Only one Oakland team advanced past the first round of the playoffs in the past two decades, and yet the 2006 A's go a little overlooked.

Is it that they were swept in the ALCS by the Tigers? Or is it that the other A's playoff teams of recent vintage made consecutive postseason appearances, while the '06 club was sort of out there alone, the only playoff club in an eight-year stretch?

Whatever the case, the 2006 A's deserve more credit: They won 93 games during the regular season and they swept a terrific Twins club in the division series, marking the best performance by an Oakland team since winning the pennant in 1990.

Newcomer Frank Thomas was the key figure, signed as a free agent after spending his entire career with the White Sox. Foot injuries had limited him to the point that there was speculation he might be done, but he had a huge year with Oakland, hitting 39 homers and driving in 114 runs, finishing fourth in the MVP race.

And with Thomas taking moody Milton Bradley under his wing, Bradley had one of his best seasons and was Oakland's top hitter in the ALCS. Thomas mentored Nick Swisher, too, and the outfielder hit 35 homers.

Veterans Mark Kotsay and Jason Kendall famously took the lead with the rest of the clubhouse.

"Kendall and Kotsay ran the show, they made sure no young guys took a lazy step," closer Huston Street said. "They'd crush you for three days if you did. I'm very thankful for those guys, that was really the last group with that old-school mentality—we didn't get away with anything. I've told Kotsay, 'Thank you for bringing me up right.'"

The lone remaining member of the Big Three, Barry Zito, was an All-Star that year and earned 16 wins. Joe Blanton also had 16 wins, and Dan Haren, 14; when healthy, Rich Harden also contributed, going 4–0.

"Rich Harden will never get the credit he deserves but when he was healthy, he was one of the most dominant pitchers I've ever seen," Street said. "That pitching staff doesn't get enough credit, period—Justin Duchscherer was an All-Star one year as a starter, one year as a reliever, and I learned more about pitch sequences from him than anyone."

The A's went into the division series against the Twins that fall with a bit of an underdog feeling, particularly with Johan Santana on the mound for Minnesota at the Metrodome. Santana, who went on to win the 2006 Cy Young Award, had not lost at home in more than a year.

And then Thomas homered to lead off the second inning, the first of his two solo homers in Game 1.

"Right before that, Frank told me he 100 percent was sitting on a changeup," Street recalled. "He said, 'If Santana throws me a changeup, I'm going to do some damage.' "

Zito, the A's Game 1 starter, didn't allow a hit until the fourth inning and just four, total, in his eight innings.

"Most people didn't give us a chance in that game," Haren said, "but I knew how much Zito wanted it."

"That game, for me, going in there and beating Santana in the Metrodome, where he hadn't lost in forever, with Frank hitting two solo shots—that was the best game for me in my career to that point," Zito said. "Santana was just such a force, untouchable. But we found a way to beat him and that set the tone."

Game 2 was all about Kotsay, who delivered one of the most memorable hits in A's history, a two-run inside-the-park homer off

Dennys Reyes in the seventh inning. Kotsay had played much of the season with a back injury so severe that he'd needed three epidural injections, and yet there he was, galloping around the bases as Torii Hunter, the Twins' Gold Glove center fielder, made an ill-advised plunge for the ball.

"They brought in the lefty to face me, which was the correct move, but at that point my arrogance, my confidence, was off the charts," Kotsay said. "It was just a line drive, and Torii broke in on it. My eyes lit up, 'Oh, he's going to go for it!' I'm going hard, and I'm thinking two bases, but when it gets by Torii, I just kept going."

Kotsay slid into home, and in one motion, leaped to his feet in celebration; he still has a photograph of the moment that he cherishes.

"When Kotsay hit that ball to the wall and slid into home, we all went nuts," Street said.

Haren was on the mound at the Coliseum for Game 3 when the A's finished off the Twins 8–3. Bradley and Eric Chavez homered, and Marco Scutaro, who had six RBIs in the series, doubled twice.

It was the A's first postseason series win since the 1990 ALCS. But Oakland—which played a full five games in every other division series appearance in the 2000s—may have taken care of business too quickly. "We played great against Minnesota but then we had too long a break," Kotsay said.

Flat going into the ALCS against the Tigers, Oakland dropped the first two games at home, with longtime postseason nemesis Justin Verlander earning the win in Game 2.

"What hurt us most was losing Game 1 at home. Then it seems like you have to win Game 2, and we lost that game and had to fly cross country to win twice to bring it back home," Haren said. "Not that we couldn't have done it, but it's a real tough way to start."

Former A's starter Kenny Rogers didn't allow a run in Game 3, and in Game 4, though Oakland took a 3–0 lead early, Detroit came back to tie it up against Haren. And with two outs in the bottom of the ninth, Magglio Ordonez sent Detroit to the World Series with a three-run homer off Street, who was working his third inning in a row.

"Even though we were down 3–0 in the series, that home run was such a shock. That's a pretty big moment, a walk-off homer to go to the World Series," Street said. "You can't escape the history of it. It was my second year in the league and I've used it as motivation ever since—you think, 'Well, I never want that to happen again.' Those moments can make you a better player. I was absolutely bummed, the hardest part is feeling like you've let your team down.

"I came in and got a double play in the seventh, pitched the eighth and came back out for the ninth. I got two quick outs and then bloop, bloop and I threw a 93 mph fastball down and in, off the plate to Magglio, and the dude took an amazing swing. That's baseball. You can rationalize and say well, we were down 3–0 at that point. I can say I felt I made good pitches, the execution was what I wanted. But I just got beat."

Despite the sweep, A's players remember that season with enormous fondness.

"Everyone liked each other," Street said. "So many of those guys I'm still in touch with, we're still friends, we call each other during big moments of our lives. You can't fake the dynamic we had on that team, and I've played for a lot of teams since then, that doesn't happen very often."

Zito, who signed a $126 million deal with the Giants after the season, said, "I knew going in it was going to be my last year with the A's, so I really wanted to soak it up and enjoy it. It was such an enjoyable team, the camaraderie was really something special."

"We just ran into a buzzsaw at the end, unfortunately," Kotsay said. "But my happiness in baseball lives in 2006 in Oakland. That collective group, we loved each other. We believed in each other."

47 Velarde's Unassisted Triple Play

Perfect games are rare in baseball. Even rarer: unassisted triple plays. It's only happened 15 times, compared to 23 perfect games.

While playing for the A's in 2000, second baseman Randy Velarde turned in the 11th unassisted triple play in big-league history, the 10th during the regular season. In the sixth inning, with men at first and second at Yankee Stadium, the Yankees put on a hit and run. Velarde caught Shane Spencer's soft liner, tagged Jorge Posada going to second base, and stepped on the bag to retire Tino Martinez, who was more than halfway to third. Bang, bang, and bang.

"When I completed the play, I said, 'That's three?' and the umpire said, 'Yeah.' I said, 'Good grief!' Velarde said. "I didn't really realize until I got back to the dugout and everyone was telling me, that I was like, 'Oh my gosh, I did that myself.'

"Everyone was saying, 'Where's the ball?' I'd left it on the field, gave it to the umpire, he was about to give it to the pitcher."

It was the first unassisted triple play ever completed in New York. It was the first and only one in A's franchise history.

The ball went to the Hall of Fame, which also wanted Velarde's glove. "They wanted the game glove on the spot, and I said, 'No sir,'" Velarde said. "I gave them my backup glove after the game. I've got the actual glove."

Velarde also homered, making him the first player to hit a homer and record an unassisted triple play in the same game. He

Fosse's Favorite Play

Ray Fosse has seen many amazing things during his time as a player and a broadcaster, but his favorite play—even over Randy Velarde's rare unassisted triple-play in 2000—came in 2005, when A's catcher Jason Kendall stuck his face right into Michael Young's spikes to record an out at Arlington, Texas.

Not just an out, but the final out of the game. Kendall scrambled to get Justin Duchscherer's pitch in the dirt, turned, and dove toward the plate, where Young was coming in feet-first.

Fosse, one of the toughest catchers in the game in his day, lost it.

"I screamed in the booth and jumped into the play-by-play," Fosse said. "I said, 'You'll never see another play like that!' That was just the instincts Jason had, when Duchscherer spiked the ball, he knew where the ball was, he knew where was the runner was—he grabs the baseball and dives in the same motion, mask off, runner coming in feet first, right into those spikes.

"The crowd was going crazy. And the umpire got right down there to call him out. That was crazy. Nowadays, the way the game is played, everyone is protected, but here's a catcher putting his face right into someone's spikes."

The other time Fosse jumped in to take over the mike? When Kendall hit his only homer in 143 games the following season. "I was yelling, 'Get up! Get up!' at the ball," Fosse said. "I still get grief about that."

was kicking himself after the game, though, rather than patting himself on the back, and he hasn't changed his feelings 15 years later.

"What people fail to realize is that I'd booted the ball right before, it would have been a routine double play right before that," said Velarde, whose error on a grounder by Posada allowed a run to score. "I'd still take the double play over the triple play."

"That triple play was the one bright spot of the game," former A's manager Art Howe recalled. "I think otherwise we were booting the ball around all day. But it is something to see—it's very rare."

Velarde also recorded an unassisted triple play while with the Yankees, amazingly enough, though that came in a spring game in 1995. "You'd have a better chance of being hit by lightning," Velarde said of pulling off the feat twice.

Triple plays can be tricky for TV and radio announcers because they happen so infrequently—sometimes, like the fielders, broadcasters need a minute to realize what happened. Not Bill King, though—Ray Fosse was working on the radio with King, and he said King nailed it.

"You talk about a perfect call. That typified Bill's brilliance," Fosse said. "A player should say, 'If the ball is hit to me, what am I going to do?' and Bill was thinking the same thing—it was like it was scripted. But triple plays are so rare, especially unassisted, and he was on target with everything. He recognized it right away and it's tough to do that, but that's Bill King's genius."

48 Fingers, Rudi Traded

After three titles in a row, free agency splintered the great A's teams of the 1970s, with Catfish Hunter leading the way.

On June 15, 1976, owner Charlie Finley continued the break-up of his dynasty by selling closer Rollie Fingers and outfielder Joe Rudi to the Red Sox for $2 million and selling Vida Blue to the Yankees for $1 million.

"It was a shock," Rudi said. "I'd been in that organization 13 years. But I always hit really, really well at Fenway. I loved that park. So I was looking forward to going."

"I was just hoping to get away from Charlie," Fingers said. "I was tired of his antics."

Finley cited "astronomical and unjustified" salary demands for the sell-off, but the public reaction was horrified—columnists all over the country wrote that the game would be destroyed if rich teams could just buy players away from those with fewer resources.

Commissioner Bowie Kuhn, Finley's old sparring partner, summoned the parties to New York to discuss the matter and 24 hours later, on June 18, he ordered the three players to be returned to Oakland. He called the sale a "spectacle" and "devastating to baseball's reputation."

"To this day, I still think Kuhn was wrong to take $3.5 million out of Finley's pocket," Rudi said nearly 40 years later. "He ended up getting nothing for us, and we would have loved to go."

The whole thing was surreal for the players involved.

"We were playing Boston, so Joe and I just picked our stuff up and went across the hallway to the Red Sox locker room," Fingers said. "For three days, I didn't pitch, but I warmed up. Joe was hurt, so he couldn't play. After the series, the commissioner nixed the sale—if I'd pitched before then, he probably wouldn't have done that. It would have been a lot harder.

"So when Boston left, we picked up our stuff and went back to the Oakland clubhouse."

Finley didn't want the three on the field, though. They sat on the sidelines, in limbo.

"The players finally had a team meeting and said, 'If they're not reinstated, we're not going to play,'" Fingers said. "We were supposed to play the Twins, and we were all in the clubhouse in street clothes 10 minutes before the game. Chuck Tanner came out, he got to Rudi's spot in the lineup and he said, 'Joe, you're in the game,' so we went out and played."

The players had voted 21–0 to strike if their teammates weren't on the diamond. Fingers and Rudi had gone 15 days without playing, total, while Blue didn't start from June 11 to July 2. The A's lost the division to Kansas City by two and a half games.

"That was kind of a bad deal. If the three of us had been used those two weeks, we could have won the league," Fingers said. "But it's nice to know you're worth $1 million, I guess. I was only making $67,000 at the time."

Said team captain Sal Bando: "We would have beat Kansas City that year except for the fact we didn't have Rollie or Rudi and Vida for two weeks. But by that time, there was no love lost between the players and the owner. I still think most people would have stayed, but he never made us an offer. If he had, we could have kept winning. We could have kept going for at least a couple of years."

Bando, Fingers and Rudi bolted as soon as the season was over. And Finley traded Blue across the Bay, to the Giants.

49 Sean Doolittle

Sean Doolittle is one of the best stories in the A's franchise history, or heck, major-league history.

Once the team's top first-base prospect, a slick fielder with some pop, Doolittle nearly quit the game because of injuries. Instead, he started pitching, following a suggestion from legendary farm director Keith Lieppman, just a little something to distract Doolittle after tearing tendons in his right wrist.

Nine months later, Doolittle was in the big leagues—as a left-handed reliever. Two years later, he was the A's closer, and an All-Star.

"Every day I come into the locker room and see my jersey, I think about the road I took to get there. It's pretty surreal," Doolittle said. "And it's maybe more so, because I can look up in the Coliseum and see high above third base where I used to sit as a kid, see the way things came full circle."

Those who knew Doolittle as a position player remain astonished at the transition.

"I remember seeing Sean in spring training at first base, and thinking, 'All right, there's the first baseman of the future.' He was so good there, he could have been a Gold Glove candidate," former A's left-hander Brett Anderson said. "Then he had knee and wrist injuries, and you're like, 'Tough break.' The last thing on your mind is that he's going to come back as a left-handed reliever throwing mid-90s. You don't see that *ever*—going from 'Maybe his career is over,' to being one of the best closers in the game."

"I played with him in the Fall League and the dude absolutely raked," former A's third baseman Josh Donaldson said. "He had a really, really nice left-handed swing, he played great defense at first base. He was right on the brink of being in the big leagues as a position player, then he gets hurt, and then he gets hurt again, and you think, 'Man, is this guy just going to fade away?'

"Then I heard he'd torn the sheath off his wrist and I thought, 'Oh, shoot, he is never going to come back.' A week later, I heard, 'Doo is pitching and throwing 95 mph,' and I was like, 'What?' It's been really remarkable because he had all the potential in the world to be a really nice, above-average major-league position player— and now he's an All-Star closer."

Doolittle was coming back from his second knee surgery in two years when he injured his wrist, and he decided he couldn't go through another surgery. He started making post-baseball plans.

"There were some dark days there for a little bit," he said. "Earlier that week, our trainer, Jeff Collins, had told me 'You're going to Sacramento,' and two days later, I swing and miss a pitch, and popped my tendon.

Sean Doolittle pitches in the ninth inning of the 2014 wild-card game against the Royals. (Ed Zurga)

"I was online looking at college courses at Virginia to go back to school. I contacted my agent to track down my athletic academic advisor to start the process to get readmitted to UVA."

At Lieppman's urging, Doolittle, a pitcher and first baseman in college, started a throwing program with rehab coordinator Garvin Alston, in part because he needed to go through rehab for his insurance to be covered.

"A lot of people were saying a lot of things about the way the ball was coming out of my hand and the carry it had on it," Doolittle recalled. "Garvin was like, 'You're going to throw really hard,' and I was like, 'Shut up!'

"It came back really naturally. It was interesting, after two weeks, I kind of knew there was something there."

Doolittle's younger brother, Ryan, also was there rehabbing, which helped immensely. Not only did Ryan, a right-handed pitcher, catch Doolittle on occasion, but he got to be the expert at times.

"We were living together, and he was able to keep me in a good place mentally. And because he'd been pitching longer, I was able to ask him all kinds of dumb questions he thought I should already know," Doolittle said. "He never lets me forget that. I always tell him that he and Garvin should get all the credit and they always refuse it."

Doolittle pitched in instructional-league games that fall, and the next season, he zipped from Class-A ball to the majors by June 4, an extraordinary time frame.

"The first time I saw Sean Doolittle throw a bullpen session that spring, they told me he was a converted first baseman who only had a fastball, and never in a million years would I have thought that we would see him up in 2012," A's manager Bob Melvin said. "I don't know if anyone could have predicted he would become an All-Star closer so quickly, but certainly we had a feeling that we had something special. Sean is a pretty strong-minded guy and he took advantage of the opportunity."

50 The $100,000 Infield

The Philadelphia A's—who were denied a shot at title in 1902, when the National League's Pirates refused to play them for the championship—made it to the World Series for the first time in

1905. But they without their top starter, Rube Waddell, and they were manhandled by the Giants' Christy Mathewson. Mathewson's final totals are considered the greatest pitching performance in World Series history: three shutouts in six days; 13 hits allowed in 27 innings, and 18 strikeouts to only one walk. The Giants gave up no earned runs in the entire series, an unbreakable record, and only one reliever was used by either club.

The A's didn't make it back to baseball's biggest stage for five years and by then, Waddell was long gone and the team was centered around its tremendous infield: third baseman Frank "Home Run" Baker, second baseman Eddie Collins, shortstop Jack Berry, and first baseman Harry Davis. Davis was a veteran, but Baker was 24 years old, Collins and Barry 23.

Chief Bender and Eddie Plank still headed up the rotation, and in 1910, the A's took the AL crown going away, winning 102 games and finishing 14½ games ahead of the runner-up Yankees.

With Plank out of the World Series because of an arm injury, Mack used only two pitchers, Bender and Jack Coombs, over the entire course of the event, and Philadelphia dispatched the Cubs easily for the first title in franchise history, winning four games to one.

Collins and Baker both had nine hits in the five games, and the team's youth led the *Sporting News* to declare that the Athletics looked like the team to beat for years to come.

The next year, 21-year-old Stuffy McInnis replaced Davis at first, giving the Athletics their famous "$100,000 infield." That tag came about after Mack told a reporter on a train trip that he wouldn't sell any part of the unit.

"Would you take $100,000 for it?" the reporter asked.

No, said Mack, not even that astronomical figure would get him to part with those players.

He was right about their value. With that foursome, Mack's club went to the World Series in 1911, 1913, and 1914.

McInnis and Barry were good players. McInnis was especially strong defensively, despite playing with a tiny glove that was the subject of ridicule from his teammates, while Barry was known as a clutch hitter who led all AL shortstops in RBIs over an eight-year span.

Collins and Baker were the standouts of that $100K infield, though.

Edward Trowbridge Collins, who played quarterback and baseball at Columbia, had played for the A's briefly after his junior year, using the name "Sullivan" so he wouldn't lose his college eligibility, but his 15 at-bats for the A's were discovered by school officials. He wound up coaching the Columbia team, instead, during his senior season.

In 1909, his second full year with Philadelphia, "Cocky" Collins hit .347 and stole 63 bases. The following year, he hit .324 and led the AL with 81 steals, then hit .429 in the World Series. In 1914, he was named the American League MVP.

When Collins tried to jump to the newly founded Federal League after the 1914 season, however, Mack quickly shipped him to the White Sox for $50,000—half of what Mack had estimated his star-studded infield to be worth.

Collins signed a contract worth a reported total of $90,000 with Chicago, and he wound up playing in two World Series with the White Sox. In 1917, he hit .409 as Chicago topped the Giants four games to two. Two years later came the Black Sox scandal, with eight members of White Sox banned from baseball for conspiring to throw the series. Collins played honestly, according to accounts, and he had no knowledge of the fix. He remained with the White Sox (who were decimated by the banishments) through 1926, managing them for three of those years, before returning to the A's in 1927 for his final three seasons.

Collins still holds the record for most games played at second base, 2,650, along with most assists (7,630) and most chances

(14,591). He's 11th on the all-time hits list, with 3,315 (he trails only Pete Rose and Ty Cobb on the all-time singles list, with 2,643) and he is eighth in stolen bases, with 741. Collins was inducted into the Hall of Fame in 1939—the same season his son, Eddie Collins Jr., began his career with the Philadelphia Athletics.

Many thought that Collins was Mack's heir apparent, because he was a favorite of Mack's and had one of the brightest minds in the game. But Mack managed another 20 years after Collins retired as a player, so after Collins' playing career was done, he became the Red Sox's general manager. And in 1937, while on a scouting trip to see Bobby Doerr in San Diego, he noticed a skinny outfielder playing for the Pacific Coast League's Padres. Collins then arranged to purchase Ted Williams from his minor-league team and signed the future Hall of Famer to a contract with the Red Sox.

Baker led the American League in home runs from 1911 to 1914, a stretch that baseball historian Bill James has called the best four-year period ever by a third baseman.

He hit only 96 for his career, however, playing in the dead-ball era. It sometimes took only seven or 10 homers a season to lead the league. Baker estimated later in life that he might have hit 50 homers a year were it not for the high wall in right at Shibe Park. His strength was unquestioned: A left-handed hitter, Baker easily swung a 52-ounce bat, 20 ounces more than most used today.

The "Home Run" nickname came after his performance in the 1911 World Series, when Baker homered off two of the Giants' dominating pitchers, Mathewson and Rube Marquard. In Game 2, he cracked a two-run shot off Marquard in the sixth inning to top New York 3–1, evening up the series at a game apiece.

The following day, he stepped up with one out in the ninth inning against Mathewson, Philadelphia down 1–0, and he smacked a long solo homer into the stands in right to tie the game. The A's went on to win in the 11th. Giants catcher Chief Meyers claimed that some of Baker's success came from the fact that A's third base coach Harry Davis always seemed to know what pitch was coming, even when the Giants stopped using signs.

With Plank back in action along with Coombs and Bender, the A's held the Giants to a .174 average and avenged their 1905 World Series loss to New York. They took the title in six games, their second championship in a row. Baker hit .375 in the series, and he hit .450 when Philadelphia won the 1913 Series, again against the Giants.

The highlights of that Fall Classic included a wild, tumbling catch by Rube Oldring in the fifth inning of Game 4 on a sinking liner by pinch-hitter Moose McCormick, which Mack called the greatest catch he'd ever seen in a World Series. The A's won in five games when Plank topped Mathewson, his old nemesis.

In 1914, the A's notched their fourth pennant in five years (in that span, only the overconfident 1912 team, which Mack described as "puffed up," failed to claim the AL title, though they won 90 games). In the 1914 World Series, Philadelphia met Boston's "Miracle Braves," who'd gone from last place on July 19 to first place by the end of the season. The Braves kept right on with their startling season, sweeping the mighty Mackmen in four games, one of the biggest upsets in World Series history.

That was the death knell of one of baseball's original dynasties, because Mack began dismantling the team. Baker was one of the few men that Mack intended to keep, but with the team a shadow of its former self, Baker held out the entire 1915 season in a salary dispute. He farmed and he played for a local semi-pro team instead.

Baker was sent to the Yankees in 1916 and continued to be one of the league's top home run hitters. He sat out another season, 1920, to nurse his terminally ill wife and, after her death, to take care of his two daughters, but he came back in 1921 and helped the Yankees win their first pennant. Baseball had a new home run king, however—Baker's teammate, Babe Ruth, hit a then-record 59 homers and drove in 168 runs that year. "He has everyone, including myself, hopelessly outclassed," Baker said of Ruth.

The dead-ball era was over. Two years later, Baker retired at the age of 37. He was elected to the Hall of Fame in 1955, joining former teammates such as Collins, Bender, and Plank.

Like infield-mate Collins, Baker is credited with discovering a Hall of Famer. While managing the Easton team in the Eastern Shore League, near his lifelong home in Trappe, Maryland, he noticed another Eastern Maryland native, young Jimmie Foxx of Sudlersville, while Foxx was still in high school. Baker invited the muscular slugger to a tryout, and he recommended Foxx to Mack.

51 Go to Ricky's Sports Theater and Grill

For the past two decades, baseball players have studied video incessantly. Modern players have their at-bats downloaded onto their iPads. Pitchers can watch their deliveries or research opponents on their phones, if need be.

In the late '70s, though, if A's players wanted to break down their performance, they went to Ricky's Sports Theater and Grill in San Leandro.

Mitchell Page, the Oakland outfielder, started the trend. He went to Ricky's in 1977 and asked owner Ricky Ricardo, who'd recently become one of the first restaurateurs to install satellite dishes, to tape the A's games for him.

Only Oakland's road games were broadcast, because teams feared attendance dips if home games were aired, so after road trips, Page would sit at Ricky's and watch his at-bats from the previous week or two. He hit .307 that season and finished second in Rookie of the Year voting.

The rest of the A's began to accompany Page to Ricky's, and soon they all wanted the games taped; Ricky Ricardo Jr. recalls the A's "Five Aces" of the early '80s coming in frequently. Eventually, the players convinced owner Charlie Finley to get a VHS machine for the Coliseum, but the team's association with Ricky's never faded—A's players, coaches and other employees have continued to be regulars over the years, as has the local media. There is a great deal of A's memorabilia on display, including a signed World Series jersey. Wally Haas held a team World Series party there.

When the A's played in Japan in 2008 and 2013, Ricky Ricardo Jr. made sure to keep the place open for viewing parties on the big screen in the middle of the night ("We opened at 3:00 AM, it was crazy," Ricardo said). During road playoff games, Oakland fans show up in full force in green and gold.

"The team's personnel changes, but the fans are still there," Ricardo said.

Ricky's, also a favorite of Raiders and Warriors players and fans for decades, is routinely voted one of the top sports bars in the nation by *Sports Illustrated*. The restaurant, first opened in 1946 on Foothill Boulevard, had to move when the 580 freeway was built, and in October 1962, Rickys moved to its current location at 15028 Hesperian Boulevard, San Leandro; check www.rickys.com for hours and upcoming events.

52 Oakland Oaks

Before the A's, there were the Oakland Oaks.

A storied team in the old Pacific Coast League, the Oaks played from 1903 to 1955 in several spots around the East Bay—and even Recreation Park in San Francisco—before settling into 10,000-seat Oaks Ball Park at Park and San Pablo Avenues in Emeryville in 1913.

The Oaks, inadvertently, were the first professional baseball team in a whites-only league to employ a black player: in 1916, Jimmy Claxton, a Canadian of African and native North American descent, pitched in both ends of a doubleheader for the club, but when the team learned of his African heritage, he was released. The Oakland had advertised him as an "Indian southpaw," but the team wasn't willing to end segregation when it came to black players.

In 1964, Claxton told the *Tacoma News-Tribune,* "I had been with Oakland for about a month when I got notice that I was released.... No reason was given, but I knew."

The Oakland won league titles in 1912, 1927, and, most memorably, in 1948, when managed by Casey Stengel, who already had held a similar post with the Dodgers and the Braves in the big leagues with little success.

The 1948 Oaks team was a special one, featuring several former big leaguers and one notable future major-league second baseman and manager, Berkeley's Billy Martin. Known as the "Nine Old Men" for their many veterans, such as 40-year-old Ernie Lombardi, the Oaks went 114–74.

"Casey was as good a manager as I ever played for and that's including Connie Mack and Jimmie Dykes," infielder Dario Lodigiani told baseball historian Dick Dobbins.

The city went nuts after taking its first title in 21 years. Broadcaster Bill Laws told Dobbins, "I remember the parade in Oakland and Casey dominating the parade. The fans just loved it."

Stengel parlayed that into a job with the Yankees, where his clubs won seven titles, including the next five in a row, still a record. He was elected to the Hall of Fame in 1966.

Oakland won two more league titles under Chuck Dressen, in 1950 and 1954, but the Oaks moved to Vancouver in 1956.

The following year, Oaks Ball Park was razed. The site was later a Pepsi-Cola plant—and now is home to the Pixar Animation Studio.

There is a terrific website dedicated to the Oakland Oaks that includes game film and other videos: oaklandoaks.tripod.com.

53 Hammer Time

Over the year, the A's have had a notable supporting cast—including a 13-year-old discovered in the Coliseum parking lot during the early '70s who went on to become a team vice president...and who later emerged as rap star MC Hammer.

Owner Charlie Finley spotted young Stanley Burrell dancing with his friends outside the stadium one day and, impressed with Burrell's splits, he called him over and asked the youth if anyone had ever told him he looked like Hank Aaron, aka, "Hammerin' Hank."

Burrell responded, "No sir, but thank you."

Finley invited Burrell, henceforth known as "Hammer," to watch the game with him, handed him a job as a clubhouse attendant, and Burrell found positions for his brothers, too. By the time

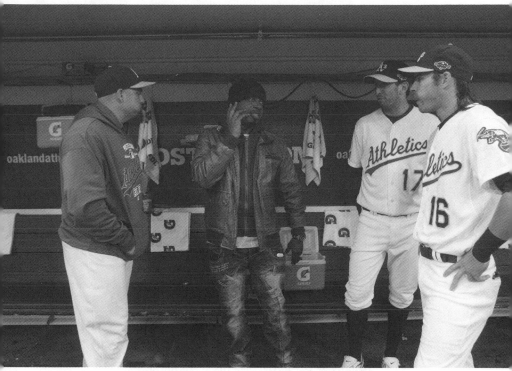

Stanley Burrell (aka: MC Hammer), talks with (left to right) Jonny Gomes, Adam Rosales, and Josh Reddick in the dugout prior to a 2012 game against the Tigers in Oakland. (Michael Zagaris)

he was 16, Burrell had been named vice president of a team that, at that point, had just six front-office employees.

Burrell often served as a go-between for Finley, who lived in Chicago, and team personnel, and he would provide Finley with play-by-play over the phone during games. They called his "broadcasts" KCOF: K-Charles O. Finley.

Finley then suggested that Hammer try the airwaves for real. Giants CEO Larry Baer, then broadcasting A's games for college station KALX, said, "Charlie called us once and said, 'I want you to put Hammer on a couple of innings.' We were 20 years old—what are we going to say? No, he doesn't have any experience?

"He broadcast an inning or two. I remember he came on a game in Seattle at the Kingdome and Mitchell Page was up. Hammer yelled, 'Here's the pitch to Mitchell Page, it's popped up...deep!' It was a home run."

When Hammer turned to music, he put out a CD that was financed in part by A's players Dwayne Murphy and Mike Davis.

"And then he became one of the biggest stars of the decade," Mike Norris said with a laugh. "He was right there with Michael Jackson and Prince. I was thinking, 'Wow...here I am remembering him on his knees in the clubhouse picking up underwear.'"

Hammer attended an '80s event at the Coliseum in 2011 and he was asked if Finley, who died in 1996, belongs in the Hall of Fame.

"Absolutely," Hammer said of his mentor. "And not as anyone's favor. Just on the facts. Just what he earned."

Hammer also said that even though everyone always credits Finley for his moniker, it was really Reggie Jackson who coined the name that eventually became part of his stage name.

54 Bobby Shantz

Even in the worst, final years of the Philadelphia A's franchise, there were some bright spots, and the brightest of all was also the least likely.

Bobby Shantz was just 5'6", 140 pounds, so small that security guards often refused to admit him into the stadium because they didn't believe he was a player. His diminutive stature, however, did not prevent the side-arming left-hander from being among the most talented of pitchers of his time.

"I was just doggone lucky even to be in the big leagues at five-foot-six," Shantz, 89, said in late 2014. "When I was at Class-A ball and I saw how big all the pitchers were and how hard they threw, I thought I didn't have a chance in the world. You've got to be lucky to be a midget and play 16 years in the big leagues."

Shantz's first victory, in 1949, was memorable: He came on in relief, worked 10 innings, and held Detroit to two hits and one run.

"The first time I saw Bobby Shantz, I assumed he was the Athletics' batboy," Cleveland's Jim Fridley said in *We Played the Game*. "He turned out to be the best left-hander I faced in the major leagues. The little guy could get you."

Shantz, who played for Connie Mack as a rookie in 1949, won the American League Most Valuable Player in 1952, at the age of 26. He went 24–7 with a 2.48 ERA that season, the best by an A's pitcher in two decades.

"Everything came together," Shantz said 62 years later. "I think it was when I learned to change speeds on my fastball. I'd never thrown many changeups in the minors—I only spent one year at Class-A ball and then I was right in the big leagues, I couldn't believe it. And hitters started hitting me pretty good, so my catcher, Joe Astroth, said, 'You should change up on your fastball.'

"I could change speeds with my curveball, but not my fastball, so I had to practice a lot. I also threw a knuckleball, but Mr. Mack thought that would hurt my arm, so he didn't let me use it, it wasn't until Jimmy Dykes took over that I could throw that again. I always had pretty good control, but I never thought I'd win 24 games. I still can't believe it.

"I was just lucky, everything went right. I'd have a couple of men on base and get a ground ball, and we had one of the best defensive infields around, they turned [a major-league record] 217 double plays when I was a rookie. That helped me a lot. I was lucky as the dickens. I give all the credit to changing speeds."

Shantz also was a terrific fielder who won eight Gold Gloves.

"I remember very well one time when Shantz and our catcher, Ray Murray, went after a slug bunt that trickled halfway up the third-base line," A's first baseman Gus Zernial said. "This little bitty tiny guy and this huge catcher went to field the ball, but Shantz was so quick, he jumped over Murray, fielded the ball, and threw to first base."

His size probably helped, Shantz speculated: He was quicker off the mound than anyone else. "I threw Phil Rizzuto out bunting twice in one game and he was the best bunter in the game," Shantz recalled. "He always used to tell me, 'I don't care what the umpire says, I was safe,' but he also told me he would never bunt against me again."

Shantz was hit by a pitch in late September of 1952 and broke his left wrist, and he was never quite as dominant again. Many speculated that his killer curveball lost some of its bite after the injury.

He returned to relief work during the latter part of his career and pitched through the 1964 season; he was selected in two expansion drafts, by the Senators in 1960 and by the Colt 45s in 1961.

In 2014, Shantz said he still finds it hard to believe he faced Hall of Famers such as Willie Mays, Joe DiMaggio, Mickey Mantle, Yogi Berra, and Ted Williams. He remembered Williams as one of the toughest lefties he faced, but, Shantz said, "I never let Ted Williams hit my fastball, I only threw him curveballs, if he was going to hit me, he was going to have to hit the curveball. He used to tell me, 'You had the best curveball in the American League,' but I don't think that was really true."

Shantz is one of fewer than a dozen surviving Philadelphia Athletics, and he has remained active at Philadelphia Athletics Historical Society events over the years.

"I'll go whenever I can if they call," he said. "I think I'm the only one left."

55 Great A's Nicknames

One of owner Charlie Finley's favorite publicity stunts was to bestow colorful nicknames as a means to create interest in players.

He was responsible for one particularly successful handle: Finley supplied the "Catfish" for pitcher Jim Hunter, and gave him a lively, if fake, backstory to go with it. Before telling the press, though, Finley had to fill Hunter in, telling him, "When you were six, you ran away from home and went fishing. When they finally found you, you'd caught two big fish...ah, catfish...and were reeling in the third. And that's how you got your nickname. Okay? Now repeat it back to me."

Hunter, known for his sense of humor, went along with it, and "Catfish" is how most people know the great left-hander.

Others, though, balked at any embellishments. Vida Blue, another sensational left-hander, flatly refused when Finley suggested he become "True" Blue.

"Vida was my father's name," he said in 1971. "It means 'life' in Spanish. I loved my father. Now that he's dead, I honor him every time the name Vida Blue appears in the headlines. If Mr. Finley thinks it's such a great name, why doesn't he call himself True O. Finley?"

Speaking more than 35 years later, Blue said, "Even today, I still meet people who say, 'Thank you for what you did, as an African American player, and thank you for not changing your name.' My name is Vida Rochelle Blue. I go to autograph shows and someone will say, 'Sign your full name,' and I'll say, 'What? Vida Blue, Jr.? Vida *Rochelle*—don't repeat that!'

Jim "Catfish" Hunter pitching in the '72 World Series against the Reds.
(AP Photo)

There are two guys who still call me 'True.' George Brett and Amos Otis. I say, 'Don't call me that!' George will shout it out across the golf course, 'Hey, True, is that you? Hey True!'"

Fellow A's starter Odom said, "Vida told me once he wished he'd changed it to 'True.' But I can't understand why, because Vida stands out anyway."

It has been widely reported that Odom was dubbed "Blue Moon" by Finley, but that was not the case, as Odom emphasized.

"Now it can be corrected: I got that name in the sixth grade during football practice," Odom said. "A guy named Joe Morris was being facetious—he said he was going to call me Moon Head because of my round face, and then he came back and said he was going to call me Blue Moon. He said, 'I can't call you Black Moon, because of your [skin] color.'

"I used to fight it, but now I love it. I called this guy recently and thanked him for it. I said, 'Because of your nickname, I'm known all over the world.' In 2004, I went into the Georgia Sports Hall of Fame, and I said I'm glad for my name. I used to hate it, but I love it."

56 Too Many Mistakes: The 2003 ALDS

In 2003, questionable baserunning bit Oakland for the second time in three postseasons—and once again after the team had taken a two-games-to-none lead in the best-of-five American League Division Series.

Two—that's right, *two*—obstruction calls played a role in Game 3 in 2003, turning the tide for Boston.

Oakland, which made four errors in the game, was down 1–0 in the sixth but had a chance to score when, with runners at the corners, Miguel Tejada hit a squibber toward third. Eric Byrnes, the team's fastest runner, took off for the plate as pitcher Derek Lowe went to field the ball.

Byrnes tripped over catcher Jason Varitek, who didn't have the ball, and Byrnes missed the plate, but instead of going back to touch it, he got up and shoved Varitek. Varitek picked up the ball and tagged Byrnes.

"I thought I'd touched the plate, and I was delirious, I thought I'd blown my knee out," Byrnes said 11 years later. "It all happened so quick, my instinct was just to shove Varitek for a B.S. and class-less move—and he turns around, picks up the ball, and tags me out. If I'd known I hadn't touched the plate, I don't care if my leg had ended up in the Red Sox dugout, I would have dragged myself back there."

"Byrnes was criticized unfairly," A's general manager Billy Beane said. "No one should ever question his desire. No. 1, the plate was being blocked without the ball, which is against the rules. And the collision was so violent, he thought he'd blown out his knee. If you can be knocked unconscious through your knee, he was. Eric was in pain. Eric has never not given 100 percent."

The craziness continued that inning when, with the bases loaded, Ramon Hernandez hit a chopper past shortstop that was ruled an error. Erubial Durazo scored on the play, and Tejada went to third—but he ran into third baseman Bill Mueller, who was right in the basepath.

Obstruction immediately was ruled, but Tejada rounded third and stopped, pointing and yelling at third, instead. Varitek, again, picked up the ball and tagged Tejada out to end the inning. The umpiring crew cited Rule 7.06 (b), which states that a runner advances at his own peril after being obstructed.

"The Tejada play—well, that's the stupidest rule I've ever heard of and I still think that," Byrnes said. "He gets run into, he gets the next base, period. Of course your natural reaction is to stop when that happens."

Tejada's confusion was understandable—in the second inning, he and Eric Chavez both had wound up at third base to cover the bag for a throw from catcher Hernandez, trying to nab Varitek (again!) in a rundown. Chavez was called for obstruction on that play—and Varitek was awarded home.

"Our team was unfairly criticized, people saying everyone should know that continuation rule, but that reaction was understandable, especially after the earlier call of obstruction," Beane said. "It was tough, because that's two runs in a very tough game and we had Keith Foulke ready to go for a couple of innings. There were a lot of what-ifs in all those series, but that one stung the most."

The Red Sox defeated Oakland 3–1 in Game 3, then scored one-run wins in each of the next two games to advance to the ALCS. The A's ran their record in potential clinch games to 0–9 over a four-year stretch.

"We played our butts off, and for whatever reason, we didn't get out of the first round of the playoffs," Byrnes said. "Sometimes it was bad luck, sometimes we didn't match up well, but I know it wasn't lack of effort. It just wasn't meant to be. In every one of those years, we could have won the World Series."

Byrnes hit .462 in the series, and he recalled that he came inches from giving the A's a big lead in Game 4 the next day, with Oakland already up 1–0.

"I came up with the bases loaded in the second inning and I hit a ball off John Burkett that was an inch from hitting the Pesky Pole down the right-field line," he said. "Talk about things that would have changed everything. This was before replay, and I've looked at it since—and you can't tell if it's in front of the pole or behind it, so the call wouldn't be changed. But it was so close."

Modern replay rules might have helped Oakland in Game 3, though, and so too, perhaps, the rules governing plays at home plate instituted for the 2014 season.

"It's funny, because if the same rules applied as they have today, the umpires would have taken one look at that sequence at the plate and would have called me safe because Varitek stuck his leg out to block me without the ball," Byrnes said. "Believe me, if he'd been in front of the plate with the ball, I would have blasted him, but he gave me the lane—and then stuck his leg out there and flipped me over.

"I wish I'd touched the plate. I wonder if the course of history would have changed if I had."

57 Pie Someone

The recipe: One aerosol can of Reddi-Wip or similar.

One pie tin or plastic plate.

One victim.

Splat!

For Josh Reddick—no, Reddi-Wip is not named after him, though the company might want to consider an endorsement deal—the list of victims is a matter of public record. Every time the A's outfielder pies a teammate, it's caught on camera. He nails every teammate who records a walk-off hit.

Reddick started the tradition his first season with the A's, in 2012. That was fortuitous, or was it some sort of impetus? Because in 2012, Oakland led the majors with 14 walk-off victories.

Reddick didn't pie the first two walk-off heroes of the season, though: He'd been hit in the face by a pitch and come out of the game right before the A's first last-second win in 2012, and he homered just before the second. But on May 8, he got Brandon Inge right in the kisser after Inge's game-winning grand slam against Toronto.

"It just felt right," Reddick said. "It got a good, positive reaction and it's just taken off. There's no reason—I just thought it added some fun."

Reddick, who has a T-shirt that reads "Come for the game, stay for the pie," used shaving cream for the pies just once, when rookie catcher Derek Norris hit a three-run blast to beat the Giants—Norris' first big-league homer. He didn't complain much, considering the circumstances, but Norris' eyes stung for days afterward and Reddick went back to whipped cream products.

He has help: Stadium workers set up the Reddi-Wip and a plate after games, but Reddick prepares the plate himself. The real key is surprising that night's hero; after three seasons, everyone is pretty much on to Reddick. He usually sprints from the visitor's side, the blind side for TV interviews, but wily teammates occasionally move quickly enough to avoid the main blast. For such instances, Reddick often has a second pie at hand.

Then there was August 3, 2012, when Reddick, dubbed Spider-Man on the previous road trip after climbing the chain-link fence at Toronto to make a stupendous catch, wore a Spidey costume— S-Pie-dy?—while smacking Coco Crisp with a 1–2 pie combo.

No one was exempt. When the A's came out of nowhere to clinch a playoff spot, Reddick creamed manager Bob Melvin with a pie during postgame interviews. Two days later, when Oakland won the division title on the final day of the season, he got GM Billy Beane.

"I like the origination of the pies very much because it was part of what made us who we were in 2012 with the walk-off wins, and that morphed into pies." Melvin said. "Guys embraced it and the fans absolutely loved it. One guy really ran with it. When fans think about that 2012 team, the pies are definitely part of that."

What happens when Reddick himself provides the winning blow in the final at-bat? Crisp does the honors, serving as the pie guy. And when Reddick was on a rehab assignment in 2014, Yoenis Cespedes was serving them up.

From a TV standpoint, the pie phenomenon is tricky. Several headsets have been ruined over the past few seasons and technicians now have a spare at the ready. Meanwhile, the broadcasters have to contend with interrupted interviews and distracted subjects—guys who have just propelled the A's to a win and whose thoughts might be of interest to the audience.

"We just know it's going to be a short interview," TV analyst Ray Fosse said with a sigh. "I don't want to take away from the celebration, but I come from a time when things like that didn't happen. Those microphones get knocked around. There are some pretty aggressive slams in the face, and when that happens, someone has to pay for a headset.

"But you know it's going to happen—and they're all in great wins. So it's hard to argue with that."

58 Joe DiMaggio

When the A's moved into their new stadium in 1968, configuring the huge field for baseball proved a bit tricky. Not much thought had been given to finding the best sightlines to the plate—until a Hall of Famer provided his two cents.

"When we went there, the Coliseum was in football configuration," former team broadcaster Monte Moore said. "Joe DiMaggio had been named the A's vice president/first base coach, which is an odd combination, but that's what he was doing. So he and I went and looked around the stadium, and it was just a concrete bomb shelter, that's what it looked like. They had some stakes in the ground to show where the baseball field would be.

"We went up and sat in some seats and Joe said, 'You know what? The people sitting here won't be able to see home plate.' And he was right: They'd put a marker down to show home plate, and an awful lot of the folks wouldn't have been able to see it. That's when they moved home plate out about 40 feet - which is why there's so much foul territory there. Joe was the first one to mention that, and if not, the people higher up would be out of luck."

To solve the problem DiMaggio had spotted, a cutout in the stands was necessary, which added to the immense amount of foul ground—the largest in the majors.

DiMaggio's chance catch of the stadium configurations might have been his key moment as a team vice president, for he was given next to nothing to do and didn't even have a desk.

George Ross, the *Oakland Tribune* sports editor, was one of the men who had urged Finley to hire DiMaggio. The legendary Yankee outfielder's roots were in the East Bay; he was born in Martinez—and DiMaggio needed two more years in the employ of a major-league team in order to get his full pension.

"Joe was one of the few guys in baseball who retained their magic," Ross said. "He was well loved by the entire baseball community…. So we presented it to Finley as a way to hire an ambassador for the city and for the A's, a Bay Area native who was well respected all over the country.

"But Finley had a penchant for hiring people for loosely worded jobs and then changing them, so we told Finley, 'Don't just make Joe a secretary or a manager, make him a vice president in charge of public relations. Make it a significant hire.'

"Charlie did, but when Joe arrived for work, he didn't have a secretary or an office or a desk. DiMaggio had a lot of baseball knowledge he wanted to spread into Finley's area of recognition, but eventually he just gave up and became a uniformed coach. That was a mistake, I thought."

In the A's first years in Oakland, DiMaggio was their most identifiable employee. The media would swarm the dugout when he was around, though he didn't spend much time on the field.

"Around strangers, non-players, he was very bashful and shy, really," outfielder Joe Rudi said. "When strangers were around, he stayed in the shadows. But with players, he was a jokester, screwed around all the time, just a great guy. A nice man, extremely classy."

"People say he was aloof—he wasn't at all," said reporter Ron Bergman, who got to know DiMaggio well. "He'd give interviews until the cows came home. And when he took some batting practice one day, he turned on it and, boom, it was gone. I remember [A's catcher] Dave Duncan said, 'The Clipper can still get around on it. That's something to see.'"

He even wore the white shoes, which many found jarring. Still, the A's green-and-gold was the only big-league uniform Joe DiMaggio ever would wear apart from his famous Yankee pinstripes.

"I've never seen a more recognizable person," third baseman Sal Bando said. "We'd go through the airport and people would stop and point at him. It was unbelievable."

"Oh my God, it was ridiculous to get in and out of town, there would be 100 people waiting for the bus, same thing getting into the ballpark." Rudi said. "It was crazy. He was the biggest thing in the world."

Bando said that DiMaggio did give some pointers. Once, when Bando was mired in a slump, he went to DiMaggio—who suggested a simple remedy.

"I was struggling, getting jammed all the time, and I asked Joe what to do," Bando said. "It's not like today, where the hitting coaches are always studying film. Joe just said, 'Ah...move away from the plate.' I said, 'Okay.'"

DiMaggio spent a lot of time working with budding star Reggie Jackson, and Jackson has said that the daily tutoring was instrumental to his development.

Furthermore, DiMaggio gave defensive tips to Rudi, who was still learning his craft after converting from playing the infield. Former A's manager Alvin Dark had told Rudi after the 1967 that he didn't think he'd ever be a major-league outfielder, but new manager Bob Kennedy and DiMaggio worked with him extensively.

"I'd never played in a huge stadium before, and it looked like the batter was three counties away, it was so different. I hit okay, but I had a hell of a time in the outfield," Rudi said. "Joe D. was here and for whatever reason, he took me under his wing. Every day, Bob Kennedy—whether it was a day game, or after a double header, night game, every day—he would stand by the coaching box and hit every kind of line drive, low fly ball, whatever you can imagine, and then Joe D. would come out and work with me. We did a lot of it in spring training and I just learned how to turn—the ball goes up, you've got to turn and go to the spot where the ball is coming down.

"At first, I'd turn and the ball would be 50 feet to my right. It took me months and months and Joe D. was really awesome. I had no idea how to keep my line. So it was just a blessing for me that he was here in '68 and '69, I learned just so much in the outfield from him."

Rudi became a Gold Glove fielder, and, using some of DiMaggio's tips about turning his back to the plate to go after deep fly balls, he made one of the most storied catches in World Series history against the Reds in 1972.

"That play against the wall was exactly the one Joe D. worked on with me all the time," Rudi said. "Man, I don't know how many balls he hit at me like that—maybe 10,000. Just like that, where you have to read it, turn and run. The ball was hit over my head and I ran back—you know if the ball is going to be that deep, you run to the fence first, and find the wall. You see a lot of kids go back and they go to jump and hit their shoulder and never get off the ground. He always told me, 'The glove is on your left hand, and as you're turning back in, you catch the ball so you knew where the wall is.'"

Another foot or so over, Rudi said, and he wouldn't have made that catch—it would have been directly in line with the sun that time of year.

59 Vida Blue

In 1971, one of Charlie Finley's self-scouted young finds burst onto the scene with one of the best seasons ever by a pitcher.

Vida Blue, all of 21 years old, had bounced up and down between Oakland and Triple-A the previous two seasons, and at the end of 1970 he'd signaled what might be in store. First came a near no-hitter against Kansas City on September 11 in which the only hit by the Royals came on a two-out single through the hole by Pat Kelly in the eighth—when second baseman Dick Green left his usual spot because he didn't think Kelly could pull Blue's fastball.

Two starts later, on September 21, Blue pulled off the real deal in Oakland against the Twins, a game in which only one Minnesota player, Harmon Killebrew, reached base, via a walk in the fourth inning.

Killebrew said later. "He wasn't giving me anything I could hit. I wouldn't have hit what he was throwing. I never saw the ball…. He wasted the walk."

Blue got a $2,000 bonus from Finley and catcher Gene Tenace a $1,000 bonus.

In 1971, Blue kept on rolling. He had a new manager to work for now; even though the A's had finished in second place in 1970, Finley had canned John McNamara because he didn't think the players respected him enough (especially when catcher Dave Duncan was quoted as saying that Finley was really managing the club).

Blue started in Dick Williams' managerial debut with Oakland, a season-opening 8–0 loss at Washington—the Presidential opener. That was a rarity that year: Blue wouldn't lose again until May 28. He won 10 decisions in a row, five of them shutouts. At that point, his ERA stood just over 1.00. He became the second-youngest man ever to record the win in an All-Star Game (and he was the only AL pitcher to win an All-Star game between 1962–1983).

"I just expected myself to do well," Blue said.

By early August, Blue had won 20 games, starting talk of a potential 30-win season—and like Reggie Jackson two years earlier, the cool young star was drawing attention from all over the country. He chatted with President Richard Nixon when the A's visited the White House, and Nixon told him he was the most underpaid player in baseball. Blue filmed Aqua Velva ads and milk ads. He was offered roles in two movies and a spot on Bob Hope's USO tour after the season. He made the cover of *Time,* which had dubbed him "The Blue Blazer."

It wasn't just the media that noticed. Fans flocked to see Blue, with attendance swelling by an estimated 15,000 every time he pitched. When he started at Yankee Stadium on August 15, the Yankees promoted the game as "Blue Sunday" and gained their biggest crowd in three years, and 100 people were allowed in for free because their last name was Blue. "After the game, I'll swing up to the stands and say hi to all the Blues," the A's pitcher joked. More than 40,000 showed up when he started at Washington—and 53,000 at Detroit. A tornado alert couldn't prevent a sellout and then some at Fenway Park.

This didn't get past Charles O. Finley, always quick to turn a buck. He ordered Williams to throw out his pitching plans and to arrange them around Blue, making sure to maximize his drawing power.

Vida Blue (center) American League MVP and Cy Young Award winner, sits at a news conference between commissioner Bowie Kuhn (left) and Charlie Finley (right), announcing that Blue had ended his holdout and signed a contract with the A's for $63,000. (AP Photo)

"Charlie did screw up the rotation," Williams said with a sigh 35 years after the fact.

Blue wasn't supposed to start on big promotional nights, because he was a promotion all by himself. When the A's were on TV, Blue was to be on the mound whenever possible. On several occasions, scheduling around Blue meant pushing back the A's established ace, Catfish Hunter, who was none too pleased about it, because he was trying to win 20 games for the first time in his career. When he pitched at home, Blue entered to the strains of "Rhapsody in Blue."

The team's most valuable asset (he brought in an estimated $1 million in extra gate receipts) was earning just $13,000 that year. Finley did reward Blue, though—he presented him with a $10,000 Cadillac.

"Charlie gave me a Carolina-blue Cadillac, a convertible," Blue said with a chuckle. "That was around the same time as *Superfly* and *Shaft* and all that B.S. I told him, 'You should have filled it with watermelons, too.'

"I told him he wasn't paying me enough for me to even get gas, so he gives me an Arco gas card. Here I am, living in the projects in Oakland, I've got a 24-gallon tank, and every time I fill it, I go ahead and fill up the tank for the lady behind me, too. I did that for two years, even after I didn't have that Cadillac anymore."

The personalized plates Finley provided meant that Blue was followed into restaurants all over town. He grew weary of signing autographs night and day.

"The license plate said, 'V BLUE.' I said, 'Mr. Finley, you just blew my cover. I can't go anywhere in this.' I had it a few weeks and my cousin came and got it, drove it across country."

Blue also talked Finley into $1,000 for a new wardrobe, saying he didn't have nice enough clothes to ride around in a Cadillac.

Over the course of his magical season, Blue never allowed more than four earned runs in a game. Slowed down in September, although not to the extent Jackson had been in his home run quest, Blue finished 24–8—more than living up to his own expectations. All year, he'd been pitching with two dimes in his pocket, which he told *Time* represented "the hope of 20 wins."

After the season was over, Blue was named the American League Cy Young winner, as expected. He was also named the AL MVP, too—the A's first MVP since another lefty, Bobby Shantz, won the award in 1952. Blue was the youngest MVP since the inception of the award.

"He was unhittable," third baseman Sal Bando said. "Just a great year. You just couldn't beat him. I will contend, then and now, I don't believe a starting pitcher should be MVP, but maybe that's sour grapes because I finished second to him."

At the time, Blue said, he was young and naïve. He knows now how special that season was.

"I was so young, I probably didn't soak it up as well as I should have at the time," Blue said. "I wish every athlete could experience that, to be at the top of their game like that. It was a lot of fun. They talk about being in the zone, that's what it was. But it's like Al Kaline said about Alex Rodriguez after his rookie year: 'You blew it. How can you ever top that?'

"Eventually, I just had to say, 'Just let me pitch and be the best I can be.'"

Sandy Koufax, to whom Blue often was compared, reportedly said of Blue that year, "I'd rather have his future than anyone else's past."

60 Spot *Moneyball* Liberties

Moneyball, the movie, earned six Academy Award nominations and made more than $110 million at the box office. The film, however, is no strict documentary of the 2002 Oakland A's season—many of the events depicted never happened or were highly exaggerated. That's show biz—as star Brad Pitt noted during the *Moneyball* press tour, the filmmakers used some "artistic license."

The discrepancies between fact and fiction in *Moneyball* generally create dramatic tension. For instance, the most obvious and to some odious break from reality is the depiction of manager Art Howe, who is played in the film by Philip Seymour Hoffman as a surly old-timer with no interest in new ideas, focused solely on getting a new contract.

The movie needed a counterpoint to general manager Billy Beane (played by Pitt), a foil, and while in real life Howe and Beane did butt heads on occasion, Howe is a kind gentleman, thoroughly respected around the game. Plus, Oakland had an option on Howe for 2003, and his employment status never was at issue. In fact, he was hired away by the Mets for a higher paying job after that season, the third in a row in which he'd taken the A's to the playoffs.

"Art Howe's portrayal bothered me a lot," said A's first baseman Scott Hatteberg, who is a central figure in the film. "Everyone liked him a lot. I guess they needed kind of a bad guy but he got the short end of the stick, which was unfair. I still feel bad for him. I know there was some volatility there with him and Billy, but we didn't know about any of it besides the occasional chair being thrown in his office."

Howe was livid after seeing the movie, and remains upset to this day. "I'm hurt by it," he said. "People who don't know me think that's me. My reputation has suffered."

In the movie, Hatteberg is played by Chris Pratt as hesitant and unsure of himself after moving from catcher to first base, while the real Hatteberg is confident, charismatic, and calm. The movie nails two portrayals, though: Stephen Bishop is excellent as veteran outfielder David Justice, and Pitt is absolutely sensational as Beane, spot-on in every way in playing the brilliant, temperamental, and larger-than-life general manager. Pitt gets every detail right, down to Beane's casual clothing, his messy snacking, and his Clash posters.

There were plenty of other liberties. One major plot point, the acquisitions of Jeremy Giambi and Chad Bradford, took place before 2002—in fact, Giambi is best known for a moment during the 2001 playoffs with Oakland, when he didn't slide coming into home plate and was thrown out on Derek Jeter's famous "flip" play.

Also wildly skewed to further the plot: A key scene depicts Beane meeting soon-to-be assistant GM ("Peter Brand") in Cleveland before the 2002 season and then "buying" him from the Indians. Former A's assistant GM Paul DePodesta, the basis for Jonah Hill's character, had been hired a full three years earlier—and front-office officials sign contracts, they aren't purchased by other teams.

Even more egregiously, the movie shows Beane firing scouting director Grady Fuson in a big to-do of a showdown. Fuson, on his own, already had left the A's before that season for a more prominent role with Texas.

At one point of *Moneyball*, Beane travels to Cleveland to discuss a deal for reliever Ricardo Rincon. That wouldn't ever happen. General managers rarely meet face-to-face to talk trades except at the winter meetings. Rarely do they go to players' houses to sign them, but in the film, Beane and first-base coach Ron Washington travel to Hatteberg's home to try to recruit him. Their first point of contact: They call him from the curb. There is no industry in which that would happen.

There are some smaller switcheroos, too. Opening Night 2002 was at night, not during the day. And Game 5 of the 2002 ALDS was played during the day, not in the evening. A's fans chuckled at the amount of time local sports-talk radio spent discussing the team in *Moneyball*—in real life, the team gets only the barest of mentions on Bay Area radio stations. And the Bay Area media never has called for Beane to be fired, as the movie suggests; he's typically seen as a media darling. His job never was in jeopardy—he was signed through 2005 at that point. Beane now has an ownership stake in the team and is signed through 2019.

And A's players never have had to pay for sodas in the clubhouse.

"The team wasn't as chintzy as they made it sound—but the color and look of the place, they captured that," Hatteberg said. "And they did a really good job of portraying Billy and how advanced the front office was."

Like the book *Moneyball*, however, the movie fails to make much mention of the A's "Big Three" starters: Tim Hudson, Mark Mulder, and Barry Zito, who were really the reason for much of the team's success—as was shortstop Miguel Tejada, who was the American League MVP in 2002.

61 Frank Thomas

Deep into his second month with the A's, Frank Thomas was doing, well, nothing.

Signed by the A's as a splashy free agent, the five-time All-Star was coming off two years in which he was limited by foot injuries, but he was healthy again. Still, 42 games into the season, he was batting .178.

"I remember specifically in the dugout in Arlington, Frank had started off the year off so horrible, and I remember telling Eric Chavez, 'We cannot continue to send this guy out there,'" former A's starter Dan Haren said of Thomas, hitting .162 at that point. "I said, 'He's done. He can't do it anymore. He's had an unbelievable career, but he's killing us.'"

Whoops.

"Fast-forward to the end of the season and he's hitting homers off Johan Santana, two of the most memorable homers ever to me, in one of the most fun games I've ever watched," Haren said. "Frank was the man. He wound up just carrying us that year, what a gratifying feel that must have been at that point in his career, coming back like that to take a team straight into the ALCS."

Outfielder Mark Kotsay recalled that just before Thomas got going with a big May series against his former White Sox team in Chicago, the A's DH decided he'd had enough of the inferior balls that Oakland used for batting practice.

"Frank had the worst April ever, and I remember so clearly, we always used these batting practice ball, 'blends,' and Frank would take BP and hit balls so hard and say, 'That ball's out of here'—and this is a guy who's taken major-league BP for 16–17 years—but those balls kept landing on the warning track," Kotsay said. "Frank finally took the whole basket of balls and threw them into the stands. He marched into [equipment manager] Steve Vucinich's office and said, 'We're not using those crappy balls anymore, we're using major-league baseballs, and I'll pay for them.' And from that point forward, he took off."

Thomas finished with 39 homers, 114 RBIs, a .270 average, and an OPS of .926. At the age of 38, he was fourth in American League MVP voting.

"No one really knew what Frank was doing when he was coming back from the foot thing—that was a lot of trust from the team," former Oakland closer Huston Street said. "And then he got as hot as any player I've ever seen, just home run after home run, big hit after big hit."

When Thomas went into the Baseball Hall of Fame in 2014, he said that it was that 2006 season with Oakland that put him over the top for the honor.

"We had a wonderful, wonderful season there, and I really think that got me to the Hall of Fame," Thomas said. "It showed I could adapt and adapt quickly."

His A's teammates cite more than just Thomas' statistics, though, when discussing his value in 2006.

"Having Frank on the team was a pleasure for everyone," A's starter Barry Zito said. "Who didn't look up to and idolize Frank Thomas?"

Temperamental outfielder Milton Bradley had his best year with the A's, and many credited Thomas' calming influence, while outfielder Nick Swisher, another player who took to Thomas quickly, hit 35 homers that season.

"So many guys benefitted from having Frank there, not just Milton and Swisher. When a Hall of Famer—and we knew he was a Hall of Famer—says to you, 'I know you were battling out there, that was good,' that means the world," Street said. "The confidence I got from playing with Frank was enormous. I consider him one of the best team guys I've ever been around. He loves the game, and he wants everyone to be good."

Thomas was not known as a leader with the White Sox, leaving under a cloud after spatting with GM Kenny Williams. His A's tenure put to rest any idea that he was a selfish player, though, according to his Oakland teammates.

"Frank had a reputation for not being a great team guy, but he was instrumental in facilitating relationships on our club," outfielder Mark Kotsay said. "He really was a huge reason for our success."

"It was fun playing with big Frank," longtime A's third baseman Eric Chavez said. "He hit 39 homers on one foot. He was huge for us, a great pickup—that's the only time we went to the ALCS, and what he meant to two of our biggest guys, Milton and Swish, the way he settled those two guys down and what he did for the team that year can't be overstated. He was rebuilding his career—and he took us to the ALCS. Frank was great. He was phenomenal."

62 The Five Aces

After their remarkable run of success in the '70s, the A's went to the postseason just once in a dozen years—led by manager Billy Martin, stolen-base king Rickey Henderson, and perhaps most important, five standout starters: Mike Norris, Matt Keough, Rick Langford, Steve McCatty, and Brian Kingman, who were featured on the cover of *Sports Illustrated* as "The Five Aces."

Most extraordinary was the quintet's ability to finish games. In 1980, Langford, Norris, and Keough combined for 72 complete games (28 by Langford; the staff had 94 altogether), and in 1981, a 109-game season thanks to a players' strike, the Oakland rotation recorded 60 complete games.

None of those promising Oakland starters ever was the same again, however. Keough was one of the few who escaped injury the following year, but he lost 18 games and had an ERA over 5.00. "We wouldn't have changed anything," Keough said. "If someone tells you that you have a chance to win if you pitch nine innings, that's what you do."

As Norris pointed out, the A's didn't have much of a bullpen in that era, either. "We didn't exactly have a Dennis Eckersley or Rollie Fingers," he said with a laugh. "So none of us ever wanted to come out of the game."

Martin always disputed the notion that he wore out pitchers' arms, saying that idea came either from owners trying to justify firing him, jealous competitors or baseball writers who didn't like him. He contended that the many arm problems that Oakland rotation incurred were a result of improper training during the seven-week strike in 1981. Martin's best argument: the starters' pitch counts were low and none of them pitched 300 innings.

"If I had the chance to do it all over, I'd do it the same way," Norris said. "We all would. We were on pitch counts and we never went over.

"What killed us was the strike. I went 72 days without pitching then came back and threw 11 innings my second time out. Then in spring training the next year, there were so many players and none of us got as many innings as we needed."

McCatty is now the Nationals' pitching coach—and Washington famously has regulated the number of games and innings for star starter Stephen Strasburg.

While the heavy workload usually is cited for the short self-life the five enjoyed in the majors, another theory has also floated around: Martin's pitching coach, Art Fowler, was rumored to teach the spitball, and because of the way the pitch is thrown—wrist firm, unbent—many believe the pitch puts too much stress on shoulders; shoulder injuries troubled McCatty, Keough, and Norris, while Langford needed elbow surgery.

Norris—who blamed his arm problems on overreliance on his screwball—appeared to have a sensational future ahead of him. He'd finished second in the Cy Young voting in 1980 after winning 22 games; and he'd tied winner Steve Stone with 13 first-place votes.

"Three rednecks left me off the ballot. Detroit, K.C. and Anaheim," Norris said. "If they'd put me third, I'd at least have tied. If they'd voted correctly, I would have won.

"My attitude was that I was really the best pitcher in the league at that time and I figured I would come back the next year and get it. I started off 9–3 and then there was the strike, and I was 3–6 the rest of the way."

Soon thereafter, Norris developed a cocaine addiction that cut short his career, but he fought to turn his life around and now he is a regular at A's alumni events. A San Francisco native, he has become a valued community member, working with youth groups and heading up the local RBI program, which is dedicated to reviving baseball in inner cities.

63 Ride a Skateboard to the Coliseum

Simpler instructions don't exist:

Grab a skateboard.

Take BART to the Coliseum.

Ride down the ramp and into the stadium…just like Johnny Damon.

"I just figured it would be easier and fun—and it's a cheap form of transportation," Damon said during his 2001 season with Oakland.

Told the front office might not love the idea of their new out-fielder rolling to work, Damon said, "I'm not going to be riding down stairwells or in empty swimming pools or anything. I think the team might have a problem with that."

Left-handed starter Barry Zito also was spotted on BART trains with his skateboard, and numerous A's players have commuted from San Francisco to the Coliseum on BART.

Several Oakland players have biked to BART and on to the Coliseum, too, including former A's pitcher Andrew Brown. And another A's pitcher, Erik Hiljus, bypassed BART altogether: He rode his bike all the way from his place in Alameda for every home game.

Sometimes BART is the only means of transportation for players in transit between teams. In 2013, when the A's and Rangers kept bouncing utility infielder Adam Rosales back and forth, Rosales' car was in Texas after Oakland reacquired him, leaving Rosales entirely reliant on rapid transit and rides from his buddies.

64 Broadcast Business

Just like much the franchise's baseball history, the A's broadcasting history veers from unusual to extraordinary.

The oddest chapter in A's broadcasting came in 1978, when the A's didn't even have a professional radio contract. And for more than a month, the games were broadcast by KALX, UC Berkeley's campus station, with students doing the play-by-play.

In an especially crazy twist, one of those announcers, Larry Baer, went on to become the Giants CEO.

"It was literally eight days before Opening Day, the A's did not have a station and Charlie Finley was talking about moving the team," Baer said. "I was at KALX, which at the time was 10 watts. I was the sports director and business manager, so I called Finley at his insurance company out of the blue and introduced myself.

"I said I was from KALX but I didn't initially mention that it was a school station. I said we'd be interested in broadcasting the games. In a gruff voice, the first thing he said was, 'Mr. Baer, B.S. walks, money talks. How much are you going to pay me?'"

Baer explained that because the FCC license was held by the UC Regents, the station was non-profit and non-commercial, "but we can put your games on the air so the fans can hear the games," Baer added.

Finley said, "Well, who would be the broadcasters?"

Baer responded, 'I'm a junior majoring in political science and my partner is a sophomore majoring in English. I'm 20 and he's 18.'

"Immediately, a light bulb went off," Baer said. "Charlie liked to get attention, and he knew this was something unique, like hot pants and bunnies. He said, 'Wait, the game would be broadcast by two kids in college? I'd like that,' and he kind of laughed."

Finley explained that he could only offer a short contract because he planned to unload the team while the A's were on the road. "On May 8, we're due to fly from Minnesota to Oakland but we're really going from Minnesota to Denver," he told Baer. "I can give you a contract for the first 23 games, because your station surely can't be heard in Denver."

"He asked me to send him $1 to make it a legal contract," Baer said. "No sooner did I hang up the phone at the station—I hadn't even told the station manager or the vice chancellor—when [Hall of Fame baseball writer] Jerome Holtzman calls, chuckling, and says, 'Is this Larry Baer? It it true you guys are going to have exclusive rights to broadcast Oakland A's games?'

"The deal was less than a minute old and Charlie was already publicizing it."

Baer and his broadcast partner, Bob Kozberg, were younger than any of the players, but Baer said the team treated them well, even if Matt Keough and Dave Revering did put bubblegum in the KALX tape recorder.

Initially, the A's new radio team got more attention than the club. The second night of the season, the CBS Evening News arrived.

"They were doing a profile on us, like, 'These kids are broad-casting games!'" Baer said. "The first inning, the umpires had to stop the game—CBS was shooting footage in our booth, and the light was bothering the players. So the umpires were waving at us and we were going, 'Should we wave back?'

"Someone said, 'No! The umpire is telling you to get the lights off!'"

The A's stint on college radio was brief, however, because the team got off to a 19–5 start and Finley, who was going through a divorce, decided against selling. He signed up with KNEW and let Baer work as a producer for Bud Foster, who tracked down free-agent pioneer Curt Flood as an on-air partner.

Flood, whose career was cut short after he challenged baseball's reserve clause, wouldn't have been Finley's first choice.

"Bud knew Curt Flood was from Oakland and he said, 'What about Curt, after all he's been through?'" Baer recalled. "Finley said, 'Curt Flood, are you kidding? He's the reason for all my problems!' And somebody said, 'Okay, that might be true, but just think what [commissioner] Bowie Kuhn will say.' Charlie said, 'Dammit, you're right! Hire him!'"

The KALX experience might have been the oddest period in A's radio/TV history—and that's saying something. The A's have employed some of the most brilliant broadcasters in baseball history, from Jon Miller to Lon Simmons to amazing multi-sport talent Bill King, but they've had some wacky on-air moments, too, especially during the Finley era.

Finley hired mainstay Monte Moore solely based on hearing him call the ABL championship between the Kansas City Steers and the Cleveland Pipers on the car radio. He didn't bother to find out if Moore had baseball experience, or if he wanted the job.

While covering one of Finley's press conferences in Kansas City, Moore ran into Finley for the first time in a hotel elevator, along with A's GM Parke Carroll.

"When I got on the elevator, Carroll said to Finley, 'Remember that guy on the radio? This is him, Monte Moore.' And without ever asking me if I'd done a baseball game in my life, Finley said, 'I want you to be my broadcaster.' In the elevator," Moore said.

"I didn't know whether to take him seriously or not. His first year, he didn't even have a radio station until two days before the season. Then he negotiated a contract for me without my knowledge. I had to call my wife and tell her I was making a little career change."

In 1964, Moore was surprised when Finley made a new addition to the booth late in the season—baseball's first woman announcer, Betty Caywood. She had no sportscasting experience, but Finley loved a gimmick.

"Betty was a weather girl in Chicago when Charlie brought her in," Moore said. "I never knew why he brought her in, exactly, but she was a good-looking lady. I got a phone call from Finley and he said, 'Go to the lobby and meet Betty, she's going to be your broadcast partner starting tonight. She doesn't have to know about baseball, she just has to talk to the ladies, let them know what they need to know.'"

Caywood wasn't allowed into the press lounge in Boston but she proved popular as a news item in New York. Mel Allen invited her on his TV show, and reporters stood in the A's radio booth, trying to hear everything she said.

"What she knew about baseball was very little," Moore said. "We played a makeup game at Minnesota and it snowed and the game went into extra innings. When we scored in the 15th inning, she jumped up and down and said, 'The game is over, we can go home where it's warm.'

"We said, 'Um, no, the team that supplies the field and the baseballs bats last.' We got a lot of mail about that."

Moore worked for the A's for nearly 25 seasons, including the championship years of the early '70s and the late '80s. He saw a lot of broadcasters come and go, including some of the game's greats.

"Harry Caray had just been fired by the Cardinals and Finley gave him a big contract in 1970, but quite frankly, he was not a success in the Bay Area," Moore said. "The Bay Area is a little different—if you get too far out on a home run call, they think you're a homer. And Harry didn't get along with a lot of people.

"I remember the first time I saw him, he said, 'Hey, take my briefcase up to the press box.' I said, 'I'm not here to be your caddy.' It wasn't a very good start. He was very egocentric, very bombastic. We didn't get along too well. No doubt, the guy was a legend, and I loved listening to him, but working with him was a different thing."

Red Rush followed Caray and lasted one season, to be followed by former big leaguer Jimmy Piersall, the subject of the book and movie *Fear Strikes Out,* based on his battle with bipolar disorder.

"Charlie hired him to do color one year and if you know his career, Jimmy was known for doing crazy things," Moore said. "He was colorful, a lot of fun, but I tell you, it was like sitting on eggs, you always wonder what's next."

During the 1972 ALCS, that became an issue when Piersall got into it with Tigers manager Billy Martin after Campy Campaneris was suspended for throwing his bat at Detroit's Lerrin LaGrow.

"The old broadcast booth at Tiger Stadium was just right there, practically on the field," Moore recalled. "Martin and Piersall had been adversaries on the field, and Martin had gotten the whole team fired up because of the Campy thing.

"So Piersall's in the booth and when Martin brings the lineup card out, Piersall sticks his head out, and, just when it's fairly quiet, he shouts, 'Martin, you're a blankety-blank bush-leaguer. You've always been a blankety blank busher.'

"Everyone could hear, and they started banging on our roof. And it was even more scary, because Finley had brought Campy into the booth and left him with us to keep him safe from the crowd.

"After the game, I told Finley, 'This guy Piersall has got to go. If he incites the crowd any more, there's going to be some real trouble.' He was too emotional. That was the crowning blow."

"That was consistent with the craziness of the team," outfielder George Hendrick said of Piersall. "This guy kind of fit with the personality of Oakland."

Just a year later, Moore uncovered a future star while sifting through job applicants.

"I had to listen to 100 tapes to find another broadcaster after the 1973 season, and I'd been listening for hours when here was one with a guy broadcasting a San Francisco Giants game," Moore remembered. "I said, 'Man, this is pretty darn good,' but I knew it wasn't one of the Giants broadcasters.

"So I looked for the name, and it said, 'Jon Miller.' He'd done the tape watching the game in the bleachers, and it was still that good. He was 22 years old. The next day, I called him to come over, he was working at a Santa Rosa TV station or something, and he came walking in and I said, 'Holy cow.' He was almost bald even then.

"I played the tape over the phone for Finley and he said, 'He is good.' I said, 'I think he'll be a good No. 2 man.' Finley said, 'Hell,

I think he'd be a good No. 1 man.' I knew he was going to be great. But Finley let him go because he wanted to hire Bob Waller. I was disappointed about that, but I helped Jon get a job in Texas. I've heard him say since, 'I've got a shrine to Monte Moore in my back yard.' I feel great about being the guy who gave him a shot, but it would have happened somewhere, he was that good."

In his second go-round with the team, beginning in 1988, Moore was teamed with former A's catcher Ray Fosse, another Moore discovery dating back more than a decade.

"He was hurt and recovering from one of those fights when we invited him up to the booth one day," Moore said. "It was a lousy game, but Ray stayed with us for a while because he was always a good interview. I said after that, 'When you get out of this business, look around, because you can do this job.'

"When the Haas family hired me, one of the things I said was, 'I want Ray Fosse with me.' He knows the game, he knows the players, and the players like him, he knows their language."

65 Chief Bender

Out of all the pitchers he managed in his 50-year career with the A's, Connie Mack had a favorite. You might think it would be the nutso Rube Waddell, or the sensational Lefty Grove.

Instead, Mack's go-to guy was Charles Albert Bender, better known as "Chief" Bender, a member of the Ojibwe tribe from the White Earth reservation in Minnesota.

"If everything depended on one game, I just used Albert— the greatest money pitcher of all time," Mack said, according to Bender's biography at the Hall of Fame. "He never let me down."

Bender, who played for the Philadelphia A's from 1903 to 1914, is considered the greatest Native American player of all-time—and he is among several potential candidates named as the possible inventor of the slider, or the "nickel curve," as it was then known.

Like Jim Thorpe, Bender attended Carlisle Indian School in Pennsylvania—and the man that first tapped his baseball potential is better known for football; Glenn "Pop" Warner, who coached both sports at the school.

Bender, according to Tom Swift's outstanding *Chief Bender's Burden,* was the victim of incessant racism in the early 20th century. Journalists and headline writers routinely referred to Bender "scalping" opponents, and fans and other teams taunted him with epithets.

At the same time, he was acknowledged as among the best of his era. Forty years after the fact, Ty Cobb, not known for his tolerance, called Bender's work in the 1911 World Series "the greatest bit of brainwork I ever saw in a ballgame" in setting up Giants catcher "Chief" Meyers for a curveball, then throwing him a fastball down the middle to strike him out looking.

Legendary sportswriter Grantland Rice called Bender one of the greatest competitors he'd ever known and quoted him as saying, "Tension is the greatest curse in sport. I've never had any tension. You give the best you have—you win or lose. What's the difference if you give all you've got to give?"

In World Series play, Bender was one of best, winning five of seven starts from 1910 to 1913. Even before that, Bender had shown his mettle, with a four-hit complete-game win in Game 2 of the 1905 World Series against the Giants, at just 21 years old. He lost Game 5 of that series, allowing only two runs in another complete-game effort—the opposing starter, Hall of Famer Christy Mathewson, threw a shutout of his own.

"The bigger the stake, the better Bender always was," Mack said.

In the 1910 World Series, with Eddie Plank out of the World Series because of an arm injury, Mack used only two pitchers, Bender and Jack Coombs, and Philadelphia beat the Cubs four games to one to win the first title in franchise history.

The next year, Bender was again terrific, winning two of three starts, putting up an ERA of 1.04, and striking out 20 men in 26 innings, as the A's beat the Giants, but the team didn't return to the World Series in 1912—Bender went just 13–8, had some injuries, and was suspended by the team for being "out of commission," a euphemism for a drinking problem.

He reverted to form in 1913, winning 21 games during the regular season and two games in the World Series against New York. Bender had helped Mack win three championships in four years. In gratitude, Mack paid off Bender's mortgage, according to Swift.

In 1914, though, things fell apart. Bender gave up six runs in 5⅓ innings against the Braves in Game 1 of the World Series, his final time on the mound for the A's. Bender, lambasted for his alcohol use in 1912, was drinking again, and Mack did not put up with that. "If the members of my team want to drink, all right, but they can't drink and play ball at the same time," Mack said. "That's settled. They can do whichever they prefer but they can't do both. There are no exceptions to my rule." Bender expected to pitch Game 4—and Mack used Bob Shawkey instead.

After getting swept by the Braves, Mack asked for waivers on Bender, Plank, and Coombs, the stars of the A's early years. Mack saw that injuries to some key players, plus age, were catching up to the team and he blew it up. He blamed former A's infielder Danny Murphy, who'd been recruiting for the new Federal League, for distracting some of his players in 1914. .

The Braves were such huge underdogs in that World Series, there is still speculation that the fix was in, but Swift finds no evidence of this. Mack, asked about it over the years, always alluded to the damage wrought by the Federal League flirtations. "Our players were simply more bitter against one another than interested in the Series," he said.

Bender was heartbroken to learn he'd been waived in a newspaper story, according to Swift, but Swift points out that Bender likely already had a Federal League contract in hand; Bender, who'd never made more than $4,000 with Philadelphia, was offered $8,500 plus a $5,000 signing bonus to join the Baltimore Terrapins.

Bender's warm relationship with Mack faltered, but more than 20 years later, Bender and Mack became friendly again. Mack employed Bender as an instructor, a scout and a coach. Bender is credited with helping turn Bobby Shantz from a mediocre 8–14 pitcher with a 4.61 ERA in 1950 into the 1952 American League MVP. Shantz said Bender taught him a knuckleball, and more important, got him to slow down.

When Bender was in the hospital that year, Shantz sent him a note that Swift reprinted.

"Chief, I'd like to take this time to thank you for all the things you taught me about pitching. I'll probably never be the pitcher you were, but I'll always be in there trying my best to do the things you taught me."

Bender was voted into the Hall of Fame that year, was inducted the following year, and he died in 1954 at the age of 70.

66 Sewage and Sprinklers

Built in 1966, the Oakland Coliseum is one of the oldest stadiums in major-league baseball, tied for fourth with Angels Stadium in Anaheim, and the building has had its share of strange happenings as it has aged.

The Coliseum's playing surface is 22 feet below sea level, and the baseball clubhouses also are below sea level, contributing to some recent havoc: Three times during the 2013 season, the A's had issues with sewage spouting forth, including one incident that rendered the bathrooms and shower areas out of bounds for both teams and the umpires.

"We came in from the field and we'd won, so we had the music blaring and after about 30 seconds, Steve Vucinich came in and turned off the music, like a record scratch—whrrrpp," A's closer Sean Doolittle recalled. 'Vuc said, 'You can't go in the bathrooms and the showers, everything's flooded with sewage.'

"It was like camping as a kid, like summer camp, take all your stuff and go to the shower. We had to walk up the stairs to the Raiders' locker room in towels and shower shoes, it was really weird. And we had to shower with the Mariners. We're all happy-go-lucky, we'd just won on getaway day, and the Mariners don't want to have to share a locker room with the team that just beat them. I've never on any level of baseball had to do that before. But that's the Coliseum way."

"When you're sharing a shower with the team you just played—'Hey Felix, you just threw a shutout, now here you are showering with us'—it's not what you expect when you come to a big-league ballpark," former A's starter Brett Anderson said. "It's

233

like something that would happen in summer-league travel ball. But it's the Coliseum, you've got to make it your own, make it a home-team advantage."

Internet wags almost immediately dubbed the Coliseum— official corporate sponsor name: the O.co Coliseum—as the E.Coli-seum.

The incident that June was blamed on a pipe blockage, but the lower level of the Coliseum has been prone to leaks and floods for more than a decade, especially during rainstorms. And in mid-September of 2013, the A's were driven out of their dugout after a bathroom flooded; bench coach Chip Hale was spotted crawling down the dugout bench to rescue his lineup card.

"I remember sitting in the dugout watching [sewage] float-ing by and saying, 'How is this even allowed to be a major-league stadium?'" former A's third baseman Josh Donaldson said.

Four days later, after rain, the coaches' facilities emptied out when water began gushing out of toilets and faucets "like lava," catcher Kurt Suzuki said. "The sound it makes is amazing."

In 2014, the plumbing at the Coliseum was upgraded and there were no major flooding incidents, but there was an unusual rainout—the tarp was left off the infield early in the season and an overnight shower left the field unplayable. With not a cloud in the sky at game time, the contest vs. Seattle was postponed until later in the season.

The real oddity during the 2014 season was a baby opossum who showed up several times during games. Dubbed the "Rally Possum" and "O.Possum," among other things, the critter wan-dered right up to Tampa Bay's Ben Zobrist at one point. Zobrist, traded to the A's after that season, said it looked him right in the eyes. "I definitely had a close encounter with a 'possum," he said.

Fans created a Twitter account for the opossum, and starter Jeff Samardzija—on the mound during two of its appearances, both A's wins—suggested the team get it a jersey.

"He likes me," Samardzija said. "I need to go find this guy. He's pretty sweet, man, he knows what he's doing—he shows up at the right time, like down times of games."

"It's on a par with everything that goes along with the Coliseum," Doolittle said with a laugh. "The players and fans took something that was kind of disgusting, when you think about it, and turned it into something funny and kind of charming,"

One infamous Coliseum incident happened on June 13, 2008, when with two outs in the bottom of the ninth against the Giants, the sprinkler system suddenly erupted, sending closer Huston Street dancing off the mound. He hung out at shortstop with Bobby Crosby until the system was shut off.

"I turned to throw the plate and—here come jets of water. You don't know what to do," Street said. "I was in total shock. 'Is this really happening?' I was trying to get out of it without getting wet because I still had to get outs. We had a four- or five-run lead, which is why it was no big deal, but if Barry Bonds was coming up with a one-run game or something, you'd be furious.

"I talked to the grounds crew and it was on a timer, the team had been on the road, someone just forgot to turn it off. It went off at exactly 10:00 PM. And they were so nice and so apologetic. More than anything, I remember talking to Crosby at shortstop and he said, 'You know you're going to be on the blooper reel for the rest of your life.'"

67 Move to Oakland

A's owner Charlie Finley never stopped looking for greener pastures. In September 1962, he asked for permission to move to the Dallas–Ft. Worth area, but was denied by the AL owners in a 9-1 vote. In 1964, he arranged a two-year agreement to move the team to Louisville, but he forgot to run it by the league, and AL president Joe Cronin enjoined him to stay in Kansas City, so Finley threatened to sue. That same year, the league also turned down Finley's request to move to Oakland, an idea that Giants owner Horace Stoneham lobbied to prevent. (Finley also asked Stoneham to share Candlestick Park while a stadium was built across the Bay. Not surprisingly, Stoneham had no interest.)

Repeatedly stymied, Finley threatened to move the A's to a cow pasture in Peculiar, Missouri. There was speculation that baseball might banish him, but as attendance plummeted to 726,000, and disenchantment in Kansas City grew with Finley, the owners finally relented to a move on October 17, 1967. The Yankees, who abstained previously, changed their vote to "aye," and the club once so closely knitted to the Athletics set them free to head west.

Kansas City might have been unhappy to see its baseball team depart, but sentiments toward Finley were quite the reverse. Missouri Senator Stuart Symington called Finley "one of the most disreputable characters ever to enter the American sports scene."

Symington then memorably called Oakland "the luckiest city since Hiroshima."

The senator made sure Kansas City wouldn't go without a major-league team very long. He threatened to contest Major League Baseball's anti-trust exemption, and that challenge ensured that the town was awarded the expansion Royals in 1969.

The Athletics' final games in Kansas City came on September 27, 1967, when the club took both ends of a doubleheader against the White Sox. Their last game as the Kansas City A's came on October 1 at New York, a 4–3 loss to the Yankees. Jim Gosger got the final hit in Kansas City Athletics' history, a single in the ninth.

The team won only 10 times in 40 games to close the season and finished last again. Finley claimed he lost $4.6 million the final four years in Kansas City

So what did the San Francisco Bay Area have in 1968 that Dallas and Louisville and all the other places Finley flirted with did not?

For one thing, the population base in the metropolitan area was the sixth largest in the country. Even with the Giants already established in San Francisco, Finley figured to draw from the growing East Bay and Contra Costa County. The broadcast market, one of the largest in the nation, also was likely to be lucrative—with a radio/TV contract worth as much as $1.3 million annually. The Kansas City broadcast rights, by comparison, were worth less than $80,000 per year.

Radio listeners rallied when asked to send in letters backing the A's move.

"One thing I think helped Oakland was that KNBR had a coordinated effort where people could mail in cards of support," play-by-play man Monte Moore said. "One day, a 55-gallon drum of cards arrived for Finley."

Finley responded by saying, "I always wanted the O. in my name to stand for Oakland."

The East Bay had a strong history of supporting baseball, including the Oakland Oaks. The Oaks memorably had won the Pacific Coast League crown in 1948 under Casey Stengel, beating out Lefty O'Doul's Seals. The area was a hotbed of talent, the weather relatively mild, and Finley found a willing group of civic leaders eager to rival San Francisco.

"Finley knew that Northern California, although it had the Giants, was probably the best marketplace for an American League team," longtime *Oakland Tribune* sports editor George Ross said. "He wasn't shopping around, he had decided on Oakland because of the population in the Bay Area and the long history of baseball success. The old Oakland Oaks had drawn very big crowds and set a record one year. He was buying into a successful territory."

Finley wouldn't have to look for a facility, either. The Oakland–Alameda County Coliseum was the biggest attraction as far as the A's owner was concerned. It had opened two years earlier, with the NFL's Raiders the first tenants of the outdoor stadium and the NHL's Seals the first to play in the adjacent arena.

When it was constructed at a cost of $25.5 million in 1966, the Coliseum's location was considered ideal. It's right next to the busy Nimitz Freeway and it boasts a Bay Area Rapid Transit (BART) subway stop. Other plusses: Parking is ample, and the outdoor stadium can hold more than 50,000 fans.

Finley wound up buying the Seals hockey team in bankruptcy court in 1970. He applied some of the same formulas he had with the A's, changing the Seals' colors to green, yellow, and white—and providing yellow skates to match the uniforms of the newly dubbed "California Golden" Seals. The following year, he introduced extremely unpopular white skates, which conjured up images of figure skaters rather than bruising hockey types. The trainers hated the skates because they got scuffed so quickly.

The Seals were dreadful throughout Finley's ownership, and he tired of them and sold them in 1974. By 1976, the franchise had been moved to Cleveland, and two years later the newly-named Barons were folded into the Minnesota North Stars' club. In 1991, in a complicated arrangement with the NHL, former Seals owner George Gund (who'd taken the team to Cleveland and was a part owner of the North Stars) was awarded an expansion team in San Jose: the Sharks, the direct heirs of Finley's Seals.

While still in Kansas City, the A's were awful, perennial cellar dwellers. Things were changing though, just as the team relocated. The talent Finley had found was just starting to show itself, and the young club knew that better times were ahead.

"There were some growing pains," third baseman Sal Bando said. "We thought we were a little better than we were, but we matured.

"In Kansas City, the history had been losing, but in the minors, we were used to winning. Once we had our feet on the ground, we knew we could improve."

Blue Moon Odom, one of the longest serving team members, really noticed the shift.

"When we were still in Kansas City, we would get to the ballpark and we knew we would lose," Odom said. "Then, in Oakland, when we got to the ballpark, we knew we would win that day. We knew we couldn't lose. We'd go into a place for four games and we'd think we'd win all four."

The A's first game in Oakland came on April 17, 1968, a 4–1 loss to the Orioles that drew an announced 50,164 (the actual total was about 3,000 fewer). Governor Ronald Reagan threw out the first pitch—and according to longtime A's equipment manager Steve Vucinich, Reagan was booed after asking the crowd, "Did everyone pay your taxes?"

The next night, the A's recorded their first victory in their new home, 4–3 in 13 innings, but only 5,304 showed up. For the rest of Finley's reign, attendance remained an issue (so much so that one year he cancelled Fan Appreciation Night out of spite).

That first season, under new manager Bob Kennedy—Finley's eighth manager in as many years—Oakland finished in sixth, moving up four spots from 1967. More important, at 82–80, the team was over .500 for the first time since 1952.

68 Great '80s Outfield

When the great outfields of the 1970s and '80s are discussed, the Expos and Reds get plenty of mentions. The best of them all, though, roamed Oakland's outfield.

The trio of center fielder Dwayne Murphy, right fielder Tony Armas, and left fielder Rickey Henderson gets overshadowed, in part, because they played together only three full years, from 1980 to '82, plus Henderson emerged as a huge star in his own right.

As a unit, though, Murphy-Armas-Henderson is worthy of its own place in history.

"As three outfielders together, it is tough to think of anyone better," former A's starter Matt Keough said. "Those Reds teams, St. Louis, Montreal—I don't think anyone had three outfielders who were as good offensively *and* defensively, all Gold Glove–level defenders who made opposing teams nuts.

"If you looked at all the WAR, the defensive zone ratings, runs saved, all the components of the modern metrics, I'm not sure you'd find a better outfield the past 50 years. They would kill everyone."

The numbers bear this out: In 1980, the trio had a mind-boggling combined WAR of 21.6.

For comparison's sake, in 1976, the Big Red Machine's outfield of George Foster, Ken Griffey, and Cesar Geronimo had a WAR of 13.2. The Cardinals' 1985 outfield of Vince Coleman, Andy Van Slyke, and Willie McGee had a WAR of 14.0. The best combined mark for the many terrific configurations of Expos' outfields, some with Tim Raines, some with Ellis Valentine, came in 1983, when Raines, Andre Dawson, and Warren Cromartie put up a sensational 14.9.

Still not even close to that 1980 Oakland outfield.

"You're talking about a guy who won six Gold Gloves; the greatest leadoff hitter in the history of the game; and a right fielder with one of the best arms in the history of the game," former A's infielder Shooty Babitt said of Murphy, Henderson, and Armas. "They were the heart and soul of that team. Everyone talks about the pitching staff, but it was that outfield—that outfield was special."

All three were true center fielders, and because Henderson and Murphy were so fast, they could play shallow, helping them throw out more baserunners; they combined for 43 assists in 1980. Armas had a team-record 17 assists that season, and Keough said that he also was the savviest when it came to knowing the league.

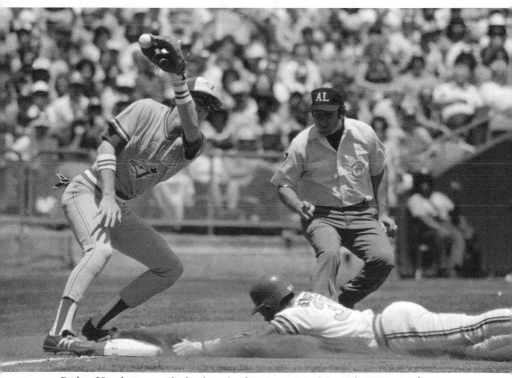

Rickey Henderson steals third in the first inning on May 24, 1981—right before Tony Armas singled to drive him in. (Paul Sakuma/AP Photo)

"Tony was just brilliant at positioning, playing pitch counts, playing hitters. Billy Martin would always position everyone else—but not Tony, because he knew the pitchers and hitters better than Billy did," Keough said. "Now they have spray charts and shifts—Tony was doing that in his head back in the day, it was uncanny.

"All three were dynamite offensive players, Murph would take pitch after pitch; he could get on with a walk, he could get on with a bunt, they could all run. And Tony was like Sal Bando or Gene Tenace—he might hit .240, but when he hit a pitch, it would be a three-run homer to beat you."

That 1980 A's pitching staff threw a record 94 complete games—and Keough said the outfielders should get a lot of the credit. He recalled a game on July 27 that year at Detroit in which he came one out from a complete game at Tiger Stadium—and 19 of the 26 outs he got came via fly balls.

"As a pitcher, you knew if you kept it in the ballpark, it wouldn't land in the grass. I remember Rod Carew would hit line drive after line drive that got caught. They took so many hits away," Keough said. "I don't get through those innings without those guys. They drove teams crazy."

69 Josh Donaldson

On the first day of full spring training in 2012, Scott Sizemore blew out his knee during defensive drills.

The A's, with no other everyday third basemen on their roster, turned to minor-league catcher Josh Donaldson, who'd played third at Auburn. The move looked like a longshot at best, desperation at worst.

And while Donaldson did have his share of struggles that season, a year later he was an MVP candidate. And in 2014, he was named to the All-Star team and was a finalist for the Gold Glove award at third.

By chance, the A's had stumbled upon one of the best young players in the game.

Donaldson was a first-round draft pick by the Cubs, acquired by the A's in the Rich Harden deal. He'd had a few brief shots with Oakland behind the plate but hadn't stuck, and by the time of Sizemore's injury, it was starting to appear as if Donaldson was no longer on the A's radar, with Anthony Recker and then newly acquired young catcher Derek Norris passing him on the depth chart.

Well aware that the team was losing interest in him, Donaldson went to the Dominican Republic after the 2011 season specifically to play third base—he figured versatility would help make him more attractive to other teams.

"It's weird how things played out in 2012," Donaldson said. "The first day of full-squad practice, I asked Bob Melvin if I should bring my glove for bunt drills—and the first ball rolled to Sizemore, pop goes his knee, that was rough.

"Bob looks at me and says, 'Yeah, go to third base.' Then the next day he told me to put my catcher's gear away, and the craziness started."

Donaldson was used to fighting the odds. He'd grown up in tough circumstances; with his father, Levon, in jail, Donaldson was raised by his mother, Lisa French, with help from Donaldson's uncle, Chuck Pyritz. Always a standout athlete, Donaldson said he was hitting perfect drives at the golf course at the age of 18 months, and in high school, he was the MVP of the Alabama All-Star football game and the state baseball player of the year.

At points in 2012, though, Donaldson was starting to lose hope, convinced the A's were done with him. He'd gotten the chance he'd so coveted, but he was sent down after hitting .094 with 13 strikeouts in his first nine games of 2012. The next time he came up, for 19 games in May and June, he hit .182. The A's had picked up Brandon Inge to play third by then and considered moving Donaldson into the back-up catcher role.

"I told my buddies, 'If at that point in 2012 you'd have told me I'd be in the big leagues and helping the team with a playoff push, I would have called you a liar,'" Donaldson recalled with a laugh.

Back at Triple-A Sacramento, Donaldson kept playing third base, and in an effort to focus his efforts at the plate, he decided to divide the plate into halves and look either middle in or middle out. Simplifying things helped, and so did the move out from behind the plate; Donaldson's legs didn't tire over the course of the season and when Inge dislocated his shoulder in August, the A's decided to give Donaldson one last chance. General manager Billy Beane said he'd have kicked himself if Oakland had let Donaldson go elsewhere only for Donaldson to turn into a star.

"When Inge got hurt, at that point, my main focus was just playing good defense because our pitchers were doing such a great job, keeping us in games," Donaldson said. "Then I even started hitting some, I think a lot of it had to do with taking pressure off myself."

Donaldson hit .301 with 24 homers in 2013 and finished fourth in MVP voting, and he hit 29 homers and drove in 98 runs in 2014 despite playing with multiple injuries down the stretch.

"To go from being a catcher and an all-or-nothing hitter to a Gold Glove–caliber third baseman and MVP candidate and one of the better run producers in the game, that's amazing," former A's left-hander Brett Anderson said. "To go from a minor prospect as a catcher to one of the best players in baseball? Wow."

"The skillset is unbelievable," A's manager Melvin said. "I can't remember another guy besides Robin Yount who moved positions and was a Gold Glove–level player, it's that dramatic."

Still, Donaldson had to prove himself time and again: He should have made the 2013 All-Star team, as manager Jim Leyland acknowledged afterward. And many people in baseball thought Donaldson was wrongly denied the Gold Glove in 2014.

"It's really been a crazy journey," he said. "Lots of ups and downs."

"The offensive ability always was there, all the parts of his game were there, it was a matter of getting the opportunity and honing his skills, gaining confidence. And he is a confident guy," Melvin said. "It's very much a football mentality—he's very focused on what he's doing. You look at his at-bats and he's into every pitch. He's always prepared. He got the opportunity a third time and he wasn't going to let it go by.

"He's one of those players that everyone else is always thinking, 'I can't stand that guy—I wish he played for us.' Those are the guys who, deep down, everyone respects."

Always on the flashy side, Donaldson is not everyone's favorite flavor; French said that's been the case all the way back to youth ball. Baltimore's Manny Machado started an odd tiff with Donaldson in 2014, angry after Donaldson tagged him out on the bases. And he's had some memorable staredowns with pitchers, including Texas' Yu Darvish and Minnesota's Glen Perkins.

"Josh knows every other team hates him," A's first baseman Brandon Moss said. "I always tell him, 'If I was on the other side, I'd hate you, too. But because you're on our team, I love you.'"

"Josh doesn't care what people think of him," former A's outfielder Jonny Gomes said. "That's okay, we're not here looking for friends—and this guy is unbelievable. He's so athletic. His work ethic is second to none. He wants to be the best, that's not something everyone can relate to, but it's something a lot of superstars have."

Now he is on the other side: On November 28, 2014, the A's traded Donaldson to Toronto for third baseman Brett Lawrie, pitchers Kendall Graveman and Sean Nolin, and shortstop prospect Franklin Barreto.

"I'm definitely a little emotional about it. Oakland is my home," Donaldson said. "But at the end of the day, it's a business, as much as it hurts emotionally. The most important thing is that Billy gave me an opportunity to be on that team and I am very grateful for that, and for all the fan support I've had. I'm so glad to have been a part of that."

70 See the A's New Spring Home

Spring training veterans will tell you: There is nothing like that atmosphere. Spring camp is relaxed, fun, and it's the best time of year to get autographs from big-league players.

This is a highly recommended experience for any fan of any team.

"If you're a fan, you've got to go to spring training," former A's outfielder/first baseman Brandon Moss said. "If you're in Arizona, you've already won the battle—you can see any team there within a 45-minute drive, you can see all the big-league players and you can see all the top prospects playing against big-leaguers. How great is that?"

Pretty great, and for A's fans, there's more: a brand-new spring-training site. Oakland's new home-away-from-home is, well, actually better than the A's regular-season home at the Coliseum. Hohokam Stadium in Mesa includes expanded seating, an HD videoboard, and plush clubhouse facilities.

In addition, the team's minor-league and training complex, three blocks away at Fitch Park, is state-of-the-art, with amenities such as hydrotherapy pools and an underwater treadmill.

"I'm addicted to spring training, I've been 20 times starting in 1993," longtime A's fan Carrie Olejnik said. "I like seeing all the prospects, it seems like there are always 60 guys running around, you'll see three guys with the same number. Some people only want to go later in the spring when all the regulars are playing, but I like the variety. I can see the regulars in Oakland."

Fan Will MacNeil also is a spring-training habitué and he has tips for first-timers. "Sunscreen is a must," he said. "Get there early if you want autographs. And try to get to two games a day and see all the ballparks."

Like everyone who attends spring training regularly, MacNeil has a favorite restaurant—he recommends Bill Johnson's, a burger place with numerous locations in the Phoenix area. Other places with several outlets that are popular: Los Dos Molinos for Mexican food, Oregano's for pizza, and gastro-pub Culinary Dropout.

Scottsdale is the center of spring-training nightlife, and it tends to be the most expensive place to stay, but bargain accommodations can be found all over the valley. Rental cars are a necessity, and while rates vary, taking a cab to off-airport rental locations can mean substantial savings.

There are numerous other attractions in the Mesa area, including casinos, historic sights, regional parks, the Mesa Arts Center, and even no-snow stand-up paddleboarding.

71 The Mike Andrews Incident

In the 1972 ALCS, the A's system of rotating second basemen nearly bit them in the rear when catcher Gene Tenace wound up at second late in the game and made a key error against the Tigers.

The same scheme caused an even bigger flap in the 1973 World Series, turning into a nasty personnel scandal that nearly derailed the entire event.

Game 2 at New York went into extra innings, leaving the A's light at second. Dick Green and Ted Kubiak already had been used, leaving Mike Andrews at a position he hadn't played since a less-than-successful three-game stint in August, after Oakland had acquired him in a trade

In the 12th, the Mets had two on and two outs when Willie Mays singled past Andrews to drive in a run. Another single loaded the bases, and Paul Lindblad got John Milner to hit a grounder to second—and the ball rolled between Andrews' legs and into the outfield, allowing two men to score. Jerry Grote then hit a ball that Andrews fielded, but his throw to first pulled Gene Tenace off the bag, with another run coming in.

Andrews was charged with an error, but many observers, including manager Dick Williams, felt that that was undeserved.

"I tell you, I've seen the highlight film a number of times, and on the throwing error, Tenace didn't have to leave the bag and he did," PR man Bob Fulton said. "It shouldn't have been ruled an error."

Andrews said afterward, "I plain kicked things around…. I haven't played much in the field this year, but that's no excuse."

Williams pointed out that had Manny Trillo be allowed to play in the series as an injury substitute, Trillo would have been out there rather than Andrews.

Finley arranged for the team doctor to check Andrews out after the game and Vida Blue heard Andrews tell them, "There's nothing wrong with me." The rest of the team got on the bus for the airport.

And the craziness began.

Fulton first got an idea something was up at the end of the game.

"I wasn't supposed to go to New York," he said. "But I'm waiting behind the screen for the game to be over to get players to the interview room and [equipment manager] Frank Ciensczyk says, 'Mr. Finley wants you on the plane. You need to be at the airport at such and such a time.' I had to rush home and pack, get to the airport.

"Then the players come on, one at a time. Reggie Jackson said, 'Have you seen Mike Andrews?' I said, 'No.' Another player gets on, and he said, 'Have you seen Mike?' I said, 'No.' Then another one. Finally, I said, 'What's going on?' And it turned out that Finley got Dr. Harry Walker to write a letter that Andrews was unfit to play."

Said Williams: "I wanted nothing to do with it. There was nothing wrong with him."

Finley ordered Fulton to write up a press release about Andrews' status, but while Fulton was making copies of the release at Shea Stadium, the players were already on the field working out. Angry about their teammate's treatment, they beat Fulton to the Andrews announcement.

"They were wearing Mike's number on their sleeves and they were being interviewed about it," Fulton recalled. "Finley was livid and he cussed the players. He said, 'They're not going to get any diamonds on their rings this time,'—and they didn't, just a script 'A,' no diamonds."

"Everyone had black tape on their sleeve with the No. 17," reliever Rollie Fingers said. "The press ate it up and blasted Charlie. We weren't going to play Game 3 of the World Series if Mike wasn't going to play."

Finley insisted that the infielder had been sent home with a shoulder injury. A statement by Dr. Walker, signed by Andrews, attesting to the shoulder injury, was met with derision by the Oakland players and media. The players were irate that Andrews presumably had been forced to sign the statement.

Jackson, the A's player representative, said, "I've never heard of firing a player in the middle of the World Series. That's what the man did. This thing is a real embarrassment and disappointment.... We're near to mutiny."

Finley was blasted by national columnists, one of whom called him "Scrooge." Commissioner Bowie Kuhn reprimanded Finley and ordered him to reinstate Andrews, who had returned to his home in Massachusetts.

"Guess who's job it is to find Andrews?" Fulton said. "I call back to the office to get his home number, but we can't track him down. Finally, I got ahold of one of the Conigliaro brothers in Boston and told him to have Andrews call me. Andrews called Jackson, and Jackson tells him to get to New York."

Meanwhile, the A's took Game 3 by a score of 3–2, and Jackson said, "I guess we're that good, that we can overcome anything Finley can do to us."

Andrews was back the following day and explained in a press conference that he was healthy and that, "embarrassed and beaten," he'd been pressured to sign the statement.

Upon Andrews' return, Fulton said, "Finley told Dick Williams, 'Don't you dare use Andrews'—so Williams used him to pinch hit as soon as he could, of course, against Finley's wishes."

Andrews pinch hit in the eighth, and, said Williams, "He got a standing ovation. Even from Finley."

Finley said later he'd been hoping Andrews would hit one out. Andrews said he was nearly in tears when the crowd of 54,000 stood. As he grounded out, they gave him another standing ovation. Joe Rudi said that the Mets fans "have a lot of class."

The A's dropped the game 6–1 and Andrews never played again.

Williams privately told many of his players he planned to resign after the series; Finley's treatment of Andrews was the last straw.

72 Satchel Paige

Twelve years after the A's integrated, the team signed one of the Negro League's greatest stars, Satchel Paige, to pitch in one game, on September 25, 1965, against Boston. Paige, then 59 years old, worked three innings and allowed only one hit, a double by Carl Yastrzemski.

"That was a wonderful experience," said longtime major-league coach Rene Lachemann, who was a rookie catcher with Kansas City that year and warmed up Paige in the bullpen. "Satchel was one of the funniest people I ever met. We asked him if Cool Papa Bell was faster than Campy Campaneris and he told us what he told everyone, that Cool Papa Bell was so fast, he'd turn the lights off and be in bed before it was dark. I said, 'We've heard that one,' and he said, 'You haven't heard this one—Cool Papa Bell was so fast, he hit a shot through the pitcher's legs and it hit him in the ass when he was sliding into second.'

"At one point that year, we had the youngest battery ever, me aged 19 and Catfish Hunter, aged 19, and at the end of the year, we had the oldest battery ever—Satchel Paige and Billy Bryan [26]."

According to Lachemann, a rocking chair was placed in the bullpen for Paige, along with "a big blonde buxom nurse" who rubbed liniment into his arm as a gag for the crowd. He had his own water boy, too, who fetched him coffee.

He chose not to sit in the dugout, according to the *New York Times,* because he was "close enough to below the surface as it is."

Paige was the oldest pitcher—and oldest player, ever—to appear in a big-league game with his three-inning outing for Kansas City. And many felt he could have continued to compete: He retired the final six men he faced—recording one strikeout in the process.

There were only 9,289 fans in attendance, but they were boisterous, according to newspaper accounts—and when Paige came out of the game, the lights dimmed in tribute and the crowd lit matches and sang "Old Rocking Chair," "I Am Growing Old," and "The Old Gray Mare."

"Old Satch has a lot of stuff left—and we'll be interested in signing him on for 1966," team owner Charlie Finley told reporters.

Paige, whose service time fell just short of a big-league pension, did not appear in another major-league game. Finley had planned to bring him back as a coach to help him get his pension, but Paige

Satchel Paige (center) shows off some of the finer points to four rookie pitchers (from left): "Blue Moon" Odom, "Catfish" Hunter, Dick Joyce, and Ron Tompkins. (AP Photo/stf)

had previous commitments to a barnstorming team and Finley had to withdraw his offer. Paige finally earned his full pension as a Braves coach in 1968.

Arguably the greatest pitcher of his era, Paige was inducted into the Baseball Hall of Fame in 1971.

73 Join Athletics Nation

Perhaps it's not surprising a team so close to Silicon Valley, a team featured in Michael Lewis' best-selling business book *Moneyball* for being on the cutting edge, wound up inspiring one of the first major fan blogs.

And by major, check this out: AthleticsNation.com, started in 2003 by *Moneyball* and A's afficianado Tyler Bleszinski, grew into the site SBNation, with more than 300 team websites, and Vox Media, valued at nearly $400 million.

Bleszinski started the site small; he attended a game with his friend, Markos Moulitsas, loved the vibe, and decided he wanted to write about the A's and GM Billy Beane, particularly because local sports-talk radio virtually ignored the team. Moulitsas, who founded the popular political blog Daily Kos, suggested Bleszinski do something similar.

"I enjoyed the energy at the Coliseum, and I wanted to talk to other people about it," Bleszinski said. "I didn't even really know what a blog was but I did a free trial at Typepad for a month and enjoyed it, so Markos gave me access to his technology.

"I wanted the blog to be more about trying to understand why Billy Beane does things rather than angry fans ranting. Billy is so smart, I was interested in the process, and that was the impetus of

AthleticsNation, trying to figure out what the front office is doing and get other fans involved. It's funny, I expected to be speaking into a vacuum but some people jumped on right away."

AN, as the site is called by regulars, is a fun stop for any A's fan, and founder Bleszinski has some tips for newbies. First among them, don't be intimidated if you don't have a background in advanced metrics.

"A Sabermetrics background is definitely not mandatory," Bleszinski said. "My suggestion is to read the community guidelines first, but one of my favorite things is going to the threads and just reading the comments as the game is going along; Michael Lewis told me the same thing. It's like sitting at the stadium and talking to a group of really intelligent, really funny fans. It's a goldmine of smart conversation. Some people don't even read the content, they just like to participate in the community."

A's players are aware of the site, and they'll check out content on occasion. (So if you're jumping on to rip a player, you might want to temper your comments—the target of your ire might actually see your post.)

"I'm not on regularly, but if I see a link or if my girlfriend points things out, it's not just fans blogging opinions—the articles I've seen are really well-written, well-reasoned," A's closer Sean Doolittle said. "They know what they're talking about, they back up whatever they're discussing with stats or metrics. It's responsible reporting, not just fans blasting their opinions. It's very interesting."

74 Charlie O. the Mule

Charlie O. wasn't just the owner. Finley also lent his name to a team mascot…a mule, briefly ending the time-honored Athletics tradition of the elephant mascot. Out with the old again, that was Finley.

The mule was the official state animal of then-heavily Democratic Missouri, and Gov. Warren Hearnes presented Finley with one for the little menagerie he'd installed down the right-field line. The collection also included goats, monkeys, rabbits, pheasants, and a horse, Warpaint, that was the Chiefs' mascot. Dyed green and yellow, sheep grazed beyond the fence, cutting down on mowing expenses; former A's manager Dick Williams recalled that Finley hired a shepherd to go along with the flock.

Finley wanted his pitchers to ride the mule in from the bullpen, offering them $50 per trip to do so, but some, like Blue Moon Odom, remember declining the offer.

Finley liked to register his four-legged version at hotels and he often took the mule into lobbies and parties. He once accompanied Charlie O. into the press room, leading one reporter to crack that you'd need a program to tell which one was the owner.

When the A's moved west, Charlie O. was part of the package. One year, according to former A's public relations director Bob Fulton, "Finley had the World Series headquarters at the Edgewater Hotel in Oakland and he had the mule there on display with bales of hay, like it was a farm, but there was some bad publicity about people eating dinner there and the mule getting its tail in their plates.

"So the hotel told the guy who was in charge of the mule, 'Keep the damn mule outside,' and an hour later, the mule's back in again—Finley's orders."

"I remember eating breakfast at the Hyatt when they brought in the mule," reporter Ron Bergman said. "It really was a nice looking animal, but still—you're trying to eat your breakfast."

Harry Caray, who broadcast Oakland A's games in 1970, told friends in Chicago that he hated working for Finley because Finley wanted him to say, "Holy Mule!" instead of his trademark "Holy Cow!"

Another short-time A's broadcaster, former major-leaguer Jimmy Piersall, had no qualms about the mule. Players and A's employees recall Piersall riding around on the mule—sometimes facing forward, sometimes backward.

"That mule had his own trailer with air conditioning," A's equipment manager Steve Vucinich said. "But Charlie wouldn't always pay his bills, and the trainer would have to call the *Oakland Tribune* to complain—then the check would be there the next day. It was a sideshow."

"Charlie O, that mule got treated better than the players, I can tell you that," A's outfielder George Hendrick said. "Damn mule. Used to make a mess all over the field, but anything that mule wanted to do was fine with Charlie."

75 Miguel Tejada

Blink and you missed Miguel Tejada in the book and movie *Moneyball.*

All he did that 2002 season was win the American League MVP Award, hitting .308 with 34 homers and 131 RBIs.

"When Jason Giambi left, Miggy became the MVP," former A's manager Art Howe said. "He took over and led the way. There

Miguel Tejada celebrates after a baserunner is gunned down at second.
(Kevork Djansezian/AP Photo)

was a fire burning in him to be the best he could be, and he was a fine shortstop, too."

Tejada drove in 72 runs in the second half of the 2002 season—including game-winning RBIs in the 18th and 19th games of Oakland's American League–record 20-game winning streak.

"Miguel was the leader of that team on the field, especially in 2002—he deserved to be MVP, he was so clutch those last few weeks of the season, as great a performance as I've ever seen," former A's outfielder Eric Byrnes said. "He was the guy."

And in an age in which playing every day is rare, Tejada was an ironman, with six consecutive seasons in a row of 162 games, three of them with the Orioles, famed for their ultimate ironman, Cal Ripken Jr.—who along with Alfredo Griffin was Tejada's idol as a child.

Tejada grew up in extreme poverty in the Dominican Republic, rendered homeless by Hurricane David in 1979, begging in the streets of Bani at the age of three, and shining shoes at the age of six, working in a garment factory at age 11. And when he was 13, his mother, Mora, died, leaving Tejada so upset he even gave up baseball for a time.

Since he was a small child, he'd played the game in the streets, using milk cartons fashioned into a glove; only a leg injury had kept one of his brothers from being considered one of the better prospects in the area. At 14, Tejada was spotted by coach Enrique Soto, who taught him the fundamentals of playing shortstop, and recommended him to A's scout Juan Marichal, the great Giants Hall of Famer.

Marichal signed Tejada, 18, for $2,000. By 23, he was in the big leagues, starting at shortstop for the A's and kicking off a career that included four 30-plus homer seasons. In 16 major-league seasons, Tejada hit 307 homers and drove in 1,302 runs—his nickname in the Dominican, where he was a longtime winter ball star with Aguilas, is "La Gua Gua" after the local buses, because he drove every one home.

He always was popular with his A's teammates, perpetually smiling and joking in a mish-mash of Spanish and English. "Even the other Dominicans couldn't understand him," former A's first baseman Scott Hatteberg said. "That made it even funnier when he told jokes; he was like Scooby-Doo, you could only make out a few words. He had his own lingo."

"Miggy was just a delight, energetic and enthusiastic," Byrnes said. "He was very soft-spoken but when he was on the field, he had some funny antics and mannerisms. He was notorious for grabbing random bats from guys to use, he liked to try everyone's, so he had a stack of about 15 bats—then one day, he struck out and he took all 15 bats and started handing them out to everyone in the crowd. I remember thinking, 'But dude, those aren't your bats!'"

Byrnes was a frequent opponent in the Dominican, where Byrnes starred with Licey, and he said that Tejada really shined in those games between the island's major rivals.

"He was a showman on the field—the greatest thing I saw was Licey versus Aguilas, the stands are packed, bottom of the ninth, two outs, and Felix Rodriguez is on the mound, throwing 100 mph. Tejada has two strikes on him—and basically, with an 0–2 count, he calls his shot," Byrnes said. "He points at Felix, Felix points at him, Miggy fouls off a ball, fouls off another one, and they're yelling at each other in Spanish, 'I'm going to get you, I'm going to get you.' And Miguel hits a ball off the fence in right center to win the game, and he's still pointing at Felix. If you knew him off the field, you'd never think it was the same guy. That was something."

76 Gus Zernial and Marilyn Monroe

Gus Zernial, who was nicknamed "Ozark Ike" after a cartoon character while a minor-league standout, was a brawny, handsome outfielder who became the first A's player since Jimmie Foxx to lead the AL in homers and RBIs, with 33 and 129 in 1951.

From 1950 through 1955, no player in the league hit more homers than Zernial's 177, and only Yogi Berra and Mickey Mantle hit more home runs in the decade. Five men, total, hit

200 or more home runs in the 1950s: Berra, Mantle, Zernial, Ted Williams, and Joe DiMaggio.

"All those guys are in the Hall of Fame," Zernial said before his death in 2011. "I can be proud to stand in the middle of that list."

Zernial drove in 100 runs or more for three consecutive years. He's also known for two other things: While with the White Sox during the spring of 1951, he posed with actress Marilyn Monroe for some publicity shots.

Joe DiMaggio first noticed Monroe when he saw those photos and he told Zernial, "How come I never get to pose with beautiful girls like that? Why should a busher like you get to meet her?'"

Zernial told DiMaggio that he should contact Monroe's press agent, Dave Marsh, who'd set up the shoot, and the Yankees star went on to marry the starlet. For years afterward, Zernial said, DiMaggio snubbed him—either mad because he thought Zernial had taken credit for introducing them (Zernial never did so but, he said, many New York sportswriters incorrectly reported that he had) or because he didn't like that particular photo of Zernial with his arms wrapped around Monroe while showing her how to swing a bat.

Zernial told *Baseball Digest* that his wife, Marla, always had been very understanding about the Marilyn Monroe episode, adding, "Besides, she came out of the same batch of women that Marilyn Monroe did! I ended up doing better than Joe did, I think."

Another photograph from that same year brought Zernial notoriety. Early in the 1951 season, he hit six homers in three games, tying a record, and for a lark, he and a photographer taped six baseballs to a bat. That shot, with Zernial flashing an 'okay' sign, wound up being Zernial's well-known 1952 Topps baseball card; *Sports Illustrated's* Steve Rushin called it the *Mona Lisa* of baseball cards because of the six balls "mysteriously affixed" to the bat. It was simple Scotch tape, Zernial said.

Later that same day, he homered again—so it could have been seven baseballs on the bat had they decided on a re-shoot.

77 The Swingin' A's

Throughout their heyday in the early- to mid-'70s, the A's lived up to their nickname, not only because of sluggers like Reggie Jackson, but because of their slugging, period.

"We had more fights than I can recall," pitcher Vida Blue said. "There should have been reality TV cameras in there—they would have made millions."

George Hendrick found out about the A's brawling ways his very first day.

"It was pretty eye-opening, but I was indoctrinated into it pretty early. I came in with a lot of fanfare, and that really bothered Reggie," Hendrick said. "We were in spring training in Mesa and I was sitting on the bench with Tommy Davis and Vida, and Reggie comes by and slaps me in the face and says, 'You're a big bag of wind.' That started a fight. That was the first fight we had.

"Reggie went and told Dick Williams and I got fined $50. So Tommy Davis went in and said, 'Hey, you fined this kid $50, you know Reggie came up and started a fight with him.' So Tommy didn't play for a while—Dick was mad that he took my side against Reggie. Then Vida went in and told him the same thing.

"So the next day Reggie comes out and we're in center field and I thought he wanted to fight, so I dropped my glove and balled up my fist, and he said, 'No, no, I don't want to fight, I just want to know if you got fined.' I said, 'Yeah, I got fined, you didn't?' And he said, 'Nope.' And the next day I got sent down to the minors.

"So it wasn't a shock for me to come in and see guys fighting all the time. After we fought, we took the field and there was nobody better on the field."

The banner year for battling was 1974. There'd been other high-profile dust-ups, especially Blue's "choking" gesture at Blue Moon Odom after the 1972 ALCS, but 1974 set a new standard.

"The people who covered the team had a unique perspective because no one was trying to hide anything," pitcher Ken Holtzman said. "As far as an act of pugilism, the best I recall was in Detroit in 1974."

Catcher Ray Fosse, an unwilling participant in that one, recalled, "Opening Day, 1974, Reggie and Billy North got into a shouting match and basically didn't talk to each other all year.

"A couple of months later in Detroit, they started fighting in the middle of the clubhouse, right in front of my locker, and Vida jumped in, but he was the starting pitcher that night so I went in to try to pull him off and basically shattered the sixth and seventh vertebrae in my neck in the fight. I was holding Vida and went back and it was like whiplash. I spent six or seven weeks in traction."

Captain Sal Bando remembers that scuffle vividly.

"The Reggie fight with Billy North in Detroit, that was unique," he said. "Baseball had just started its chapel program, and in Detroit, my locker was right where you came in from the concourse. So the chaplain came in before one game and told me, 'I'm looking for Reggie because we have chapel.'

"No sooner does he say, 'Where's Reggie?' than Reggie is right there and he's in a fight with North. I said, 'There he is.' This guy wants to talk to Reggie about chapel, and here he is, fighting.

"The best part was, Dick Green and Darold Knowles, Ken Holtzman and Rollie Fingers always played bridge and they're right to the side of North and Reggie fighting—and they didn't move.

I said, 'Guys, do something,' and they kept playing. Dick Green said, 'Sal, this is the best hand I've had this year. I'm not moving.'"

Holtzman confirmed that, saying, "We were playing bridge when the fight started and it wasn't a push and pull fight, it was punching. I had a good hand, so did Green. So we said, 'Let them beat the hell out of each other.' Even Fosse didn't get in there right away—it was the second time it started that Ray went over there, and then he's the one who wound up getting hurt. There were so dang many fights, another one wasn't out of the ordinary."

Tempers didn't subdue once the season ended. Fingers and Odom got into a scuffle at Dodger Stadium during the 1974 World Series that left Fingers with stitches in his head.

"Blue Moon Odom and Rollie got into it in the clubhouse before Game 1 at the workout, and someone picked up [the equipment manager's] shopping cart and threw it," Fosse said. "The second I saw that, I sprinted to the trainer's room. I was not breaking up any more fights. I've done my job. I was shaking like a leaf, remembering what I'd gone through.

"Then we're taking photos in the press room after the series, and Rollie and Blue Moon are sitting down at the bottom of the podium with their arms wrapped around each others. Five days earlier, they're throwing shopping carts and fighting each other."

Said Fingers, "It was a matter of pick a ticket—who would it be that day? A lot of stuff happened. Guys would be standing there, and the next minute, they'd be rolling around, swinging. Then that night, they'd be out to dinner together."

Ron Bergman covered the team for the *Oakland Tribune,* and he was a witness to most of the fisticuffs. Asked if reports of the club's brawling were overblown, Bergman laughed and said, "No, they were underblown. If I'd written about every fight, I would have been a boxing writer, not a baseball writer."

Bergman recalled Odom hitting Tommie Reynolds in the nose with a Coke bottle at a hotel in Boston, and that the room sustained $25,000 in damage. The next day, they were walking arm in arm.

Owner Charlie Finley got in on the act, too. He took swipes at at least two reporters over the years.

Not even the manager was entirely safe. Blue didn't get physical with Alvin Dark that season, but he got his point across strongly after a bad start in New York.

"Dark came out to get me and I said, 'No, I can get this guy out,' Blue said. "He said, 'Give me the ball.' So I threw the ball about the height of an NBA basket and when it hit the ground, I walked away. He said, 'That cost you $500.' I said, 'I don't care.'

"So I thought, 'I'll fix him,' I got $500 in nickels and dimes, and I looked like one of those bank guys, carrying three bags of coins. I came in and dumped them on his desk when he wasn't there.

"He called me in later and said, 'Vida, is this from you?' And I said, 'Yeah, are you going to count it?'

"He said 'No,' and kind of laughed. And he had one of the batboys give it to charity."

78 Debbi Fields

Along with MC Hammer, another famous name worked for the A's in the '70s: Debbi Sivyer, who at the age of 15 became one of the team's first ballgirls.

"They announced they were looking for ballgirls in the *Oakland Tribune* and that experience wasn't required," said Debbi—now better known as Mrs. Fields, of Mrs. Field's Cookies,

Inc. "My sister worked in the A's offices as a secretary and that helped because there were hordes and hordes of candidates.

"The fans who sat behind me were like my adoptive parents, they always worried if I was cold. It was a real community. The players, some of them were talkative and some of them weren't, but they were all nice to me; the ones I got to know were mostly the ones who sat in the bullpen, and Sal Bando, because third base was on my side. He was always very kind."

Her glovework wasn't memorable. ("I never made any spectacular plays," she said. "I tried, but those balls were coming way too fast. If anything, I was dodging them.") Her culinary skills were much more appreciated, and she wound up with her first clientele.

"I would bring my cookies and share them with the fans," Fields said. "Charlie Finley said, 'Why don't we have a milk-and-cookie break during the game?' So I would bring cookies and milk to the umpires. The umpires were older gentlemen and they were always very happy to have a cookie and milk during their break."

The ballgirl position funded Debbi Sivyer's first foray into first-class baking. Her previous efforts weren't that special.

"When I started making cookies, I used what we could afford: margarine, ordinary chocolate, imitation vanilla," she said. "With my first check from the A's, I purchased real butter, good chocolate and real vanilla, and whipped up the cookies using real ingredients. I was awestruck how much better they were. It really made a big difference. I decided from then on I would always use the best ingredients."

With her savings from working the lines at the Coliseum, Debbi bought her first car, her transportation when she opened her original cookie shop in Palo Alto.

She never forgot the man who gave her her first job.

"Charlie Finley was bigger than life," Fields said in 2006. "I called him about 12 years ago to thank him for giving me the opportunity—he was getting older and his health was failing but he still remembered me. He said he was so proud of giving me a job, and MC Hammer. I told him my being part of the Oakland A's was so wonderful for me moving forward."

Another celeb who worked at the Coliseum as a teen: Skyline High School's Tom Hanks, who was a popcorn and peanut vender before going onto Hollywood stardom—and eventually a baseball role, as a manager in *A League of Their Own*.

79 The Longest Game

Brett Anderson was scratched from a start on April 19, 2013, against the Angels—and several hours later, he wound up pitching in the same game.

Over the course of April 19 and April 20, the A's and Angels played 19 innings and Anderson, initially held out with a foot injury, worked 5⅓ innings—longer than starter Dan Straily. He allowed three hits and one run, "probably my best outing of the season—and it came in relief," the left-hander cracked.

And six hours and 32 minutes after the game began, the A's finally won 10–8 on a walk-off homer by Brandon Moss.

The team was too tired to celebrate. Josh Reddick, who usually slams teammates in the face with whipped-cream concoctions after last-second wins, just handed the tin to Moss—and Moss, on live TV, pied himself.

Moss said the next day that his young son Jayden loved that clip so much, he asked to watch it over and over. "Not me hitting the homer," Moss said of Jayden's preference. "Me hitting myself in the face with the pie."

It was the longest Oakland A's game by 32 minutes, and it was the longest game in Angels history, topping a 6:06 game. Moss' wife, sister, and two children had spent four and a half hours waiting for him in the parking lot after arriving to pick him up at the reasonable time of 9:45 PM.

The teams threw a total of 598 pitches and 40 players participated. Jed Lowrie set an A's record with nine at-bats.

And the A's even had to come back in extra innings—the Angels took the lead in the 15th when Anderson walked in a run; Adam Rosales provided a two-out RBI single in the bottom of the inning to keep things going.

Oakland left fielder Yoenis Cespedes had sent the game into extra innings in the first place, also with a two-out hit in the ninth, a single off the wall in left that scored Coco Crisp. Chris Young then nearly ended things in the 10th with a drive that appeared to strike a sign beyond the wall in left but that was ruled a triple, instead. The play was reviewed by the umpiring crew but was not changed.

Anderson did not wind up with the win, despite his heroics pitching while injured. Reliever Jerry Blevins, working his third day in a row, was the beneficiary of Moss' blast—and the left-hander also got his first career at-bat, and struck out.

"The fans were all chanting 'Jerry, Jerry,' like in the *Rocky* movie," former A's third baseman Josh Donaldson recalled. "He fouled a ball off and we were all so happy about that."

"If Jerry had gotten a hit there, he'd have been a cult hero for years and years," manager Bob Melvin said.

Donaldson said that game, which ended at 1:41 AM, left him wishing there were still a curfew in the major leagues, though. "It was terrible because we had a day game the next day on 3–4 hours of sleep and you're trying to play baseball at a high level," he said. "It would have been tougher if we'd lost though."

As for Anderson, he missed the next four months with a fractured navicular bone in his right foot.

"Around the 10ᵗʰ inning, they asked me if I could pitch and I told them I'd give it my best shot," he remembered. "And 5⅓ innings later I could barely walk off the field, and a few days later I was in a walking boot. It was pretty much all on adrenaline and being competitive. And it helped that we won the game."

80 Doc Powers

The Shibe Park opener in 1909 was marred by tragedy: Mike "Doc" Powers, who caught the ceremonial pitch that day—and who had started the Athletics' very first game, back in 1901—came out of the stadium's inaugural game after collapsing with what was thought to be food poisoning.

Powers, himself a doctor at a Philadelphia hospital in the off-season, was taken to Northwest General Hospital, but his condition worsened. The following morning, he had surgery, which determined that his lower intestines were twisted, causing gangrene, so a foot-long section of intestine was removed.

Peritonitis set in, however, and despite two more surgeries, Powers died two weeks later, at the age of 38.

Flags flew at half-staff at all major-league stadiums following Powers' death, and Philadelphia and Washington postponed their game so the players could attend his funeral. The following year, four teams participated in "Doc Powers Day," which raised $8,000 for Powers' widow and three daughters.

Reports from the time indicated that Powers first complained of abdominal pain after diving for a foul ball (some accounts say he crashed into a wall), which might make him the first player in major-league history whose death was the result on an on-field injury. Others argue that the problem was pre-existing. Author Norman Macht calls it "a fluke," a blockage caused by the telescoping of the intestines.

Rumors long have persisted that the character of "Bump" Bailey in Bernard Malamud's *The Natural* was based on Powers.

Powers, who played baseball at Notre Dame has another claim to fame: According to the Society for American Baseball Research, when Powers caught Jim Newton of the New York Highlanders (eventually the Yankees) in 1905, they formed the only all-M.D. battery in baseball history.

The A's had another death in the early years of the organization—in late 1915, their batboy and team mascot, Louis Van Zelst, died of Bright's Disease at the age of 20. Van Zelst had had a twisted spine since a fall at the age of eight, and the players rubbed his "hump" for good luck—he was enormously popular while working for the club from 1910 to 1915, known for his mimicry skills, including imitations of batters' stances.

While Van Zelst was Philadelphia's batboy, the team won four pennants and three World Series—and opposing teams even accused him of stealing signs for the team. The A's players, according to Macht, believed their good-luck charm died of a broken heart after the team lost to the Braves in the 1914 World Series.

After he died, the Athletics had what is widely considered the worst season ever by a major-league club. Philadelphia went 36–117, a modern-era low winning percentage of .235. Even the 20th century's most famous losers, the 1962 Mets (who set a record with 120 losses) still won 25 percent of their games.

Most amazing, the Athletics finished 40 games out of *seventh place*, behind the next-to-last place Senators, and they wound up 54-½ games behind AL-best Boston. Among some of their other notable failures, the 1916 A's set an AL record with 19 consecutive road losses and they went 2–28 in July.

The 1916 A's had three 20-game losers: Joe Bush (15–24 despite a 2.57 ERA), Elmer Myers (14–23), and Jack Nabors, who went a dismal 1–20. Nabors' roommate, Tom Sheehan, was 1–16.

The lowest point of the season may have come during a series at Boston. Sheehan pitched a one-hitter in the opener, but lost 1–0. Nabors had a one-hitter going into the ninth in the second game, but after the Red Sox tied the game, according to several accounts, he threw the next pitch well over the batter's head and the winning run scored easily from third.

Afterward, one of his teammates asked what happened.

"Look," Nabors is said to have replied. "I knew those guys wouldn't get me another run, and if you think I'm going to throw nine more innings on a hot day like this, you're crazy."

81 White Shoes

Always colorful, owner Charlie Finley put his team in vivid green and gold uniforms when he bought the team in late 1960—then made an even more striking change: Finley ditched the black spikes that every team had worn since the inception of organized baseball in favor of white shoes.

Many in baseball couldn't get used to the footwear; more than 40 years later, they still have detractors.

Bucking a longstanding tradition wasn't enough for Finley, though. He had to add a story to go along with it.

"The white shoes, well, Charlie told me to tell the listeners that they were made exclusively of albino kangaroos from Australia," broadcaster Monte Moore said. "Of which there were none."

The announcement led to complaints from animal rights groups, even though the white kangaroos were a Finley invention.

Immediately, the white cleats were an issue, according to Moore, who said, "The first year of the white shoes, 1967, Joe Adcock was the opposing manager and after the first pitch, he came out and said, 'I'm playing this game in protest. My players won't be able to see the ball with those white shoes.'"

Outfielder Joe Rudi recalled, "Adcock was a mountain of a man, he was huge, and after Lew Krausse threw the first pitch, Adcock comes charging out like a wild bull to protest. It must have delayed the game 20 minutes."

"The umpire just said, 'Duly noted, the game is being played under protest,'" Moore said. "The next day, the A's gave up seven runs and that was pretty much the end of the protest."

Finley made certain that the white shoes were constantly associated with the A's. Moore said that when he and seven players attended functions in the Bay Area after the 1967 season, drumming up interest in Oakland's new team, "Finley had us look around until we found white dress shoes for all those banquets. They made fun of us a few places, especially those events when the Giants were there, too."

Eventually, the white spikes wound up on the A's logo, at the suggestion of Finley's secretary, Carolyn Coffin.

"People forget that three other teams wore white shoes—the Angels, the Astros, the Senators, but never for very long," longtime A's equipment manager Steve Vucinich said. "It was tough to get them because there weren't many manufacturers, and it was very hard to clean them and preserve them. And we always had guys who would say, 'We just can't get used to them—when are we going to change to black?'"

Blue Moon Odom was one of those. "I didn't like the white shoes when I got called up," he said. "They make your feet look twice their size. People called us Barnum and Bailey clowns.

"But they grew on us. I like them now. Charlie O. said the women would come out to the game because of the uniforms and the white shoes, that they were going to bring some attention to the team."

Third baseman Sal Bando also was there for the white shoes' debut, and he said, "They took some getting used to. They felt like you had boats on. But we liked the colorful uniforms, being a young team. We didn't want to be in the same mold as everyone else. It was fun."

The A's swapped around uniform colors, around, too, as the years went on, sometimes wearing unheard-of combinations such as yellow jerseys with yellow pants or green jerseys with green pants.

"At the All-Star Game in Kansas City in 1974, nine of us, counting coaches, were there from Oakland—and we had nine different possible ensembles with the California gold and the wedding white and the Kelly green," former A's manager Dick Williams remembered before his death in 2011.

There were no road grays; Finley wanted colors that showed up well on television. For old-fashioned baseball, this was tantamount to revolution.

"When they first came out, Norm Siebern was an All-Star for us in 1963 and Ralph Houk was the American League manager," Moore said. "Houk put every player in the game except Siebern, and when he was asked why, Houk said he didn't want Siebern to be embarrassed in front of a national audience wearing that softball uniform."

Now major-league jerseys come in all sorts of shades, including teal and purple, and can change even from season to season.

"You see the alternate jerseys are a huge marketing tool for clubs," A's catcher-turned-analyst Ray Fosse said. "Charlie started all that. Before that it was all gray and white."

Finley wasn't shy about wearing the A's vivid colors himself. He was often photographed in a bright green sports coats and a green cowboy hat, or in plaid jackets that boasted the team's hues. He once claimed that he'd chosen green and yellow because they were his wife's favorite colors, and said, "If it's good enough for my wife, it's good enough for my players."

"I loved the white shoes, oh I loved them, and all the different color uniforms," former A's outfielder George Hendrick said. "You know what? Say what you want about Charlie Finley, but he was way ahead of his time, you see his influence around baseball everywhere. Until he came in, it was all pretty much black and gray."

82 Stadium Search

Few franchises are as well traveled as the Athletics, who hopped from Philadelphia to Kansas City to Oakland.

They've now been in Oakland nearly as long as their original city; the A's were in Philly for 54 years and the 2015 season will be No. 48 at the Coliseum. And yet, the A's have spent more than a decade talking about moving—and even back in the 1970s, Charlie Finley was trying to move the club, twice trying to park the A's in Denver.

Only one Oakland ownership group, the Haas family (1980–1995), never explored a potential move, and they stipulated to the next owners, Steve Schott and Ken Hofman, that the team must stay in the Bay Area. Under the two developers, though, the A's started talking to Santa Clara County about a possible stadium site, even though the area is considered part of the Giants' designated territory. During Schott and Hoffman's tenure, Portland, Las Vegas, and Sacramento were all rumored as possible destinations.

John Fisher, a Gap clothing company heir, became the principal owner in 2005, with developer Lew Wolff a minority owner and spokesman for the ownership group. The group initially looked at southern Alameda County, within the A's territory, for a stadium site, settling on Fremont. There was some investment, including land purchase, before the plan was scuttled for a number of reasons, among them the fact that the A's owners did not believe accompanying development—housing, retail—would work in the location.

Again, the A's turned toward Santa Clara County, this time to San Jose, despite the territorial rights issue with the Giants. The 10th biggest city in the country and the heart of Silicon Valley, San Jose appeared a prime location for a ballpark, and the city offered up a ballpark site right near a transit hub and the arena where the NHL's Sharks play.

The Giants protested, vigorously, and in March 2009, commissioner Bud Selig appointed a panel to look at the A's stadium matter, acknowledging that the club does need a new ballpark.

Oft-mocked, the panel never issued any public report during Selig's five-plus remaining years in office, though by the end of his tenure, things had been complicated by San Jose's anti-trust lawsuit against MLB for denying the city the right to do business with the A's. The Ninth U.S. Circuit Court of Appeals upheld the dismissal of San Jose's lawsuit in January 2015, and the city announced plans to appeal that decision to the Supreme Court.

Were it not for the territorial rights, assigned in 1993 for a Giants stadium ballot measure in San Jose that failed, the A's doubtless would have tried to get a new ballpark built in the South Bay long before now.

The pro–San Jose side points out that no other two-team markets have defined territories within their areas, as well as the fact that the Giants were assigned five counties, the A's two. In terms of land mass, population and income levels within the territories, the Giants are the clear winners, and they also have a gorgeous, baseball-only stadium right on the Bay (and they've won three World Series in a five-year stretch in it), while the A's play in a multi-use stadium that is nearly 50 years old and that has had infrastructure issues.

The Giants argue that both the San Francisco and Oakland ownership groups bought their teams with the territorial rights in place and that the San Francisco team took on significant debt with the understanding that San Jose was part of its market. Many around baseball believe the rights should have reverted back to the mutual-shared area enjoyed before the Giants' failed ballot measure, but that ship has sailed and the Giants owners purchased their club with San Jose included—and the A's owners without.

And what of Oakland, always overshadowed in the Bay Area? The A's have won four championships there, the fans are loyal and passionate. The team does not regularly sell out, but many fans believe that that's because the owners have alienated longtime ticket holders.

Major League Baseball has hinted that an alternate Oakland location might be the best bet, perhaps even a new baseball-only stadium at the Coliseum site. But until the San Jose lawsuit is settled, everything is on hold, while the Warriors' plans to leave for San Francisco and the Raiders' rumored search for a new home further complicate things. Were cash-strapped Oakland somehow to make a big push to keep the Raiders, the A's—who signed a 10-year lease at the Coliseum in 2014—might have to look elsewhere altogether.

83 Integration

The A's had only two black players in Philadelphia. First was Bob Trice, a rookie pitcher, came up in 1953, six years after Jackie Robinson broke baseball's color barrier with the Dodgers. Trice appeared in 26 games over three seasons with the A's; at one point in 1954, however, he asked to be sent back to Ottawa, according to author Mark Stang. He told reporters that the game wasn't fun anymore; "it was work."

At one point during 1954, Trice was part of an all-star Negro Leagues barnstorming tour that included Jackie Robinson, Roy Campanella, Larry Doby, Don Newcombe, and Minnie Minoso.

The team's second black player was Vic Power, a flashy first baseman from Puerto Rico who, in the book *We Played the Game,* recounts in great detail his experiences with racism while playing in the U.S., especially in the minor leagues in the South.

Power made it to the majors when the team was still in Philadelphia (he was part of the 11-player deal with the Yankees that Eddie Joost hated in 1954), but the bulk of his race-related trouble with the A's came in Kansas City, where he felt that he was targeted by police because he openly dated white women.

"I'd be driving my Cadillac 25 mph and the police would pull me over, and I'd have to give them the name of the dealership where I bought it," Power said. "When I'd tell them, 'I'm Vic Power, the ballplayer,' they'd say, 'Okay, we were just making a routine investigation.'

"The editor of the black paper in Kansas City wrote that he saw 50 policemen while driving by the ballpark, but when he saw a man beating a screaming woman two blocks past, there were no cops around because they were back at the ballpark 'waiting for Vic Power so they could make a routine investigation.'"

During spring training of 1958, while with the K.C. A's, Power wasn't allowed to use the restroom at a gas station in Lake Okeechobee, Florida, when the team bus stopped there. The gas station attendant wouldn't let Power go in because he was black, then he got mad when Power didn't return the Coke bottle he'd purchased because he wasn't finished with it. Power offered him the quarter deposit, he said, but the attendant insisted on the bottle, so Power pushed it at him.

"He then ran and called the sheriff and told him to arrest 'that black bastard in the back of the bus,'" Power recalled.

The players wouldn't let the sheriff on the bus, though, and scraped up $500 on the spot to settle the matter. After that, Power said, the A's left him behind when they went to play in small towns during the spring.

Power, who died in 2005 at the age of 78, was best known for being one of the first players to catch everything one-handed—and for stealing home twice in one game in 1958 while playing for the Indians.

In his second season with the A's, Power hit .319 and was the runner-up to Detroit's Al Kaline for the batting crown.

84 Balfour Rage

Even during spring training, reliever Grant Balfour was spitting fire, swearing up a storm on the mound, generally behaving like a madman.

Kind of scary for a young catcher, borrowed for the day from minor-league camp, a memory that still tickles former A's lefty Brett Anderson.

"I remember in 2011, a minor-league catcher was out there for the first time and Grant told him, 'Poke me in the eye. Piss me off. I need to get fired up,' and the kid was like, 'Dude, I'm just over here from minor-league camp, I'm not poking you in the eye and hurting you and getting in trouble,'" Anderson said. "But Grant just needed that adrenaline, needed to get that intensity—he is wired a little differently."

Balfour already had a reputation for R-rated hollering and vein-popping anger before he got to Oakland—he had a memorable postseason shouting match with White Sox infielder Orlando Cabrera in 2008, telling Cabrera to "sit the [expletive] down."

"Balfour always had that mentality," former A's outfielder Jonny Gomes said. "It rubbed some people the wrong way, but he has an electric arm and I'm all for it—I'd rather have to dial a guy down than dial him up. If you have to try to get a guy amped up, there's a problem. Not ever an issue with Balf."

The fiery Aussie didn't earn the A's closer role until 2012 with Oakland, in his second crack at it that season. Balfour fit in nicely with the tradition of wacko relievers such as Al "The Mad Hungarian" Hrabosky, pacing around the mound and cussing at himself. The fans in the right-field bleachers at the Coliseum loved it—they started a "Balfour Rage" phenomenon, head-banging and hair-spinning to Balfour's warmup music, Metallica's "One."

Once installed as Oakland's closer, Balfour flourished. He was on the mound when the A's clinched the division title on the last day of the 2012 season, and the next year, he really took off. He established a franchise record with saves in 44 consecutive opportunities, eclipsing the mark set by Hall of Famer Dennis Eckersley, and he was named to the 2013 American League All-Star team.

Balfour left as a free agent after the season, heading back to Tampa Bay, but he remains popular with his ex-teammates and with the Coliseum fans, who went nuts when Balfour made his first appearance back in Oakland with the Rays.

"There were definitely times the Balfour Rage got my hair standing up," former A's third baseman Josh Donaldson said. "I love Balfour, I do, he's one of my favorite guys I've played with. I hated playing behind him because he worked so slow, but I loved the result, and at the end of the day, he was getting the job done.

"He broke the franchise record and there have been some pretty good closers in Oakland history. He's an absolute beauty and I don't mean his looks—his personality, his intensity, his passion, I absolutely loved him."

85 Crash Davis

Thanks to the movie *Bull Durham,* every longtime minor-leaguer gets dubbed "a real-life Crash Davis," after Kevin Costner's wise old catcher.

But there was a real Lawrence "Crash" Davis—who played for the Philadelphia Athletics from 1940 to 1942 and hit .230 with two homers in 148 games. His big-league career ended when he was drafted into the Navy during World War II.

Davis was a second baseman, not a catcher, but Davis was the model for Costner's character and he served as a consultant on the set of Ron Shelton's 1988 film. A legend in the Carolina League (where he did play with the Durham Bulls, among other teams), Davis liked to tell the Philadelphia Historical Society that he was "the consultant for all those love scenes" with Susan Sarandon.

Davis, who got his nickname after a major collision going after a pop-up when he was 14 years old, also played Hall of Famer Sam Crawford in another of Ron Shelton's movies, *Cobb*.

Davis played at Duke, where his coach was former A's pitcher Jack Coombs.

"Coach Coombs was kind of the type of manager Mr. Mack was," Davis told authors Hank Utley and Scott Verner. "He didn't wear a baseball uniform, at least when I was there. He sat on the bench with his hat and suit. He didn't get out on the field either. Just like Mr. Mack, he always sent one of the assistant coaches out to change pitchers and he didn't argue with the umpires. But he had a great, great knowledge of baseball."

Davis shared an experience with many other Philadelphia A's players—he was lured to the team by Connie Mack only to be underwhelmed by the contract offer.

He told Utley and Verner: "When I got to Shibe Park in Philadelphia, Mr. Mack said he was going to give me $300. I said, 'Mr. Mack, I won't play for that. I'm making about that much now. He said. 'Well young man, if you don't want it, just go home.'

"I couldn't go home; I didn't have any money. So I signed."

Davis admitted in *The Independent Carolina Baseball League* that he wasn't much of a big-leaguer—but his first big-league at-bat came against Bob Feller (he popped up) and he was on the field for an important day. Ted Williams came to Philadelphia chasing the .400 mark in the final series of the season.

"On Saturday he went none for four and went down right on the .400 mark," Davis told Utley and Verner. "He could have sat out the double header the next day and still hit .400 but he elected to play. I played in both of those games. I played second base in the first game and first base in the second.

"People used to think that maybe we would try to throw those games and Mr. Mack told us, 'This is baseball and if I ever find out anyone is letting down, I'm going to get you kicked out of baseball.' But Porter [Vaughan] was a left-handed pitcher and Ted Williams was a left-handed hitter and he'd never seen Porter. Porter was just brought up, you know. It's very difficult for a guy to hit against anybody if he's never seen them before. But it didn't stop Ted Williams, though, because he got six for eight in the double header. He's the greatest hitter who ever lived."

Davis also had an unusual experience his first time playing first base for the A's after a career spent at second base.

"We were riding down the elevator and Mr. Mack said, 'Davie, can you play first base?' I replied, 'Never played it but I can.' So that day I played first base against the Chicago White Sox in Comiskey Park," Davis said. "And…when you play second base and a ball goes through your legs, you don't chase it. Anyway, a ball went over my head that day at first. I didn't really hustle. My cap came off and I went over to pick it up before I picked up the ball. The next day's paper said, 'Davis retrieves cap before ball.'"

Chuck Hartman, the longtime coach at Virginia Tech, played for Davis at Gastonia (S.C.) High School, and Hartman told *Baseball America* his favorite Crash Davis story: "The whole stadium was full of ladies, and he came to bat and shook his rear and did a little can-can dance in the box," Hartman said. "He said the place went crazy and he had phone calls from women all over the place."

Davis might have been forgotten entirely except for Shelton, who told Davis that he was going through the Carolina League record books and saw that Davis led the league in doubles in 1948. He liked the sound of "Crash Davis," but for the movie, Shelton changed the doubles to homers.

Suddenly, near the end of his life, Davis was famous.

"Like anywhere I go in America, they call my name, they know me," Davis told the *Washington Post* in 2001, the year he died. "Then they step back and they look at you like a different person."

86 Eric Chavez

In the first decade of the new millennium, there was no better fielding third baseman in the game than Eric Chavez.

The longest-serving A's player in the Billy Beane era, Chavez earned six consecutive Gold Gloves, taking full advantage of the huge foul ground at the Coliseum with an endless array of sprinting, diving, rolling catches.

"He was so magical, I was blown away by that guy," former A's first baseman Scott Hatteberg said, "It was like watching Xbox action, he'd get to balls he had no business getting to. His reactions were like a video game."

"He was signed as a shortstop, and that's the kind of great hands he showed," former Oakland manager Art Howe said. "With Eric and Miguel Tejada, it felt like we had two shortstops on the left side of the infield. I mean, Chavvy rarely even had a bad bounce off him, and he had a very accurate arm. He seemed to get better and better as the years went on."

That, Chavez said, was because of one man: Former A's third-base and infield coach Ron Washington. Chavez appreciated Washington's work so much, he gave Washington his 2004 Gold Glove trophy. And when that trophy was too damaged by Hurricane Katrina to be salvaged, Chavez presented Washington, by then the Rangers manager, with a duplicate trophy in a ceremony on the field at Texas.

"As they say, there's no crying in baseball, but sometimes, you get close," Washington said. "This is one of those moments."

Chavez, a first-round pick in 1996, spent 12-plus seasons with the A's and hit 230 homers and drove in 787 runs, putting up an OPS of .821, but injuries, particularly back problems, plagued his

Eric Chavez shows off his 2003 Gold Glove Award. (Justin Sullivan)

final years after he'd signed the largest deal in team history, six years and $66 million.

"The thing I think that gets lost toward the tail end of Chavvy's career was how great he was during his prime," former A's outfielder Eric Byrnes said. "At one time, Eric Chavez was the most talented baseball player I had ever seen. When I first came up, he was younger than me, maybe 22, and the way the ball came off his bat was like few others, there was not a quicker bat around. He was far and away the best defensive third baseman I'd ever seen. He was a very good baserunner. Everything came so easily to that guy.

"All around, he was one of the best players in the game, but not many people outside of Oakland know that—people just say, 'Oh, yeah, he had a solid major-league career.' I'm telling you: If Eric Chavez had been healthy throughout his career, he would have been a Hall of Famer, there is no doubt in my mind."

87 Join the Historical Society

For nearly two decades, a museum in suburban Philadelphia housed exhibits from the Athletics' half century in that town, but sadly, lease issues led the facility to close in 2013. With only a handful of surviving Philadelphia A's players, interest had dwindled.

"All the players are dead," said Philadelphia Athletics Historical Society founder and executive director Ernie Montella. "We couldn't afford the space anymore."

Some of the Society's artifacts remain on display at Spike's Trophies on Grant Avenue in Philadelphia, and the Philadelphia History Museum in downtown Philadelphia has featured the A's in past exhibits.

The Society still holds live auctions several times a year; 1952 American League MVP Bobby Shantz is a regular at the events.

Fans who would like to help keep alive the legacy of the Philadelphia A's, however, can still join the Philadelphia Athletics Historical Society, which puts out an annual newsletter. Send $20 to P.O. Box 42, Hatboro PA. 19040.

There is also a Facebook group dedicated to saving the Philadelphia Athletics Historical Society—as well as a Facebook page called Bring Your A's Game, which is dedicated to restoring the A's to their original city.

88. Voos and Mickey

One man has worked for the A's throughout the team's entire time in Oakland—and a Hall of Famer endorsed his initial hire.

Steve Vucinich, now the clubhouse manager, started in ticket services in 1968. He worked there all of one night—Opening Night.

"When the team moved out from Kansas City in 1968, they hired five guys to work in the clubhouse—and I knew four of the five, even though they didn't know each other," Vucinich said. "After the first game, the one kid I didn't know quit, so the other guys told me I should go see the equipment manager, Al Zych."

That's when one of the game's greats stepped in.

"Joe DiMaggio was standing there when I said I'd like to work in the clubhouse," Vucinich said—DiMaggio was an A's coach and advisor at the time—"And Joe asked where I went to high school, and I told him St. Joe's in Alameda.

"He told Zych, 'A Catholic, hire him.'

"That's not why I got the job, but it is a true story."

Vucinich, widely known as "Vuc" (pronounced "Voos"), worked as a ballboy and clubhouse attendant, then as the visiting clubhouse manager before moving to the home side in 1994. He has more institutional knowledge than almost anyone in baseball.

"I call him the historian," A's broadcaster and former catcher Ray Fosse said. "Duane Kuiper [the Giants broadcaster and long-time major-leaguer] calls him the Godfather. You see how former players always come over to see him, say hi—he's loved by everybody. You see the pictures in his office, there's Vuc, there's the great Joe D. I don't think anyone knows more about the history of the game and the A's."

There is only one A's player that Vucinich did not meet—the team acquired Ryan Langerhans while on a road trip in 2007 while he was with the team, and they traded him three days later. Vucinich made sure to introduce himself to Langerhans at the first opportunity after that, when Langerhans was with Seattle two years later.

"Catfish Hunter was my favorite player of all time—I have an All-Vuc team from my years with the A's, including 20 years on the visiting side," Vucinich said. "You didn't have to be a superstar, but a lot of them are because you see how well some of those guys handle all of that attention. Guys like Cal Ripken Jr., Allen Trammell, Dave Righetti, Jason Giambi, Dwight Evans, Kuiper, Buddy Bell, Dave Henderson—the guys who go above and beyond."

The A's second-longest serving employee is, like Vucinich, a legend in the business: Mickey Morabito, the director of team travel. The one-time Yankees PR man arrived with manager Billy Martin in 1980, and he was an easy sell to then-owner Charlie Finley, who hated to spend money.

"He came over to be our PR director and travel secretary—of course Finley loved that because that was two positions and he only had to pay one guy," Vucinich said. "Mickey had a good under-standing of how to deal with Billy, which helped—Billy had just gotten fired for getting in a fight with a marshmallow salesman, and everywhere he went, people would get drunk and challenge him, 'I'll go fight the tough guy.'"

Morabito, who'd started as a Yankees batboy in 1970, said he'd had to handle some media crises for Martin in New York, so they'd developed a good relationship. And anyone who could somehow finesse Yankees hotheads Martin, Reggie Jackson and George Steinbrenner was special.

"I'm the only Yankees PR guy who had Reggie, Billy, and George at the same time, and it was always two of them against the third—Billy and Reggie were mad at George, George and Reggie were made at Billy, whatever it was that day," Morabito said with a chuckle. "I used to call it the Vicious Triangle."

The first person to meet Morabito when he joined the A's during the spring of 1980? Vucinich, who whisked Morabito to a legendary lounge in Scottsdale.

"He was the guy who picked me up at the airport—I thought we'd go to the team hotel, but we went straight to the Pink Pony," Morabito said. "I'd never been to Arizona before and the first place I went was to the Pony—and Billy's already there, sitting in a booth, holding court. I wound up spending a lot of time there."

Vucinich reckoned that the reason both men have lasted so long is that they've been able to adapt as the business of baseball evolved. Big-league clubhouses are much different than they used to be—the players make huge sums, the demands can be much greater—and team travel has changed drastically.

"We used to take 100 percent commercial flights—50 people changing planes, all of that," Morabito said. "Once when Milwaukee was still in the American League, we missed a commer-cial flight after a game, extra innings or something, so we had to go to Chicago to fly out of O'Hare.

"I'm trying to get 50 tickets on a commercial flight, and I was so proud of myself when I did, but then we had a city transit bus that was supposed to take us to the airport in Milwaukee. I told the driver, 'We're going to O'Hare,' and he said. 'I can't go to Chicago!' So here I am on a Sunday afternoon trying to find a bus to get to Chicago. I did it, but can you imagine putting players on a commercial flight now?"

They may be in the background, but with Vucinich and Morabito, the A's are in extraordinarily good hands, spoiled even.

"I don't think anyone's better than Mickey," Fosse said "I will say I've never seen a more conscientious person in my life—I don't think there's ever been a screwup. He's the best at what he does, just like Vuc. The A's are fortunate to have had those two together."

Marco Scutaro

Even before Marco Scutaro provided the game-winning single to give the Giants the 2012 championship—and earned MVP honors in the NLCS that year—he had made a name with the A's for his clutch performances.

In less than three years, from June 26, 2004, to April 15, 2007, Scutaro had eight walk-off hits for the A's, plus a sacrifice bunt-error vs. the Angels to give Oakland another last second win.

"Marco just had a knack for driving in runs late, like, 'You've got to be kidding me,'" former A's outfielder Eric Byrnes said. "I've thought about this a lot, especially after what he did with the Giants. He has such a short, compact swing, so that helps—and Scoot is just totally unfazed. The bigger the moment, the calmer

Scutaro Walk-Off Hits/Bunt With A's

Date	Play	Result
6/26/04	RBI single in 10th	8–7 vs. Giants
8/25/04	3-run HR in 9th	3–0 vs. Orioles
4/16/05	Sac/error in 10th	1–0 vs. Angels
4/27/05	RBI single in 9th	2–1 vs. White Sox
6/15/05	RBI single in 9th	3–2 vs. Mets
7/27/05	RBI single in 10th	5–4 vs. Indians
4/4/06	RBI single in 9th	4–3 vs. Yankees
9/22/06	RBI single in 12th	5–4 vs. Angels
4/15/07	3-run HR in 9th	5–4 vs. Yankees

he gets. Most players, the bigger the moment, the more excited you get. He was just even-keel, it made the situation easy for him, he slowed it all down. I'd be surprised if there are many players with more game-winning hits per at-bats than Marco."

Scutaro was the only batter ever to hit an 0–2 pitch off Yankees great Mariano Rivera for a walk-off homer—a three-run shot with two outs in the ninth inning on April 15, 2007. Afterward, Oakland second baseman Mark Ellis said by that point—it was Scutaro's eighth walk-off hit with the team—the A's players would have been more surprised if Scutaro hadn't gotten a hit in that situation.

Never projected as a starter, Scutaro bailed the A's out time and again when there were injuries to regulars, including playing much of 2004 at second after Ellis tore the labrum in his right shoulder and much of the following two seasons at shortstop while Bobby Crosby was hurt. And in 2006, Scutaro was instrumental in helping Oakland get past the first round of the playoffs for the only time in the Billy Beane era, hitting .333 with four doubles and six RBIs in a three-game sweep of the Twins.

"Scutaro—what an asset," former A's first baseman Scott Hatteberg said. "You could put him in any situation and he'd do something. He was so smooth with the glove at so many spots and underrated with the bat, just a heck of a baseball player."

The A's traded Scutaro to Toronto after the 2007 season, for two minor-leaguers.

"I think he was undervalued because he wasn't a guy who walked a lot, so they didn't view him as an everyday guy," former A's third baseman Eric Chavez said. "It's funny, because once he left us, he became much better at that, his on-base percentage got a lot higher. He really became that player we all knew he was.

"He was like a .240-.250 hitter but every time he stepped into the box late in games, it always worked out if we needed a hit, he got it. The Giants found that out."

In 2012, the Rockies traded Scutaro to the Giants, and he worked his magic on the big stage.

"When the Giants got Scutaro, a friend of mine who is part of their ownership group called and asked me what to expect," Byrnes recalled. "I said, 'The one thing I promise you is you will get one of the most clutch performers ever. I don't know if he'll hit .300—but he will win you games.'"

90 Other Hall Of Famers

Throughout their history, the A's have employed more than their fair share of Hall of Famers who are far more associated with other clubs.

The first of those—Nap Lajoie—wound up having a large impact on the game, in a legal sense, just as the early modern era was beginning.

Many of the eight new American League clubs fielded teams in 1901 by raiding National League clubs, luring more than 100 players away even though they were already under contract. Lajoie was the most high-profile team-jumper; A's manager Connie Mack convinced him to leave the Phillies with an offer of $4,000 that nearly doubled his salary.

Lajoie became the central figure of Philadelphia's new club, providing it with immediate credibility. So it hit the team hard when on April 21, 1902, two days before Opening Day, the Pennsylvania Supreme Court invalidated Lajoie's contract with his new club and ordered him to return to the Phillies.

The case, Philadelphia Ball Club v. Napoleon Lajoie, is still cited in sports law. The state supreme court upheld the National League's reserve clause and concluded, in part, "The services of the defendant are of such a unique character, and display such a special knowledge, skill, and ability as renders them of peculiar value to the plaintiff. The action of the defendant in violating his contract is a breach of good faith, for which there would be no adequate redress at law."

Mack started Lajoie on Opening Day at Baltimore, but after receiving a telegram informing him that there was an injunction barring Lajoie from participating, Mack removed him from the game.

The great second baseman sat for two months as appeals were filed and debates raged, but the league was desperate to keep its top player. So when lawyers determined the ruling only applied in the state of Pennsylvania, AL president Ban Johnson transferred Lajoie to Cleveland, where he rescued a failing franchise and was so popular that the team was dubbed "the Naps." Whenever the club played at Philadelphia, Lajoie remained in Cleveland (though some said he headed to Atlantic City when left behind).

The initial injunction covered several other A's: Chick Fraser and Bill Bernhard, who had been two of the Phillies' best pitchers in 1900, were transferred to Cleveland, too. Elmer Flick and Bill Duggleby, who went from the Phillies to Athletics before the 1902 season, were returned to their original club, and shortstop Monte Cross stayed with the A's because the Phillies apparently didn't mind his relocation.

"I felt as though they had swept my ball club right from under me," Mack said after the ruling.

In 1903, the two leagues came to an agreement that allowed all players who had jumped to the American League to remain there, and the Phillies let the injunction against Lajoie lapse.

He did not return to the Athletics until 1915, when he was 40 years old. He spent his final two major-league seasons in Philadelphia, the city he'd once been barred from entering.

Lajoie, who is most associated with the Indians, was the sixth man voted into the Baseball Hall of Fame, elected in 1937 along with Tris Speaker and Cy Young.

Ty Cobb, who was part of the Hall of Fame's first class in 1936, also played for the Philadelphia A's, finishing his career with the team in 1927 and 1928. The Georgia Peach, the early game's greatest hitter, still had something left: he hit .357 in 1927 and .323 in 1928.

Tris Speaker, age 40, played in 64 games with the A's in 1928 and he also went into the Hall in 1937 along with Lajoie—and with Connie Mack. He and Cobb both joined the A's after allegations of fixing games while acting as player/managers; they were exonerated by commissioner Kenesaw Mountain Landis, the accusations chalked up as attempts at personal revenge by former Detroit pitcher Dutch Leonard. Speaker was reinstated to the Indians, Cobb to the Tigers but their teams declared them available to other suitors.

Told both men were free, Norman Macht writes, Mack was elated and said, "I certainly would like to have both Cobb and Speaker, also Babe Ruth and a few others."

In 1928, former Philadelphia star Eddie Collins returned after 12 years in Chicago. Age 39, he hit .338 in a bench role and led the league in pinch hits.

Mack always had a soft spot for the game's old heroes, and, from a baseball standpoint, he hoped all three—Cobb, Speaker and Collins—would be role models for the A's rising stars, such as Jimmie Foxx.

That proved to be the case. The 1928 team, with the three greats, won 98 games but finished in second place in the American League.

Over the next three seasons, Philadelphia won 313 games and played in three World Series, winning titles in 1929 and 1930.

Philadelphia came close to acquiring Ruth before he was a big name. In 1914, Mack decided to break up his first championship club. The main reason he spurned Baltimore's offer of Ruth, at the time the Orioles' top pitching prospect, along with two other players for $10,000? Mack allegedly told Orioles owner Jack Dunn, "Sell him where you can get some money. You could use it as well as I."

Cincinnati passed on Ruth, too, so Dunn, whose International League team was suffering because of Federal League competition in Baltimore, sold Ruth to the Red Sox.

Two other big names played for Mack briefly—but he discounted them too soon: Tigers' Hall of Famer George Kell began his career in Philadelphia, where he played well at third. Mack was never convinced he'd hit in the majors, though, and traded him in 1946. Kell, who was batting .299 at the time of the deal, won the AL batting title in 1949.

Another man who made the Hall of Fame despite Mack's doubts was second baseman Nellie Fox. Fox was signed by Mack at the age of 16, came up at the age of 19 and played briefly with the A's in 1948 and 1949. Mack was so underwhelmed he convinced his friend, Senators owner Clark Griffith, not to spend $10,000 to pick him up on waivers. Instead, Mack traded Fox for back-up catcher Joe Tipton.

Fox went on to lead the league in hits four times with the White Sox. He was the AL MVP in 1959 and made 12 All-Star teams—none with the A's, who struggled throughout Fox's fine career.

91 Josh Reddick

Josh Reddick is many things to the A's: Gold Glove defender. Thirty-plus home run hitter. And marketing genius.

When Reddick arrived in 2012 after coming over from Boston in exchange for closer Andrew Bailey, he got his first chance to be an everyday player in the big leagues. He crushed 32 homers and was named the Gold Glove right fielder. He was a key figure as the A's chased down Texas the final weekend of the season to win their first division crown in six years.

Since then, Reddick's offense has fluctuated, but his defensive ability remains first rate.

"Watching him play every day, I don't understand how he doesn't win the Gold Glove every year," former A's outfielder Brandon Moss said in late 2014. "He's the best defender on our team, and it's not even close. His arm is incredible. And as an outfielder, I know how hard it is to get to some of the balls he runs down, and Josh makes it look easy."

Reddick has made some storied catches, like the "Spider-Man" catch in Toronto in 2012—he clambered up the chain-link fence in right, turned, clung to the wall and waited to grab a drive by Travis Snyder.

"Why yes, I am part spider," he told reporters afterwards.

Reddick's best catch, though, came in a spring-training game against the Giants in 2014, when he scaled the wall in right at Scottsdale Stadium and extended his glove well over the fence to rob Michael Morse of a homer. Morse's next time up, Reddick nabbed another would-be homer.

The first of those was the stuff of legends—even in a spring game. Reddick has made a habit of robbing homers, but he called that catch—easily found on YouTube and on MLB.com—the best of his career "by far."

"That was nuts," former A's third baseman Josh Donaldson said.

"Twelve on a scale of 10," A's pitcher Jesse Chavez said.

Reddick has one of the best arms in baseball. Over his first three seasons with Oakland, he had 29 assists, including 15 in 2012, but the number keeps dropping as opponents stop testing him. "I don't know why anyone ever runs on him at all," Donaldson said, "but guys do it and you go, 'Why?'"

Reddick, a natural showman, revels in attention. Within days of his Spider-Man catch, he was wearing a Spider-Man costume in the clubhouse, and he donned it one night to deliver a whipped-cream pie to Coco Crisp's face during the postgame TV interview.

"Josh asked me one day if he could put on his Spider-Man costume and pie someone," A's outfielder and team leader Jonny Gomes said. "I was like, 'Oh, my, the questions you never think you'll be asked,' and said, 'No chance.'

"But he really wanted to do it, and I started thinking about it. It's all in fun. I'm not a principal on yard duty, I'm not a dream-crusher. So I said, 'On further review, do whatever you want to do, have fun.'"

Reddick's love of professional wrestling has earned him a lot of notice, as has his facial hair, which at times has engulfed him caveman-style. In 2014, he made national news with his selection of walkup music: George Michael's "Careless Whisper," a 1980s pop ballad.

"Careless Whisper" became something of a sensation, with fans going nuts for it and dancing in the aisles. TV cameras caught A's reliever Sean Doolittle swaying to the song in the bullpen.

"That was a bombshell. For something that was just so simple—something I heard one day and thought that might be good—it just took off," Reddick said. "I didn't think it would get national attention, but *Rolling Stone* magazine, who'd have ever thought I'd be in that? Every team loved it, every media person. It would have been nice if we could have gotten ol' George to come to the Coliseum though. I started hitting when I was using it and then fans started swaying to it, bringing saxophones, that was neat to see."

Reddick started the A's signature whipped-cream walk-off-pie routine, and he said that he never has received proper credit for another of the team's popular celebratory rituals, 2012's "Bernie Lean" dance.

"I'm the one who came up with the whole 'Bernie Lean' thing, that's never come out before," he said. "Coco and Jerry Blevins always take credit for it, but I'm the one who was playing it in the clubhouse. Blevins is going to give me hell for saying it, but I'm the one who started that."

Throughout the latter portion of the 2014 season, Reddick sported superhero underoos in the clubhouse after games, never failing to get a chuckle out of his teammates and the coaching staff. The kid-style underpants were revealed to the public during the A's wild-card clinching celebration when a teammate posted a photo online.

"I bought them five years ago and had them in Georgia, and I went home on an off-day and was leaving for a rehab assignment. I looked around for some boxers, found those and thought, 'This could be a funny clubhouse thing,'" Reddick said. "I wore them for the rehab assignment, I hit well, then wore them at Florida, hit well—and before that, I'd been hitting terrible.

"They seemed to be working and they're surprisingly comfortable so I wasn't going to switch it up. If you believe in it, you don't switch it."

As always, Reddick was just ahead of the curve; national magazines began writing about the popularity of adult underoos two months later.

"Redd sometimes gets too caught up in making people happy and trying to make them laugh," close friend Moss said. "I love him to death, he's one of the most genuinely nice and respectful guys around, and sometimes you wouldn't know that from his public persona because it looks like he's all about making people notice him.

"That said, Redd does like attention and he does do things for it. And when you think about it, there's nothing bad about good publicity, he loves it, and he ain't hurting anybody. He's just having fun."

92 Move to K.C.

By 1954, the A's attendance was down around the 300,000 mark. Playing at the same ballpark, the Phillies drew more than double that. "They were the kings of Philadelphia," Athletics outfielder Gus Zernial said.

It came as no surprise, then, when the Mack brothers, who'd heavily mortgaged the team, finally sold. A's player Eddie Joost said he heard that prominent Philadelphian Jack Kelly (father of actress Grace Kelly) was in line to buy the club for $1.5 million, but the deal fell through because the Macks wanted to keep control of the front office.

Another bid was made by Chicago insurance man Charles O. Finley, who put in a bid of $3 million. Just an hour before that, however, Chicago businessman Arnold Johnson—who specifically arrived early to beat out any competition—had offered $3.5 million, and the Macks agreed.

"I had a check as big as Johnson's," Finley told author Bill Libby, "but I never got a chance to wave it."

A "Save the A's" campaign in Philadelphia couldn't stop the sale. Connie Mack, now 91, reluctantly approved the deal and an era was over. Johnson moved the Athletics to Kansas City the following season.

"The writing was on the wall," first baseman Lou Limmer said. "The team wasn't going well, there were financial problems. They were nice guys, but even the coaches were stabbing each other in the back. It wasn't a nice feeling. And they wanted to cut everyone's contracts. We had a few players who didn't care, just wanted to see how many hits they could get, but most of us tried.

"We knew they were going to K.C. They took as many people as they could, and got rid of the rest. It was an unhappy feeling in Philadelphia. A lot of history went down the drain. Even now there are a lot of A's fans there and they're fantastic, just fantastic. I'm not sure the city has ever had the same connection with the Phillies."

Kansas City, on the other hand, was overjoyed to get a big-league team, and attendance quadrupled.

"We all heard about the big welcome parade, and that is just what happened," Gus Zernial wrote in his memoirs. "Thousands welcomed us. And we felt pretty good about that.... The fans were more enjoyable to watch than the team on the field. I had never played before a more enthusiastic bunch of fans for one season. I had a fan club that wore letters on their sweaters spelling out Z E R N I A L.

"The fans in Kansas City should have a book written about them. I can't praise the fans any more than to say they were great."

Under Lou Boudreau, the former Indians great, the Athletics went 63–91 and finished in sixth place that first season in Kansas City. It was the best they'd do while in Missouri. They'd lose 90 games or more nine times during their 13 seasons in K.C., and attendance tailed off dramatically.

93 Roy Steele

The most storied public address announcer in baseball history is, of course, Bob Sheppard of the Yankees.

Right behind the legendary Sheppard, though, is Roy Steele, who was at the microphone at the Oakland Coliseum from 1968, when the A's moved from Kansas City, to late 2005, when an esophageal illness prevented Steele, then 73, from working a full schedule. Dick Callahan has filled in for Steele much of the time since then, though Steele has returned, to great fanfare, several times—including on his own bobblehead-giveaway night in 2007, an honor few PA announcers can claim.

In 2006, Steele told Gwen Knapp of the *San Francisco Chronicle* that he got his start in public speaking as a minister, a vocation he held for 17 years. He was working a part-time gig as a water-ski-show announcer at Marine World when Charlie Finley brought the A's to Oakland, and he got the job at the Coliseum as soon as he applied.

Jon Miller, the longtime national broadcaster and Giants radio play-by-play man, gave Steele his "Voice of God" nickname when Miller was working for the A's in 1974.

Few players got to know Steele well during his time with the A's—he was way up in the press level—but they all knew who he was and loved hearing his baritone reading the lineup.

"That's when you know when you're in the big leagues, that deep, authoritative voice announcing your name," former A's outfielder Eric Byrnes said. "That always blew me away."

94 Visit Stadium Sites

Before moving to the Oakland Coliseum in 1968, the A's played in three other stadiums—none of which still stand.

North Philadelphia was the site of the Athletics' original stadium, a vacant lot that Connie Mack found at 20th Street and Columbia Avenue in a residential area that also featured several beerworks—enough of them that the neighborhood is known as "Brewerytown." He obtained a 10-year lease and had a structure quickly erected for $35,000.

Columbia Park was a small, wooden building that held only 9,500 fans. There was so little space, visiting players changed into their uniforms at their hotel. There were no dugouts, only benches in front of the stands.

The first game in Mack's tiny stadium was on April 26, 1901, a home opener twice postponed by rain. A crowd of 10,547 turned up, testing the ballpark's capacity, and more fans watched from nearby rooftops. Philadelphia major Samuel Ashbridge threw out the ceremonial first pitch, but the hometown fans did not enjoy a victory: The Washington Nationals won 5–1 despite three hits by Athletics second baseman Nap Lajoie. The *Philadelphia Inquirer* noted, "The game itself will never be recalled as a sample of the National pastime at its best estate."

Though Columbia Park was expanded to hold 13,500 in 1906, the stadium was not fireproof, and as demand for tickets grew, the overflow crowds topped 20,000. The Athletics needed a new facility, and they played their final season at Columbia Park in 1909. Five years later, it was gone, demolished to make way for housing.

Fittingly for a man who had helped develop modern baseball equipment, Benjamin Shibe's new stadium at 21st Street and Lehigh Avenue was the first to be constructed of steel and concrete. It was also the first with folding chairs, drinking fountains, and a parking garage, and was, in time, the first with a public address system and the first to display lineups on the scoreboard. In 1939, it became the first AL park with lights.

Always a savvy businessman, Shibe had bought the land in North Philadelphia at a reduced rate, for just over $140,000, because it bordered a hospital for infectious diseases. Shibe apparently was tipped off that the hospital was slated for closing, which it did during the 1909 season. The site was five blocks away from the Phillies' Baker Bowl, and it was conveniently located near trolley lines in an area Shibe thought ripe for an economic upturn.

Construction cost $315,248.69, and the park held 23,000 fans, plus an additional 10,000 in standing room areas. It was a lovely building, terra cotta and brick with French Renaissance arches, columns and scrollwork and a copper-trimmed mansard roof. The most impressive feature was a Beaux Arts tower, complete with cupola, that stood at the main entrance and housed the team offices.

During the team's first season, bleacher tickets were 25 cents, and grandstand tickets 50 cents to a dollar. Nearby rooftops, like those near Columbia Park, allowed free viewing. A game program cost a dime.

The park opened on April 12, 1909, and Philadelphia mayor John Reyburn threw out the first ball. This time around, the Athletics won their opener, beating the Red Sox 8–1. The *Evening Bulletin* wrote, "It was a great day for Philadelphia in the baseball world, it was a great day for the fans [and] a most profitable one for the owners of Shibe Park." The stadium was bursting at the seams, with a paid admission of 30,162, and it's estimated as many as 5,000 more squeezed in without paying. Outside, 30,000 more tried to storm the gates, according to the Philadelphia Athletics Historical Society, and it took police action to clear the area.

In 1953, Shibe Park was renamed Connie Mack Stadium, but by then, the Phillies were the hot ticket in town and Mack's sons, Roy and Earle, had run the team into the ground. They often feuded with each other and other relatives—and when attendance plummeted, they opted to sell the club to Arnold Johnson, who moved the franchise to Kansas City.

After Mack died in 1956, a statue was commissioned to commemorate him in Reyburn Park, later renamed for Mack. The statue was moved to Veterans Stadium when it opened in 1971 and now stands at Citizens Bank Park.

The Phillies played at Shibe Park through 1970, and a fire damaged the building beyond repair in 1971. It was razed in 1976, though elements of Shibe Park were incorporated into the design of Citizens Bank Park. In the 1990s, a church was built on the site where Shibe Park once stood.

New Athletics owner Johnson also owned Yankee Stadium, as well as Blues Stadium in Kansas City. Once he bought the A's, however, he sold Blues Stadium (the former home of the Negro League's famed Monarchs) back to the city and signed a three-year lease to play at the revamped minor-league park. The short timeframe led some to believe Johnson had designs on eventually heading to Los Angeles, but the Dodgers moved there after the 1957 season, quashing that idea.

Kansas City was thrilled to be considered a big-league town at last and embraced its new team, at least initially. The A's drew 1.4 million to the newly named Municipal Stadium in 1955, the second highest total in the league and an increase of 1.1 million from the final season in Philadelphia.

The team made its debut on April 12, 1955, with President Harry Truman throwing out the ceremonial first pitch and Commissioner Ford Frick and former manager and owner Connie Mack also on hand; during the sixth inning, a woman ran into Mack's box in the front row, planted a kiss on the 92-year-old's forehead and thanked him for allowing the team to move to Kansas City. Then the A's beat the Tigers 6–2 to kick off a new chapter in franchise history.

After the A's left in 1968, the Royals and Chiefs both played at Municipal Stadium, as did other professional sports teams throughout the building's existence, and the Beatles played there in 1964.

The structure was torn down in 1976, but a plaque marks the site at 22nd and Brooklyn in Kansas City—and the Negro Leagues Museum is just a few blocks away, complete with exhibits about Kansas City's baseball history.

95 Eric Byrnes

Anyone who'd known Eric Byrnes in college, high school, or even as a small child, would not be surprised by what happened on May 15, 2005, when Byrnes chased after a fan who'd run onto the field and hauled the man down from the fence in left.

While at UCLA, Byrnes had sprinted down a would-be robber and pinned him until police arrived. He'd played linebacker and running back at St. Francis High School in Mountain View, California. And even as a tiny tot, Byrnes was climbing the tallest trees in his San Carlos neighborhood, occasionally needing rescue from the fire department.

So in the third inning against the Yankees, when two men hopped onto the field and eluded Coliseum security personnel, Byrnes leaped into action.

"For whatever reason, that year it was en vogue to run on the field, it seemed like it was happening every other day. It was annoying," Byrnes said. "I had no interest in going after the guy, but that day, it was two guys and they were doing figure eights in the outfield—and one of them started running directly at me, so my high-school football instincts kicked in and I put myself in a position to defend myself. Then he turned and made a beeline for the fence, so I chased him and grabbed him and pulled him down."

The other man, shirtless and wearing what the *San Francisco Chronicle* reported "appeared to be a giant diaper," was apprehended by five officers.

After the game, A's manager Ken Macha said that Byrnes should have left the fan alone. Told that, Byrnes—who'd been lifted for a pinch hitter later in the game—responded, "I don't really care what he says."

"I knew there was something wrong the next morning when I had phone calls from both my mom and my dad and it wasn't about going after the fan—well, my mom [Judy] was a little concerned about that, but my dad [Jim] loved it. It was about me saying, 'I don't care what the manager thinks.' They were both upset about that and if there's anything I wish I could have taken back, it's that," Byrnes said. "I didn't mean it, it was just that a lot of things had caught up with me. I wasn't happy with my playing time, and there was this seemingly endless supply of people running on the field.

"My parents said, 'Get your rear in Ken Macha's office and apologize right away,' and that's what I did. I walked into the stadium, went right to his office and said I was sorry, that didn't come out the right way, and he absolutely let me have it, which he should have. That's the one time I knew I was absolutely wrong."

Major League Baseball sent security officials to the Coliseum to emphasize that players should not to interfere with fans, which is a safety issue and a potential liability problem for teams.

"I don't think MLB was too happy with him doing that," former A's third baseman Eric Chavez said. "But Byrnes was a nut—like [manager] Art Howe always said, 'Byrnsie played with his hair on fire.'"

Eric Byrnes tackles a streaking fan during a game against the Yankees in 2005.
(Michael Zagaris)

The Oakland Police Department, however, didn't rebuke Byrnes—they presented him with a baton and a pair of handcuffs.

Byrnes' top highlight with the A's actually took place on the other side of the Bay. A lifelong Giants fan, Byrnes hit for the cycle against San Francisco on June 29, 2003.

He needed a triple in his final at-bat to complete the feat, and Giants center fielder Carlos Valderrama slipped while coming in on Byrnes' sinking line drive in the ninth.

"I was just happy because I was going to be 5-for-5—but Valderrama was going to dive for it, his feet came out from under him and boom, it fell in and I had a stand-up triple," Byrnes said. "How does it get much better? I had all my best friends in the crowd, we'd all grown up Giants fans, and there were 10 or 15 of them there, heckling me. To do that in that park—and to get an ovation at third base after the triple, a visiting player, that was amazing."

96 Yankees Farm Club

Arnold Johnson, who moved the A's to Kansas City, had made another major baseball purchase before obtaining Philadelphia's American League club.

A longtime business associate of the Yankees' ownership group, Johnson had bought Yankee Stadium the previous year. As a condition of the A's sale, Johnson had to divest himself of that investment to avoid a potential conflict of interest—but Johnson's links to the Yankees remained, and the Athletics' reputation for supplying their AL rival with players grew.

Even before the move, New York had dumped unwanted players on the Athletics, and when Johnson took the team west, there was even less doubt about what was happening.

Eddie Joost, who had to deal with an influx of such New York rejects while managing the team in 1954, said more than 50 years later, "Everybody knew the A's were a Yankees farm team by that point. The newspapers, the fans. That's what was intended [with the sale]. I don't know how they did that, it seems like it should have been illegal, but we knew that would happen."

Adding to the connection: The Athletics relocated to the same town where the Yankees' top farm club, the Kansas City Blues, had played, and as the A's seemingly took over that role, they became known as the "stepchildren" of the Yankees. The disparity in deals was noted, with young talent flowing from K.C. in exchange for cash and players on the decline or in the doghouse—Billy Martin was sent to Kansas City after a notorious nightclub fight, for instance.

While Johnson was the owner, his team made at least two trades every season with New York—and the Athletics parted with one-time ace Bobby Shantz as well as Clete Boyer, Hector Lopez, and Art Ditmar, among others. Ralph Terry was the quintessential example of how the Yankees made use of K.C.: The right-hander was sent to the Athletics in 1957, at the age of 21—then two years later, when he was more seasoned, New York reacquired him (and Lopez) for Jerry Lumpe and two others who were essentially spare parts.

"The truth is, nobody else was willing to trade with [the Yankees] because they were afraid of making them stronger," shortstop Joe De Maestri said in *We Played the Game*. "None of us gave it a second thought about our trading with them."

From March 1955 to June 1957, the two teams made 12 deals that involved 32 players—including Enos Slaughter, twice.

The most famously poor deal of the bunch didn't seem entirely lopsided at the time. On December 11, 1959, the Yankees sent Don Larsen, Hank Bauer, Norm Siebern, and Marv Throneberry to Kansas City for De Maestri, first baseman Kent Hadley, and outfielder Roger Maris, a promising 24-year-old who'd hit .273 with 16 homers and 72 RBIs, making the All-Star team and becoming a fan favorite.

Two years later, when Maris hit 61 homers to break Babe Ruth's single-season record, the folly of the trade was clear. It's often cited as the worst in franchise history.

Larsen, he of the World Series perfect game, went 1–10 with the A's in 1960 and made just one start the following year. Throneberry was traded to Baltimore halfway through 1961. Bauer, who was 37 years old in 1960, played in just 95 games in 1960 and 43 the year after before becoming the A's manager.

Siebern did make two All-Star teams while in Kansas City, and he hit .308 with 117 RBIs in 1962.

Everything turned around when Charlie Finley bought the team from Johnson's estate in 1960. Johnson may have enjoyed a cozy relationship with the Yankees, but the man he sold the club to was not a fan. Finley especially disliked Yankee Stadium. He felt the dimensions were unfair, especially the fact that the foul pole in right was just 296 feet from the plate.

So Finley constructed his own "pennant porch" in right at Memorial Stadium, mimicking Yankee Stadium. The A's played two exhibition games with the "pennant porch" in place before the league made Finley restore the previous alignment or risk forfeiting games.

In response, Finley had a white line painted on the field where the porch had stood and he made the PA announcer note whenever balls were hit that distance, "That would have been a home run at Yankee Stadium." That didn't last long, because opponents reached the line with so much more regularity than the home team.

The next year, Finley extended the roof past the stands and out to 296 feet, saying it was to provide more shade. According to Bill Libby's *Charlie O. and the Angry A's,* Finley was ordered to move it back to the edge of the seats and complied half an hour before the game.

97 Brandon McCarthy

One of the most frightening moments of A's history, one of the scariest moments of any recent baseball season, happened on September 5, 2012, at the Coliseum, when starter Brandon McCarthy was struck in the head by a line drive off the bat of Angels shortstop Erick Aybar.

After getting checked out on the field for several minutes, McCarthy left under his own power, but several hours later, he was taken to a nearby hospital for emergency surgery to relieve pressure on his brain caused by an epidural hemorrhage.

"It was so surreal to see that happen—you think, 'Oh no, that's awful,' and then you see him walk off the mound and everything seemed fine," said former A's starter Brett Anderson. "I remember talking to Brandon in the clubhouse and he was holding a normal conversation.

"Three or four hours later, he's having major brain surgery. I'm not the most emotional guy but that thing was hit really hard, and Brandon is one of my better friends in the game—that was a life or death situation. That brings you back to reality. This is just a game, someone's life and health are more important."

"That was scary, that play was nasty, something you never want to see," former Oakland third baseman Josh Donaldson said. "I went to the mound, and it seemed like everything was okay, they said, 'He's just coming out as a precaution.' He was talking.

"Then it turns out he didn't remember any of that, and the next thing you know, he's getting his skull operated on. He's very fortunate. It's one of those things where you don't worry about his career, even—you just hope he's going to be okay and can live a normal life."

McCarthy, then 29, spent six days in the hospital, and things initially were touch-and-go; it was a life-threatening situation. Three days after his surgery, however, McCarthy was joking on Twitter, he and his wife, Amanda, having already built a huge following as one of the best comedy teams on social media.

Among other things, told that the stadium scoreboard in Seattle had flashed "Get well soon, Brandon McCarthy," McCarthy responded from his hospital bed, "Nice, but sorta bossy?"

McCarthy, of course, was out the remainder of the season, but he was able to sit in the dugout with his teammates during the playoffs, and he even began to play some catch before games, hoping he might be okayed to participate if the A's made it to the World Series.

"It was crazy, he was pushing so hard to do anything to come back and pitch in the playoffs, that was impressive," Anderson said. "For him to get back to where he is today is and to be able to pitch every day is a testament to his mental fortitude."

In mid-November, McCarthy was cleared to resume baseball activity by concussion expert Dr. Micky Collins, and less than a month later the Arizona Diamondbacks signed him to a two-year, $15.5 million contract. He was traded to the Yankees in the middle of the 2014 season and made 14 starts with New York to finish the 2014 season, putting up a 2.89 ERA in pinstripes. And on September 17, 2014, McCarthy became the 77th pitcher in history to throw an immaculate inning, three strikeouts, nine pitches.

98 Mt. Davis

In 1995 and 1996, the Coliseum underwent a major revision, as part of an agreement to induce the Raiders to return to Oakland from Los Angeles.

Until then, there was an extensive iceplant-covered area beyond the outfield fences, plus a view of the East Bay hills and the BART trains chugging past. As far as multi-purpose facilities went, the Coliseum was among baseball's best and most attractive.

The $200 million renovation ruined all that.

The A's had recently changed hands, when the Haas family sold the club to local developers Steve Schott and Ken Hofmann. Oakland finished in last place that year and Tony La Russa left to become the Cardinals' manager. Everything was changing, including the team's ballpark.

"It was a dilemma," GM Sandy Alderson said. "We all knew that the city and the Bay Area wanted the Raiders to come back from Los Angeles but we knew it would destroy the Coliseum as a baseball facility and undercut our ability to market and grow."

Construction delays forced the A's to play their first six home games of 1996 at a Triple-A field in Las Vegas. An Elvis impersonator introduced the A's and Blue Jays before the opener. "It's a circus," Oakland pitcher Jim Corsi cracked to the *San Francisco Examiner*. "In fact, it's Circus Circus."

"As a major-league team opening in a minor-league park in Vegas—we didn't have a particularly good team, but we still felt like second-class citizens," said then-assistant GM Billy Beane. "We had to grind our teeth. Even now, there's a sense of bitterness to look at it."

The project included a four-tier concrete grandstand that obliterated the iceplant-swathed slope beyond the outfield, as well as the lovely views of the hills. And the consensus was that the changes ruined the Coliseum for baseball.

"There was always something special about attending an Oakland A's game in the summer, with the nice weather, the white uniforms, and those hills beyond the outfield," Beane said. "Something special was lost."

"It was a gorgeous stadium before that," then-Oakland manager Art Howe said.

The massive structure, which became known as "Mt. Davis" for Raiders owner Al Davis, went up throughout 1996 season. During day games, workers swarmed the area, and they occasionally had to dodge balls Mark McGwire sent their way.

"I remember McGwire knocking some workers off the scaffolding a couple of times," Howe said with a laugh. "It got so they'd stop and watch if he was up. Then they had construction workers dancing to 'YMCA' after the fifth inning."

An already somewhat dingy gray building (dubbed "The Mausoleum" by, among others, former A's third baseman Sal Bando) became even more oppressive. And hitters, already contending with all that extra foul territory at the multi-sport stadium, felt as if the ball no longer carried as well.

"It's really a football stadium," Bando said. "It always has been."

The extra seating capacity hurt the A's season-ticket sales because fans could walk up and purchase tickets so easily on game day. The team began to close off the upper portion of Mt. Davis and then, for the 2006 season, the top of Mt. Davis and the third deck of the old Coliseum were tarped off, giving the stadium a capacity of 35,067.

That's approximately the same size the team is eyeing for its next facility, wherever it might be.

The A's removed the tarp from some sections during the 2013 Division Series against the Tigers and planned to remove all of them for the ALCS, but did not make it that far. They also planned to take the tarps off for home playoff games in 2014, however the team did not advance past the wild-card game at Kansas City.

99 Nick Swisher

Nick Swisher was a name to know even before he was called up to Oakland, because he was one of the *Moneyball* draft picks in 2002. With that notoriety came a little extra pressure, so not every A's minor-leaguer enjoyed having a connection to the best-selling book.

Swisher, though, loved the spotlight. Always has, always will. With the Yankees later in his career, the loud and lively first baseman/outfielder was in his element.

His swagger didn't necessarily go over so well when Swisher was in his youth, however. The A's brought him to AT&T Park to shag fly balls and meet the media after he signed his first pro deal, and the big-league players were astonished by his brashness.

"They bring the first-round picks out to work out on the field with the team, sort of show 'em off before shipping them off to the bushes, but the day Swisher came out I thought we must have made a trade, he didn't have the aura of a new draft pick," former A's first baseman Scott Hatteberg said with a chuckle. "I didn't know who this guy was—Mr. T starter set with all these gold chains, bare-chested, giving everyone the bro-hug thing. I was saying, 'Oh my God, who did we trade for? Who is this guy?'

"He gives me the bare-chested hug and then I find out this is our first-round pick. I was like, 'I hate him already.' Then on the field, he's catching balls in the outfield and throwing every other one into the stands, and we don't have enough balls as it is. But that was Swish. I grew to love him."

"Swisher didn't make the best impression at first," third baseman Eric Chavez said. "I remember Billy Beane loved him, he said, 'He's like another Jim Edmonds!' but they brought him in to shag balls one day and I always remember how great Jason Giambi was to me when I first came up, so I went out there to say hi, introduce myself, and Swisher started telling me about how he was going to put on 30 pounds, be a home run hitter. I was like, 'Oh, man, this guy really likes himself.' He rubbed a lot of people wrong his first year, especially the older guys."

When Swisher was called up at the end of 2004, second baseman Mark McLemore immediately began hazing Swisher, writing "rookie" on a batting helmet and making Swisher wear it during batting practice. Swisher also was fined $1,100 his first day for various offenses ranging from his "Brady Anderson sideburns" to "being called up because of working the count."

Swisher hit 21 homers as a rookie in 2005 and 35 in 2006, helping Oakland win the division, and he had three hits and scored three runs in the A's three-game sweep of the Twins in the division series.

"I would take Swish on my team 10 out of 10 times," said Huston Street, the closer for that 2006 team. "When he's not around, you really appreciate him. When he's around every day, you're like, 'Okay, bro, can we get a filter?' But everything was always very positive."

Always a fan favorite because of his all-out playing style and vibrant personality, Swisher made headlines off the field for charitable efforts such as growing his hair out for Locks of Love to honor his late grandmother.

After the 2007 season, he was traded to the White Sox for pitchers Gio Gonzalez and Fautino de los Santos and outfielder Ryan Sweeney.

He has put together a solid big-league career: In his first 10-plus seasons, Swisher hit 239 homers and drove in 778 runs, becoming a respected veteran and a team leader with the Yankees and Indians.

"When I went back to the Yankees with Swisher, I started to appreciate what he was about more," Chavez said. "He always has a smile on his face, he's always ready to play, he's high energy, he's laughing.

"I remember you'd get to first base or third base, and so many guys would say, 'What's up with this Swish?' but I always told people, 'If you played with him, you'd love him, he always brings a positive energy.'"

100 Go to Fanfest

Here is a no-brainer for any A's fan: Attend FanFest, which usually is held in late January or early February at the Coliseum complex, most recently in the arena.

Tickets usually go on sale in early January, and in 2014 they were $10 for general admission, $5 for season-ticket holders. The event is limited to 10,000 and usually sells out quickly, so purchase tickets as soon as they are available. There is no fee for parking.

Q&A sessions with players are popular events, and often take strange turns. In 2013, one female fan asked starter A.J. Griffin if she could touch his shaggy blond mane. He cheerfully obliged.

It's a child-friendly event, too, with lots of kids' activities, and it's free for children six and under. Just be careful when it comes to infants—closer Sean Doolittle may be a sure-handed fielder, but he's still worried he might drop your child.

"Last year, this couple came up with this baby and they were like, 'We'd love your picture with our son,' and I said, 'Absolutely,' thinking they'd be holding the baby," he said. "But they just handed me the baby, and I don't know how to hold babies. I was looking at the security guy like, 'What do I do? Help!' They trusted me with their newborn son—I was not comfortable. I would love to see how the picture turned out, there's no chance I was smiling. The panic had to show on my face.

"That happened to me a couple times, and I was asking the A's people shepherding us around, 'What do I do with a baby? Hold it like a football? Hold it up like Simba in the Lion King?'"

Also make sure not to snub any players. Doolittle remains a little scarred from 2013.

"My first year, I was signing autographs and there was a line waiting for me, and Coco Crisp walked by and probably a third of my line left," Doolittle recalled. "Then Yoenis Cespedes walked by and another third of my line left. I had so few people left, people could walk right up. Not great for my self-esteem."

Even so, Doolittle recommends FanFest emphatically.

"If you're a fan, that's something that should be on your bucket list," Doolittle said. "It's a way to see the players, interact with players, take a picture with some players, ask some questions at Q&As.

"And we feel the same way—it's a cool way for fans to see you more as a person, you're not in game mode. It's nice to break down that wall."

Acknowledgments

All a sportswriter really needs is a constant supply of great stories—and that makes the Oakland A's a reporter's dream.

Colorful characters, check. Fascinating decision-makers, check. Lots of success, check, check, check.

Some fun common themes run throughout the course of the A's franchise, making this project particularly rewarding. From Rube Waddell straight through to Josh Reddick, from Connie Mack to Billy Beane, the cast of big personalities and important baseball figures is hard to match in pro sports history.

I'm lucky to have had such vivid figures to chronicle and even luckier that so many of them are gracious with their time, including the many current and former players, coaches, managers, staff members, broadcasters, owners, and front-office people who helped with this project. Special thanks to Ken Korach, Ray Fosse, Steve Vucinich, and Mickey Morabito.

To the A's public-relations staff, past and present, my undying thanks, especially stats-wiz Mike Selleck for answering all my non-stop, last-second questions over the years and for contributing so much information for this book.

The media-relations crew at Major League Baseball—Pat Courtney, Mike Teevan, John Blundell—deserve a big shout-out, as does Phyllis Mehrige of the club-relations office. I'd also like to recognize Jack O'Connell of the Baseball Writers' Association of America for all his hard work and his support.

Were there space, I'd thank dozens upon dozens of baseball writers and major-league scouts for their friendship and their help, but since I can't, I'll single out one of each, my dear pal David Lennon of *Newsday* and the late, great Jim Fregosi, forever missed in every press box.

Roger Angell of the *New Yorker* always will serve as inspiration, and no one has ever had a better teacher than Forbes Keaton or a better editor than Mark Smoyer. And to all my former and current colleagues at the *San Francisco Chronicle*, with a special tip of the cap to national baseball writer John Shea, I say that it is an honor and privilege to work with you. Ditto Jesse Jordan at Triumph Books for shepherding this project.

To all my friends and relatives, thank you for putting up with my strange schedules. I've missed many weddings and other big moments for baseball, but I love you all, especially my uncles, Mike and Matt, and my godsons, Michael Gerlach and Dugan Ellin. And I'm lucky to have the best best friend in the world, Christine Winge.

This book could not have been written without two people: stats guru David Feldman, whose knowledge of the A's is unmatched, and my kind, patient, and hilarious husband, Dan Brown of the *San Jose Mercury News*, a phenomenal writer who authored the *100 Things* 49ers book, giving us a matching set. The *A League of Their Own* references are for you, Brownie.

Bibliography

Newspapers
The San Francisco Chronicle
Associated Press
The Dallas Morning News
The New York Times
The Washington Post
The Tacoma News-Tribune

Magazines
Baseball America
Sports Illustrated
The Sporting News
Time

Websites
BaseballReference.com
Baseballhall.org
PhiladelphiaAthletics.org
SABR.org

Books
Ron Bergman, *The Mustache Gang,* Dell. (1973)
Robert P. Broadwater, *Lefty Gomez and the 1931 Philadelphia Athletics*, McFarland. (2014)
Tom Clark, *Champagne and Baloney, the Rise and Fall of Finley's A's,* Harper and Row. (1976)
Donald Dewey and Nicholas Acocella, *The New Biographical History of Baseball,* Triumph Books. (2002)
Paul Dickson, *Baseball's Greatest Quotations,* HarperCollins. (1991)

Dick Dobbins, *The Grand Minor League, An Oral History of the Old Pacific Coast League,* Duane Press. (1999)

Dick Dobbins and Jon Twichell, *Nuggets on the Diamond,* Woodford Press. (1994)

Rickey Henderson and John Shea, *Off Base: Confessions of a Thief,* Harper Collins. (1992)

Donald Honig and Red Smith, *Baseball Between the Lines, Baseball in the Forties and Fifties Told By The Men Who Played It,* University of Nebraska Press. (1993)

Reggie Jackson and Mike Lupica, *Reggie: The Autobiography,* Random House. (1984).

Jim Kaplan, *Lefty Grove: American Original,* Society for American Baseball Research. (2000)

Leonard Koppett, *The Man in the Dugout,* Temple University Press. (2000)

Michael Lewis, *Moneyball,* W.W. Norton and Company. (2003)

Bill Libby, *Charlie O. and the Angry A's,* Doubleday. (1975)

Norman L. Macht, *Connie Mack and the Early Years of Baseball,* University of Nebraska Press. (2007)

Norman L. Macht, *Connie Mack, the Turbulent and Triumphant Years, 1915–31,* University of Nebraska Press. (2012)

Billy Martin, *Billyball,* Doubleday. (1987)

Daniel Okrent and Steve Wulf, *Baseball Anecdotes,* Oxford University Press. (1989)

Danny Peary, *We Played the Game: Memories of Baseball's Greatest Era,* Black Dog and Leventhal. (2002)

Lawrence S. Ritter, *The Glory of Their Times,* William Morrow and Co. (1984)

Mark Stang, *Athletics Album, a Photo History of the Philadelphia Athletics,* Orange Frazer Press. (2006)

Tom Swift, *Chief Bender's Burden,* Bison Books. (2010)

Hank Utley and Scott Verner, *The Independent Carolina Baseball League,* McFarland. (2005)